STUDY GUIDE

Susana Urbina

PSYCHOLOGICAL TESTING

Seventh Edition

ANNE ANASTASI
Fordham University

SUSANA URBINA
University of North Florida

Pearson
Education

PRENTICE HALL, Upper Saddle River, NJ 07458

© 1997 by PRENTICE-HALL, INC.

A Pearson Education Company
Upper Saddle River, NJ 07458

10 9 8

ISBN 0-13-257321-0

Printed in the United States of America

CONTENTS

PREFACE

This *Study Guide* has been prepared to provide a useful supplement for students of *Psychological Testing* (7th ed.). Its primary purpose is to be a user-friendly companion to that text and a learning tool. It contains material versatile enough to be used in different ways, and at different levels, by beginning as well as advanced students.

The Guide begins with a section, addressed to the student, on how to make the most effective use of its contents. The chapters that follow contain some common features: Chapter Outline; Chapter Summary; Study Questions that cover the major topics of each chapter; Multiple-Choice self-test; and Miniprojects/Suggested Homework Activities. In addition, each chapter has a number of items tailored to the content of the respective textbook chapter. These structured activities include: Statistical exercises; Fill-in-the-blanks; Matching items; and True/false questions—with answers provided for all. Appendix A contains the Table of Areas under the Normal Curve, needed for many statistical exercises, and directions on how to use it. Appendix B presents a suggested outline for test evaluation.

I wish to express my appreciation to Anne Anastasi for the contribution she made to the preparation of the previous edition of this Guide. Her comments and suggestions, at every step of the process, were invariably helpful.

Susana Urbina

TO THE STUDENT

This Guide has been prepared as a companion to the seventh edition of *Psychological Testing*. Because of the comprehensive scope of this textbook and the relative complexity of its subject matter, a supplement of this kind should prove helpful. Before you begin, read this section of the Guide thoroughly, familiarize yourself with its contents, and devise a personal plan so that it can best serve your purposes.

Each chapter of the *Study Guide* follows the respective textbook chapter closely and contains five major sections:

I. <u>Chapter Outline</u>

○ Contains the headings for all of the sections of each chapter.
☞ Should be reviewed before you read the textbook chapter.

II. <u>Chapter Summary</u>

○ Condenses the most important ideas presented in each chapter.
☞ Note ideas and terms that are new to you and study them in the textbook.
○ Serves as a review in preparation for tests.
○ Conveys only a small portion of the information in the text.
☞ Cannot substitute for reading the book.

III. <u>Comprehensive Review</u>

○ Contains a variety of items for use after you have read the textbook chapters. Activities in this section include the following:

❶. <u>Study Questions</u>.

○ Provided in every chapter of the Guide.
○ Chapter contents broken down into topical areas.
○ Useful in listing learning objectives.
☞ Write down answers to each as though they were essay questions in a test or select a few study questions and prepare answers to those.
☞ Make the study questions a central part of your reviews.

❷ Exercises.

- o Included in all chapters containing statistical material.
- o Chapter 3—Norms and the Meaning of Scores—includes a brief review of basic statistics.
- o Appendix A contains the Table of Areas under the Normal Curve, and directions on how to use it. *Understanding that table is indispensable to psychological testing.*
- o Statistical concepts encompassed are basic and unavoidable in this field.

  ☞ Survey all the exercises in a given chapter and attempt those that seem most manageable.

  ☞ As the level of difficulty increases, look at the answers and explanations provided and rework the solutions to make sure you have understood the process.

  ☞ You may need to review material in a basic statistics textbook.

❸ **Fill-in-the-Blanks and Matching Items.**

- o Aimed at helping you understand the key terms, concepts, and names in the textbook chapter.
- o Matching items typically cover test titles and are relatively easy.
- o Fill-in items provide a clue by showing the same number of blank spaces as the number of letters in the answer.
- o Can help you learn key material in three ways:

  ☞ Try to answer after your initial reading of the textbook chapter; if you cannot do so, reread the text.

  ☞ Use the items to help commit the information to memory.

  ☞ Gauge your knowledge of the important terms, concepts, names, and tests by looking over the lists of answers to the fill-in items, and making sure you can identify or define them.

❹ **True/False and Why? Items**

- o Highlight important issues or research findings related to testing.

  ☞ First, decide whether the statements are true or false.

  ☞ After you have studied the text in greater depth and are preparing for a test, answer the question "Why?"

  ☞ Write down the reason(s) for your true/false responses to clarify your understanding of the issues involved and to prepare for essay tests.

IV. Multiple Choice: Test Yourself

- ○ Multiple-choice items are the most common type of examination questions.

  ☞ Best reserved for your last review before a test to gauge your knowledge of the chapter.

  ☞ Responding to the self-test will be a good "dress rehearsal" for the real test.

  Multiple-choice self-tests sample the content of each chapter sparsely, as a real examination is likely to do, and are more appropriate as a minitest than for a systematic review.

  ☞ Leave the self-tests for the last part of your review, to get an idea of how prepared you are for upcoming tests. (If your score on the minitest is below 75 percent, you need to do more studying prior to the real test.)

V. Miniprojects/Suggested Homework Activities

- ○ Addressed to students who want not only to do well in the psychological testing course but also to begin a professional preparation in the use of psychological tests.
- ○ Many activities involve readings of outside sources that are important in the field.
- ○ A number of miniprojects encourage you to get actively involved in experiences that will deepen your knowledge of how testing is applied.
- ○ Choice of miniprojects is varied and enjoyable.

  ☞ Try to follow through with one or two from every chapter. *If you go beyond the text, your knowledge of what is in the text will deepen and increase.*

PART I   Functions and Origins of Psychological Testing

∞ 1 ∞

NATURE AND USE OF PSYCHOLOGICAL TESTS

Chapter Outline

Uses and Varieties of Psychological Tests

What is a Psychological Test?
    Behavior Sample
    Standardization
    Objective Measurement of Difficulty
    Reliability
    Validity

Why Control the Use of Psychological Tests?
    Qualified Examiner
    Role of the Test User
    Security of Test Content and Communication of Test Information

Test Administration
    Advance Preparation of Examiners
    Testing Conditions
    Introducing the Test: Rapport and Test-Taker Orientation

Examiner and Situational Variables

A View from the Test-Taker's Perspective
    Test Anxiety
    Comprehensive Investigation of Test-Taker Views

Effects of Training on Test Performance
    Coaching
    Test Sophistication
    Instruction in Broad Cognitive Skills
    Overview

Sources of Information about Tests

Chapter Summary

Psychological tests are tools. They were developed in response to the practical need to select or classify people in such settings as schools, clinics, industry, and the military. This fact is largely responsible for the popularity and growth of psychological testing and for many of the weaknesses that became inherent in their use. Testing has also been applied in counseling individuals with regard to their life choices, as well as for self-understanding and personal development. In addition to their applications in the solution of practical problems, tests play a significant role in psychological research. This chapter examines the characteristics that define psychological tests and differentiate them from other tools.

A psychological test is defined as an objective and standardized measure of a sample of behavior. The adequacy of coverage of a test depends on the number and nature of its items, whereas its predictive or diagnostic value depends on the empirical relationship between its items and the behavior in question. Standardization of a test consists of developing uniform procedures for its administration and scoring, as well as generating normative data on which to base the interpretation of scores. Tests are primarily evaluated in terms of reliability, or consistency of their scores, and in terms of validity, or the extent to which we know what they measure.

The use of psychological tests needs to be controlled in order to ensure that they are employed only by those people who are qualified to select and apply them properly. The person who employs test scores as a source of information in reaching decisions about people, or test user, has increasingly been recognized as having primary responsibility for the proper use of tests. Furthermore, in order to preserve the integrity and usefulness of most tests, access to their content needs to be carefully monitored by test publishers and purchasers.

One of the most important objectives in psychological testing is to reduce or eliminate the influence of any variables extraneous to what the test is measuring. To this end, good testing practice requires the examiner to be prepared to deal with all eventualities related to the administration of the test and to establish rapport with the individuals to be tested. In addition, attention should be given to ensuring that the testing environment and other testing conditions do not interfere with the performance of examinees. Skilled examiners try to detect, and whenever possible eliminate, the operation of extraneous influences in a testing situation, whether such influences arise from their own expectations, from the context of the testing or from special characteristics of examinees. One such characteristic is the amount of anxiety experienced by some test takers. This variable has been studied extensively and, although its operation appears to be quite complex, it has generally been found to correlate negatively with scores on tests of achievement and intelligence. Treatment programs that address both test anxiety and study skills appear to be the most promising in this regard.

Recently, efforts to gather information about many other important aspects of test takers' reactions have been made by investigators in several countries. The results of such

2

surveys promise to enhance the testing enterprise by increasing the level of mutual understanding between test users and test takers.

An extraneous variable which can affect performance on psychological tests, and thus potentially alter their validity, is the extent of training individuals receive prior to the testing. Training can encompass activities that range from coaching, which is specific to the test and may reduce validity, to instruction in broader skills, which falls in the realm of education and does not affect validity. Many procedures designed to orient examinees and to equalize their test-taking experience are also available now. Such procedures may actually enhance validity by reducing the influence of test sophistication as an extraneous variable.

The rapidity of changes in the area of psychological testing requires familiarity with the major sources of information in the field. Organizations such as the Buros Institute—which publishes the *Mental Measurements Yearbook* (MMY) series and *Tests in Print* (TIP)—as well as the Educational Testing Service (ETS), monitor the publication of new tests and changes in existing tests to keep test users abreast of developments. In addition, test publishers provide information directly to test users through their catalogs and test manuals. An indispensable guide for anyone wishing to evaluate psychological tests is the *Standards for Educational and Psychological Testing*, currently under revision.

Comprehensive Review

STUDY QUESTIONS:

1. Identify the traditional function of psychological tests and describe how that function has affected their development and their role in contemporary psychology.

2. Define what a psychological test is and explain the meaning of each term in that definition.

3. Identify and describe the two principal ways in which psychological tests are currently evaluated.

4. Discuss the major reasons why the use of tests needs to be controlled.

5. List and discuss the reasons why testing information needs to be communicated effectively to test takers, concerned professionals, and the general public.

6. Discuss the function that advance preparation of examiners and knowledge and control of conditions serve in testing.

7. Describe the ways in which the process of establishing rapport may vary with different types of tests and test takers.

8. Identify the major examiner variables which might affect test results.

9. Discuss the effects of test anxiety on test results, in light of the research findings cited in the text.

10. Contrast coaching with education in terms of how each might affect testing.

11. Describe various types of test familiarization materials.

12. List the major sources of information on testing that are currently available.

FILL IN THE BLANKS: Key Terms and Concepts

1. A(n) _____ _____ is an objective and standardized measure of a sample of behavior.

2. A(n) _____ is a small portion or subset selected from a population or universe.

3. A test is _____ when control of testing conditions is established through uniformity of procedures in administration and scoring.

4. The average performance of a representative sample of the types of persons for whom a test is designed is called the ____.

5. Although _____ refers to a determination of a present condition based on test results, the term also implies a prediction regarding behaviors in situations other than the present test.

6. A test's norms are based on a group that is called the _____ _____.

7. A(n) ___ _____ is an objective measure of test performance that is, by itself, meaningless.

8. _____ refers to the consistency of test scores across time, forms, or scorers.

9. _____ refers to the degree to which a test fulfills its purported function.

10. A(n)_ _ _ _ _ _ _ _ _ is an independent measure of performance on the function assessed by a test that can be used to validate the test.

11. A(n)_ _ _ _ _ _ _ _ _ _ _ _ _ _ _ _ _ _ is a measure of correlation between test scores and a criterion.

12. The _ _ _ _ _ _ _ _ _ group is a representative sample of persons on whom a test's validity is investigated.

13. The _ _ _ _ _ _ _ _ _ _ _ _ _ _ is an empirically established measure of how hard a test item is and it is used to determine whether an item is selected for a test and where it is placed.

14. A person who uses test scores as a source of information in reaching practical decisions is a _ _ _ _ _ _ _ _.

15. _ _ _ _ _ _ _ is a term that refers to the examiner's efforts to arouse interest in, and elicit cooperation from, test takers.

16. The _ _ _ _ - _ _ _ _ _ _ _ _ _ _ prophecy is an effect on the test taker's responses that can occur as a function of the examiner's expectations.

17. _ _ _ _ _ _ _ _ is a term that refers to intensive drills on items similar to those on a test to be taken.

18. The difference between coaching and _ _ _ _ _ _ _ _ _ is that the results of the latter extend to the broader behavior that the test is designed to assess whereas the effects of the former are limited to the test.

19. _ _ _ _ _ _ _ _ _ _ _ _ _ _ _ _ _ is an examinee variable that consists of test-taking practice and generally results in score gains.

20. _ _ _ _ _ - _ _ _ _ _ _ _ _ _ _ _ procedures are techniques designed to rule out or equalize differences in the prior test-taking experience of examinees.

21. _ _ _ _ _ _ _ _ _ _ _ _ is an examinee variable that consists of cognitive and emotional components and generally results in score decrements.

22. The _ series, originated by Oscar Buros, is one of the most important sources of information about tests.

1. psychological test
2. sample
3. standardized
4. norm
5. diagnosis
6. standardization sample
7. raw score
8. reliability
9. validity
10. criterion
11. validity coefficient
12. validation (group)
13. difficulty level
14. test user
15. rapport
16. self-fulfilling (prophecy)
17. coaching
18. education
19. test sophistication
20. test-orientation (procedures)
21. test anxiety
22. *Mental Measurements Yearbook* (series)

TRUE/FALSE and WHY?

1. The goal of psychological testing is to obtain a direct measurement of the behavior sample covered by the test. (T/F) Why? _____
   _____

2. In personality testing, responses are usually evaluated in terms of norms that represent the most desirable pattern of performance. (T/F) Why? _____
   _____

3. In individual assessment an experienced examiner may occasionally depart from standardized test procedures provided that the information thus elicited is not used in arriving at scores. (T/F) Why? _____
   _____

4. In general, children are more susceptible to examiner and situational variables than are adults. (T/F) Why? _____
   _____

5. Studies of the relation between anxiety and test performance indicate that even a slight amount of anxiety is detrimental to performance. (T/F) Why? _____

_____

_____

6. Promoting some sense of mystery about tests is an effective device that examiners may use to build rapport. (T/F) Why? _____

_____

7. Proper interpretation of test scores cannot proceed without some background data on the test taker. (T/F) Why? _____

_____

8. The state laws regarding disclosure of testing information enacted in New York in the late 1970s have been quite effective in accomplishing the goals that prompted their enactment. (T/F) Why? _____

_____

9. The test user may or may not be the examiner who administers and scores the test. (T/F) Why? _____

_____

10. Empirical verification of equivalence is necessary when any test materials, such as answer sheets, differ from those used with the standardization sample. (T/F) Why?

_____

_____

11. The single most important requirement for proper test administration is the advance preparation of the examiner. (T/F) Why? _____

_____

12. General motivational feedback has been found more effective than corrective feedback in improving the performance of low scorers on subsequent tests. (T/F) Why?_____

_____

_____

13. In order to be qualified to administer most group tests some supervised training in the administration of the particular test is usually essential. (T/F) Why? _____

_____

14. The results of recent surveys of attitudes toward testing reveal that the public's views on testing issues are quite biased. (T/F) Why? _____

_____

15. The need to establish *Testing Standards* that concern the effect of testing on the welfare of the individual has been recognized since the 1940s. (T/F) Why? _____

_____

_____

ANSWERS TO TRUE/FALSE:

1. False	4. True	7. True	10. True	13. False
2. False	5. False	8. False	11. True	14. False
3. True	6. False	9. True	12. False	15. False

MATCHING: Sources of Information about Tests (One letter per number)

_____ 1. One of the earliest and most important sources of information on published tests.

_____ 2. Source which should provide essential information for administering, scoring, and evaluating a particular test.

_____ 3. Major professional association for psychologists which is responsible for publishing the Testing Standards.

_____ 4. Current publisher of the MMY series.

_____ 5. Best source of information for purchasing a published test.

_____ 6. Source of current information on unpublished tests.

_____ 7. Comprehensive guide for evaluating practices in psychological testing.

_____ 8. Buros Institute publication that serves as an index for the MMY.

A. *Tests in Microfiche* (ETS)
B. *Tests in Print* (TIP)
C. *Standards for Educational and Psychological Testing*
D. *Mental Measurements Yearbook* (MMY)
E. Test publishers' catalog
F. Test manual
G. American Psychological Association
H. Buros Institute of Mental Measurements

ANSWERS TO MATCHING ITEMS: 1-D   2-F   3-G   4-H   5-E   6-A   7-C   8-B

Multiple Choice: Test Yourself

1. All psychological tests fundamentally depend upon the measurement of _____.
    a. basic mental processes
    b. aptitudes

c.   behavior samples

d.   traits

2. In the final analysis, the worth of a test item or an entire test depends upon_____
_____.

a.   how closely the material covered by the test resembles the behavior that is to be predicted

b.   the norms that are published in the test manual

c.   the standardization procedures

d.   its empirical correspondence with the criterion

3. The major distinction between "diagnosis" and "prediction" centers upon _____.

a.   time factors

b.   whether behavior external to the test is involved

c.   whether a physician is involved

d.   accuracy

4. Standardization in testing basically refers to _____.

a.   a printed test form

b.   the use of trained examiners to evaluate performance

c.   measurement against a proven standard

d.   complete uniformity of procedure

5. A ten-year-old boy takes an intelligence test and gets only 8 out of 40 questions correct. Based on this we can say _____.

a.   that the test was too difficult for him

b.   that he is definitely below average in IQ

c.   that he should be retested

d.   nothing, since we do not know the norms

6. A person scores exactly at the norm on an aptitude test. This means that the person
_____.

a.   achieved an "average" score

b.   had the highest score possible

c.   answered 50% of the questions correctly

d.   showed "ideal" performance

7. The standardization sample is used in test development to _____.

a.   test the test

b.   generate test items

c.   establish the norms

d.   determine test validity

8. Reliability in testing is best defined as _____.
   a. objectivity
   b. exactness
   c. consistency
   d. accuracy

9. The most important consideration regarding any test is its _____.
   a. norms
   b. accuracy
   c. reliability
   d. validity

10. It has been said that persons who score well on a medical aptitude test also do very well in medical school. This would mean that the medical aptitude test is _____.
    a. reliable
    b. valid
    c. qualified
    d. standardized

11. A test is designed to predict success in graduate school. Success in graduate school is therefore the _____.
    a. criterion
    b. validation factor
    c. empirical validity
    d. objective

12. Some controls must be placed on the availability of psychological tests in order to _____.
    a. protect the content from disclosure
    b. ensure that the test is administered by qualified people
    c. prevent test misuse
    d. all of the above

13. Rapport is best defined in the testing situation as _____.
    a. ensuring total objectivity
    b. arousing the examinee's interest and cooperation
    c. making special efforts to motivate those students who do not show normal interest
    d. being especially friendly with the examinees

14. Test anxiety _____.
    a. is always detrimental to test performance
    b. generally causes an examinee to work harder

c. is more of a problem for some examinees than others
d. should be eliminated on good objective tests

15. Most criticisms of psychological tests are directed to _____.
a. intrinsic features of the tests themselves
b. the publishers and developers of tests
c. professional associations concerned with testing
d. misuses of test results by poorly qualified users

Miniprojects/Suggested Homework Activities:

1. Two of the most useful sources of information on psychological tests—available in many libraries—are the *Mental Measurements Yearbook* (MMY) series and *Tests in Print* (TIP). Locate the latest editions of these works and familiarize yourself with them by reading their respective introductions. These sections are only a few pages long and should not take much time to read. However, they are as good an investment of time as possible for students starting to get acquainted with the field of testing. If time allows, look up the entries of one or two tests in each source to become even more familiar with these works.

2. One fringe benefit from the study of psychological testing is, or at least ought to be, an increase in one's test sophistication. Chapter 1 contains a good deal of information which, if followed up, could prove useful in that regard. The activities listed below may be more or less appropriate, depending on your individual circumstances, but either one of them would serve to deepen your understanding of the material in the chapter and might also increase your success as a test-taker.

   (A) If you are prone to experience test anxiety to an extent that is bothersome, find out the resources available in your area, perhaps in the Counseling Center in your school, to help you deal with that problem. First, you may want to assess objectively the extent to which test anxiety is a problem by taking the Test Anxiety Inventory or a similar instrument. Afterwards, if the results warrant it or simply for the sake of the experience, you could go through a test anxiety reduction treatment program, preferably one that addresses the cognitive and emotional aspects of test anxiety.

   (B) If you are planning to enter a graduate or professional school, a worthwhile investment of your time would be to investigate what materials are available in your area to prepare for the appropriate entrance examinations. Test-preparation software packages, such as the one available for the GRE General Test that is mentioned in the text, would be among the most useful. In addition, there is an ample supply of book such as the Barron's series, available in most college bookstores. These guides con helpful information and practice items for every major entrance examination u' universities and professional schools. As you go through the practice items, keep track of the time they take, as well as your scores, and try to gauge "practice effects" by noting any improvements in your speed and accuracy.

3. An excellent and concise guide for locating information about published and unpublished psychological tests is available in the booklet entitled "Finding Information about Psychological Tests." A single copy of this booklet can be obtained, at no cost, by writing to the Science Directorate of the American Psychological Association (APA) at 750 First Street, NE in Washington, DC 20002-4242. The text of this document is also available from the APA's World Wide Web site:

    http://www.apa.org/

    The title of the document—accessed by selecting science information from the APA's home page—is "Frequently Asked Questions (FAQ) on Psychological Tests."

4. A great deal of additional information on tests and testing is available on the Internet. The Buros Institute of Mental Measurements has a web site that is eminently worth exploring, including a Test Review Locator, at:

    http://www.unl.edu/buros/home.html

5. For a brief overview of the advantages of psychological tests over other methods for making decisions about people, see W. Grant Dahlstrom's article "Tests: Small Samples, Large Consequences" in the April 1993 issue of the *American Psychologist* (Vol. 48, pp. 393-399).

6. The most direct way to learn how the use of tests is controlled is to obtain one or more of the catalogs of test publishers and look up the sections dealing with restrictions on sales of their tests, qualifications purchasers must meet, and issues of test security. Some catalogs are more explicit than others in outlining their policies and some—for example, Consulting Psychologists Press, Inc.'s catalog—even contain sections outlining the elements of good testing practice discussed in Chapter 1. Catalogs can be obtained by writing to some of the publishers listed in Appendix B of the textbook, through your professor, or from a local testing center.

ANSWERS TO MULTIPLE CHOICE/TEST YOURSELF ITEMS:

1.	c	4.	d	7.	c	10.	b	13.	b
2.	d	5.	d	8.	c	11.	a	14.	c
3.	a	6.	a	9.	d	12.	d	15.	d

HISTORICAL ANTECEDENTS OF MODERN TESTING

Chapter Outline

Early Interest in Classification and Training of Mentally Retarded Persons

The First Experimental Psychologists

Contributions of Francis Galton

Cattell and the Early "Mental Tests"

Binet and the Rise of Intelligence Tests

Group Testing

Aptitude Testing

Standardized Achievement Tests

Assessment of Personality

Chapter Summary

An overview of the antecedents of psychological testing and of its beginnings offers a useful perspective for understanding present-day developments in the field. The precursors of psychological testing date back at least two milennia to the Chinese empire and the ancient Greeks.

The major historical influences that led to and shaped the development of modern psychological testing, however, can be traced back to the late nineteenth century. These influences consisted of the awakening of interest in the humane treatment and training of mentally retarded persons, as well as the emergence of psychology as an experimental discipline. Francis Galton, in England, and James McKeen Cattell, in the United States, pioneered in the attempt to measure intellectual functions through tests of sensory discrimination and reaction time. However, it was Alfred Binet, in France, who devised the first successful tests of intelligence which centered on tasks that directly assessed functions such as judgment, reasoning, and comprehension.

Further developments in psychological testing came around the time of World War I, when the need to classify a large number of recruits into the armed forces in the United States gave rise to group testing which, among other things, introduced "objective" types of items. The need to differentiate among an individual's performance on various types of abilities, along with the development of factor analysis, led to aptitude testing. In the meantime, standardized achievement tests were also being developed for the purpose of assessing the outcomes of school instruction. Techniques for the assessment of personality or nonintellectual aspects of behavior, including self-report inventories and projective devices, were also developed around the time of World War I but, on the whole, they have lagged behind tests of abilities in terms of their accomplishments.

Since the late 1980s and early 1990s, a great deal of activity has been aimed at the integration of alternative approaches to mental measurement. A prime example of this trend is the recognition that human abilities can be properly assessed at various levels of breadth, depending on the purposes of testing. In addition, there are unifying trends aimed at reintegrating the artificially imposed distinction between affective ("personality") and cognitive ("ability") traits. The results of this activity can be seen in the emergence of comprehensive theoretical models, as well as in test development.

Comprehensive Review

STUDY QUESTIONS:

1. Describe the historical precursors of psychological testing that existed prior to the nineteenth century.

2. Identify three historical events that propelled the development of modern psychological testing in the nineteenth and early twentieth centuries.

3. List the two major ways in which the first experimental psychologists influenced the development of the testing movement.

4. Discuss the contributions of Francis Galton to the development of psychology and testing.

5. Describe the role that James McKeen Cattell played in the history of "mental" testing.

6. Outline the content of the Binet-Simon scales and the procedures used in their development.

7. Identify the major differences between individual and group testing.

8. Discuss how aptitude testing developed and identify the two major types of tests that fall in that category.

9. Discuss the ways in which achievement tests resemble and differ from intelligence and aptitude tests.

10. Describe three major approaches to the assessment of personality.

FILL IN THE BLANKS: Key Terms and Concepts

1. A major legacy of the early psychological labs to the field of psychological testing was an emphasis on rigorous control of experimental conditions; in testing, this feature became known as _ _ _ _ _ _ _ _ _ _ _ _ _ _ _ of procedures.

2. The term _ _ _ _ _ _ _ _ _ _ was used for the first time by Cattell to describe measures of sensory and motor processes.

3. The term _ _ _ _ _ _ _ _ _ _ was used by Binet to express a child's score on his entire test.

4. Tests that are supposed to be administered to only one person at a time are called _ _ _ _ _ _ _ _ _ _ _ _ _ _ _ _.

5. The testing movement underwent tremendous growth after the development of _ _ _ _ _ _ _ _ _ _ made large scale testing programs possible.

6. _ _ _ _ _ _ _ _ _ _ _ _ _ _ _ _ _ tests were developed especially for use in vocational counseling and in the selection and classification of personnel, in order to supplement global intelligence tests.

7. _ _ _ _ _ _ _ _ _ _ _ _ _ _ _ _ batteries are especially suitable for intraindividual comparisons because they provide separate scores on several traits.

8. _ _ _ _ _ _ _ _ _ _ _ _ _ _ _ is a statistical method for studying the interrelatedness among scores obtained by many persons on a variety of different tests.

9. _ _ _ _ _ _ _ _ _ _ _ tests are educational tools that were originally devised to assess the outcomes of school instruction.

10. The term _ _ _ _ _ _ _ _ _ _ _ _ tests refers to measures concerned with nonintellectual aspects of behavior, such as emotional states, motivation, and interests.

11. The term used to describe the use of the questionnaire technique in personality testing is _ _ _ _ – _ _ _ _ _ _ inventory.

12. In the context of personality measurement, a task that simulates everyday-life settings is called a _ _ _ _ _ _ _ _ _ _ _ _ test.

13. The approach to the study of personality that consists of presenting a person with a relatively unstructured task meant to assess characteristic modes of response is known as _.

FILL IN THE BLANKS: Key People

1. _ _ _ _ _ _ _ _ was a French physician who established the use of language as the main criterion of intellectual level.

2. _ _ _ _ _ _ was a French physician who pioneered sense- and muscle-training techniques for mentally retarded persons.

3. _ _ _ _ _ was the originator of the first successful scale of intelligence.

4. The founder of the first major psychology laboratory established in Leipzig, Germany in 1879 was _ _ _ _ _.

5. _ _ _ _ _ _ was an English biologist who contributed to the testing movement through his interest in the study of heredity.

6. _ _ _ _ _ _ _ was an American psychologist whose work merged experimental psychology with the testing movement.

7. _ _ _ _ _ _ _ _ _ was a German psychologist whose pioneering work in testing grew out of his interest in the clinical examination of psychiatric patients.

8. _ _ _ _ _ _ _ _ _ _ was a German psychologist who advanced testing through his use of sentence completion, memory span, and arithmetical tasks in the lab.

9. In the United States, the first translation of the Binet-Simon tests was the one prepared by _ _ _ _ _ _ _ at the Vineland Training School for mentally retarded children.

10. The American psychologist who prepared the most famous revision of the Binet-Simon scales was _ _ _ _ _ _.

11. _ _ _ _ _ _ was the director of a committee formed by psychologists to assist the United States government in the World War I effort.

12. The psychologist who introduced multiple-choice items to testing was ____.

13. _____ was an Englishman who pioneered studies of trait organization through the use of correlational analysis.

14. _____ was the American psychologist whose work spearheaded the development of standardized achievement tests.

ANSWERS TO FILL-IN-THE-BLANKS:

Key Terms and Concepts

1. standardization
2. mental test
3. mental level
4. individual scales (or individual tests)
5. group tests
6. special aptitude (tests)
7. multiple aptitude (batteries)
8. factor analysis
9. achievement (tests)
10. personality (tests)
11. self-report (inventory)
12. situational (test)
13. projective techniques

Key People

1. Esquirol
2. Seguin
3. Binet
4. Wundt
5. Galton
6. Cattell
7. Kraepelin
8. Ebbinghaus
9. Goddard
10. Terman
11. Yerkes
12. Otis
13. Spearman
14. Thorndike

MATCHING: Early Tests   (One letter per number)

_____ 1.   Early procedure for the assessment of intelligence through nonverbal channels.
_____ 2.   Prototype of the personality questionnaire.
_____ 3.   Group test for general routine testing developed during World War I.
_____ 4.   The first test to use the intelligence quotient (IQ) as a score.
_____ 5.   First nonlanguage group scale of intelligence.
_____ 6.   First successful individual intelligence test.

   A.   Stanford-Binet
   B.   Seguin Form Board
   C.   Binet-Simon Scale
   D.   Army Alpha
   E.   Army Beta
   F.   Woodworth Personal Data Sheet

ANSWERS TO MATCHING ITEMS: 1-B   2-F   3-D   4-A   5-E   6-C

Multiple Choice: Test Yourself

1.   Intelligence testing began in the early twentieth century from Seguin's and Binet's work with _____.
   a.   retarded children
   b.   gifted children
   c.   mentally ill individuals
   d.   normal children

2.   The early experimental psychologists in Germany were primarily concerned with___
   _____.
   a.   establishing the uniformities in human behavior
   b.   establishing the range of individual differences in human behavior
   c.   investigating the reasons for individual variability
   d.   studying human behavior in naturalistic settings

3.   Francis Galton believed intelligence could be assessed by _____
   _____.
   a.   evaluating a child's verbal development
   b.   using the method of free association
   c.   measuring sensory discrimination and reaction time
   d.   testing for memory span

4. According to the Binet test, if a child had a mental level of six, his performance
   _____.
   a. was definitely retarded
   b. matched that of the average six-year-old
   c. indicated a readiness for school
   d. showed he was incapable of making judgments based on reason

5. The Binet scale placed most of its emphasis on _____.
   a. reasoning
   b. comprehension
   c. judgments
   d. all of the above

6. The first group tests of intelligence were prepared for _____.
   a. identifying mentally retarded persons for special educational programs
   b. research conducted at the Columbian Exposition of 1893
   c. quickly assessing the intelligence of army draftees
   d. the evaluation of normal school children

7. Compared with the Army Alpha, the Army Beta placed more emphasis on
   _____.
   a. nonlanguage items
   b. verbal items
   c. discrimination items
   d. reading

8. Multiple aptitude test batteries _____.
   a. were among the first group tests developed
   b. are based mostly on numerical reasoning items
   c. were a practical outcome of factor analysis
   d. are not suitable for differential diagnosis

9. The major difference between aptitude and achievement tests is that aptitude tests
   _____.
   a. place more emphasis on performance-type skills
   b. go through more rigorous technical development
   c. depend less on specific content learning
   d. none of the above

10. Which of the following is the best example of an achievement test? _____.
    a. The Stanford-Binet
    b. A final exam in Physics
    c. The Army Alpha

        d.   A sentence completion test

11.   Some persons are placed in a setting in which it would be very easy for them to cheat.
       They do not know that their behavior is being closely observed. This type of test is
       best classified as a _____.
       a.   situational test
       b.   self-report
       c.   projective test
       d.   free association evaluation

12.   The Woodworth Personal Data Sheet was developed to _____.
       a.   identify mental retardation in school children
       b.   summarize an individual's life history
       c.   predict student success in college
       d.   screen military recruits for severe emotional disturbance

Miniprojects/Suggested Homework Activities:

1.   Although many of the terms and concepts essential to psychological testing were listed
      in the comprehensive review, there are other important terms in this chapter that you
      may not know. Many of these words are part of the basic vocabulary of psychology
      and related disciplines. As a vocabulary-building exercise, underline any unfamiliar
      words and look them up in a good, preferably unabridged, dictionary. Here is a
      sample of terms with which you may not, but ought to, be familiar:

      anthropometric
      intraindividual (versus *interindividual*)
      stimulus (singular) and *stimuli* (plural)
      phenomenon (singular) and *phenomena* (plural)
      kinesthetic
      reaction time
      aesthetic
      psychopathology
      homogeneous and *heterogeneous*
      psychometrics

2.   Chapter 2 contains many names of people important in the history of testing; the
      more you know about them, the easier it will be to remember them. A quick way to
      learn more about the people mentioned in this chapter is to look up their names in the
      second edition of the *Encyclopedia of Psychology,* edited by R. J. Corsini (New York:
      Wiley, 1994). A more time-consuming, but highly enjoyable, way to learn about the

pioneers of psychological testing is to read Raymond Fancher's book *The Intelligence Men: Makers of the IQ Controversy* (New York: Norton, 1985), which is available in paperback.

3. Additional insight into the role that psychological testing played in the United States in the early part of the twentieth century can be found in an excellent volume on *Psychological Testing and American Society, 1890-1930*, edited by Michael M. Sokal (New Brunswick, NJ: Rutgers University Press, 1987). The same period is examined by Paul Davis Chapman, from the viewpoint of educational testing in *Schools as Sorters: Lewis M. Terman, Applied Psychology, and the Intelligence Testing Movement, 1890-1930* (New York: New York University Press, 1988).

4. Some worthwhile, and briefer, follow-up readings on the history of testing can be found in the *American Psychologist (AP)*, which is the flagship journal of the American Psychological Association. For a nice bit of historical research on testing in ancient China, see M. L. Bowman's Comment on the subject in the March 1989 issue of the *AP* (Vol. *44*, pp. 576-578). A short review of some of the difficult issues faced by the pioneers of intelligence testing is presented by R. T. von Mayrhauser, in an article entitled "The Mental Testing Community and Validity: A Prehistory", which appeared in the February 1992 issue of the *AP* (Vol. *47*, pp. 244-253).

ANSWERS TO MULTIPLE CHOICE/TEST YOURSELF ITEMS:

1. a
2. a
3. c
4. b
5. d
6. c
7. a
8. c
9. c
10. b
11. a
12. d

PART II Technical and Methodological Principles

∞ 3 ∞

NORMS AND THE MEANING OF TEST SCORES

<u>Chapter Outline</u>

Statistical Concepts

Developmental Norms
      Mental Age
      Grade Equivalents
      Ordinal Scales

Within-Group Norms
      Percentiles
      Standard Scores
      The Deviation IQ
      Interrelationships of Within-Group Scores

Relativity of Norms
      Intertest Comparisons
      The Normative Sample
      National Anchor Norms
      Specific Norms
      Fixed Reference Group
      Item Response Theory

Computers and the Interpretation of Test Scores
      Technical Developments
      Hazards and Guidelines

Domain-Referenced Test Interpretation
      Nature and Uses
      Content Meaning
      Mastery Testing
      Relation to Norm-Referenced Testing

Minimum Qualifications and Cutoff Scores
      Practical Needs and Pitfalls
      Expectancy Tables

Chapter Summary

Raw scores on psychological tests are meaningless and can only be interpreted in terms of a clearly defined and uniform frame of reference. The most commonly used frame of reference for score interpretation consists of norms derived from the performance of representative samples of individuals against which a test taker's own performance can be compared. In order to allow for meaningful use of the information extracted from tests, raw scores typically are converted into derived scores which express test results in ways that permit comparisons of an individual's performance to the standardization sample and also of an individual's performance across various tests.

Statistical methods used to organize and summarize quantitative score data for normative purposes begin by grouping the data into frequency distributions and plotting them graphically in distribution curves that frequently approximate the mathematical model of the normal curve. In addition, score distributions are described in terms of measures of central tendency, such as the mean, and measures of variability, such as the standard deviation.

Developmental regularities, such as chronological age, progression through school grades, and invariant sequences in the unfolding of certain behaviors, allow for the use of developmental level attained as a frame of reference for the interpretation of test scores. Developmental norms, which include mental ages, grade equivalents, and ordinal scales based on developmental stages, are derived by gathering data on the typical performance of individuals who are at various points within a given sequence. Although these norms have popular appeal, they tend to be either qualitative or psychometrically crude and thus do not lend themselves to precise statistical treatment.

On the other hand, within-group norms—which evaluate an individual's performance in terms of the most nearly comparable standardization group—have a uniform and clearly defined quantitative meaning, and can be used in most statistical analyses. The main types of within-group norms are percentiles and standard scores. Percentile scores express an individual's relative position within the standardization group in terms of the percentage of persons whose scores fall below that of the individual. Standard scores express the distance between an individual's score and the group mean in terms of the standard deviation of the distribution of scores. The most basic type of standard scores, which are called "z scores," can be derived linearly, through an equation that uses the mean and the standard deviation of a normative group to set up the new scale. They can also be "normalized," i.e., obtained by matching the cumulative distribution of scores of a normative sample to the percentage of cases at various points in the normal curve. Both types of standard scores can be transformed further into scales that are more convenient, such as T scores or deviation IQs.

The comparability of test scores depends not just on the use of comparable scale units, but also on test content and on the composition of the groups from which norms are derived. Norms can be derived (a) from large samples representative of broadly defined populations (e.g., national norms for elementary school children), (b) from more narrowly defined subgroups (e.g., gifted children), or (c) locally in a particular setting (e.g., a single school)—depending on the purpose of the test. Comparability of scores can also be achieved without the use of a normative sample. This can be done either by scaling a test in terms of a fixed reference group or—with the use of item response theory (IRT) models—by deriving a common scale unit from item data representing a wide range of ability and item difficulty.

The use of computers has had an impact on every aspect of psychological testing, including test construction, administration, scoring, and interpretation. The speed and flexibility that computers bring to data-processing also allows the exploration of new approaches to testing, such as IRT models of sample-free scaling and interactive computer systems. However, computerized testing procedures also have given rise to new concerns regarding the proper evaluation and use of the computer-generated test data.

Domain-referenced test interpretation is an approach that uses a specified content domain, rather than a specified population of persons, as its interpretive frame of reference. This approach, which has been applied primarily in educational settings, requires the delineation of a clearly defined content domain of knowledge or skills to be assessed by the test as well as a determination of what constitutes mastery of that domain. Both of these requirements limit the range of applicability of domain-referenced testing.

Many decisions in everyday life call for the specification and implementation of minimum qualifications. In some cases, safety concerns require the setting of cutoff points in test performance that are, in turn, linked to minimum levels of skills essential to the performance of certain functions. Whenever practical considerations require the use of such cutoffs, the latter should be based on multiple sources of data as well as on empirically established relationships between test scores and criterion performance. Expectancy tables and expectancy charts are two of the methods used to represent the relationship between scores on a test or predictor and the outcome on a criterion. Further discussion of procedures for setting cutoff scores and of decision models for the fair use of tests can be found in Chapter 6 of the textbook.

Comprehensive Review

STUDY QUESTIONS:

1. Define three measures of central tendency and three measures of variability that are used to describe a group of scores.

2. Describe mental age units and grade equivalents and discuss their similarities and their shortcomings.

3. Describe the approach to developmental norms exemplified by ordinal scales and cite two areas of development in which this approach can be applied.

4. Define and compare percentile scores and standard scores in terms of how they are derived and how they are interpreted.

5. Describe the traditional ratio IQ score and contrast it with the deviation IQ.

6. List and discuss the major factors that need to be taken into consideration if test scores are to be compared.

7. Discuss the issues that are pertinent to the selection of a normative sample.

8. Describe two ways in which score comparability can be achieved through nonnormative scales.

9. Discuss two examples of testing innovations that have come about through the use of computers.

10. Contrast and compare domain-referenced testing with norm-referenced testing.

11. Outline the arguments in favor of and against the use of cutoff scores.

12. Describe how test scores can be interpreted in terms of expected criterion performance.

EXERCISES: Review of Basic Statistics and Standard Scores

NOTE: All of the following exercises, as well as those in subsequent chapters, are based on the formulas given in the textbook and use the same notations that the textbook uses.

Table 1 — Results of a Test Taken by 50 Students (N = 50)

70	74	80	86	89	90	60	41	62	51
67	63	65	66	59	66	69	55	72	73
75	80	82	83	94	97	47	54	63	71
66	70	76	80	75	77	78	78	81	57
68	69	71	72	74	74	84	85	89	93

❶ In order to make the data in Table 1 more manageable, set up a grouped frequency distribution through the following steps:

A. List all of the scores in descending order.
B. Determine the range of the distribution by subtracting the lowest score obtained from the highest one and adding 1.

C. Divide the range by 12, which is an arbitrary but appropriate (i.e., between 10 and 20) number of groups to cover the score distribution in Table 1. Round the result to the next whole number which will then be the interval size or i.

D. Build the grouped frequency distribution from the bottom, making sure that the lowest class interval starts with a multiple of the interval size, i, and includes the lowest score obtained. Continue building additional class intervals, all with the same i, until you reach a group that includes the highest obtained score.

E. Tally the number of raw scores that occur within each class interval in the distribution and place the sum of the tallies for each interval in a column labelled "f", for "frequencies", next to the respective intervals. The sum of the f column should equal N, the number of cases.

❷ Draw a frequency polygon to represent the data in the grouped frequency distribution based on Table 1 by following these steps:

A. On quadrille ruled paper, draw a perpendicular axis, or ordinate (usually labelled the "Y" axis) to present all the frequencies in column f from zero to the highest one.

B. Draw a horizontal axis, or abscissa (usually labelled the "X" axis) to present the midpoint or middle score of each interval from the lowest to one above the highest one in the grouped distribution. Note that the length of the Y axis should be approximately 60% of the length of the X axis.

C. Place a point on the graph at the appropriate frequency for each point on the X axis and connect these points with straight lines. The lowest and highest points should be connected with the baseline at the next lowest and highest X values.

❸ Draw a histogram to represent the same data by duplicating the X and Y axes used for the frequency polygon and drawing a bar with the midpoint as its center for each score interval. The height of each bar will be the frequency, on the Y axis, that corresponds to each interval.

❹ Set up a cumulative frequency distribution from the grouped version of the data in Table 1 that you prepared in Exercise 1. In order to do this you will need to:

A. Start a column for cumulative frequencies, labelled "cf." The cf column will consist of the total number of scores up to and including each class interval, starting from the lowest one to the highest one. The cf for the highest interval should equal N.

B. Add a cumulative proportion column, labelled "cp," by dividing each cumulative frequency value by N. Then create a cumulative percentage column, labelled "C%," by multiplying each cp value by 100.

C. Prepare a cumulative percentage distribution graph by creating an X axis listing the upper real limit for each interval, which is the top score in each interval plus .5. The Y axis should list the cumulative percentages, C%, from zero to 100% at intervals of 10. Plot the C% values corresponding to each of the values on the X axis and connect all the points with straight lines.

5. For the following set of raw score data:

52   54   56   58   60   61   61   63   67   68

A. Describe the central tendency by finding the mean (M), median, and mode;
B. Describe the variability by finding the range, standard deviation (SD), and variance; and
C. Express each score in terms of its distance from the mean in standard deviation units by calculating the z score for each raw score.

6. Assume that a large tenth grade class took achievement tests known to be highly reliable and valid in the areas of Geography, Spelling, and Mathematics. The scores on all three of these tests were normally distributed, but the tests differed in the following respects:

	Number of Items	Mean	Standard Deviation
Geography Test	75	60	10
Spelling Test	150	100	20
Math Test	40	25	5

Assume that you are particularly interested in comparing three of the students who took these tests (Alan, Betty, and Carlos) in terms of how they did in relation to each other, in relation to their classmates, and also in terms of designating the one who performed best in all areas. The students' scores are as follows:

	Alan	Betty	Carlos
Geography Test	46	72	60
Spelling Test	110	100	140
Math Test	30	33	37

A. Prepare a table showing the percentage scores for each student on each test. Note, however, that since the percentage scores on each test come from different distributions, they cannot be justifiably averaged across tests or otherwise compared with the percentage scores from the other tests.

B. Prepare a table showing linearly derived z scores for Alan, Betty, and Carlos. Note that although z scores can be averaged, the presence of decimals and negative values will make it more difficult to do so than it would be otherwise.
C. Using the Table of Areas under the Normal Curve in Appendix A of this guide, look up the percentile equivalents for each z score.
D. Convert each of the z scores into T scores (Mean = 50, SD = 10) and make up a table showing them and showing the average T score for each student. The initial goal of obtaining scores that are intra- and interindividually comparable will have been achieved most suitably with this final step.

❼ Convert the z scores you prepared for Exercise 6 B into the types of scores designated below—through linear transformations—by using the following formula:

$$\text{New score} = (\text{z score} \times \text{SD}) + \text{Mean}$$

A. Deviation IQs (M = 100 and SD = 15);
B. College Entrance Examination Board (CEEB) scores (M = 500; SD = 100).

❽ Convert each of the percentile scores you obtained in Exercise 6 C into stanine scores by using the information in Table 2.

Table 2 — Normal Curve Percentages for Use in Stanine Conversion

STANINE	1	2	3	4	5	6	7	8	9
Percentage	4	7	12	17	20	17	12	7	4
Cumulative %	4	11	23	40	60	77	89	96	100

Note: The cumulative percentages have been derived by adding the percentages allocated to each stanine (see Table 3-4 in the textbook), starting with 1 and going from left to right. These are the first nonlinearly derived standard scores you have obtained thus far in these exercises.

❾ Assume that the scores and cumulative percentages given below were taken from a distribution whose shape deviated somewhat from the normal curve. Obtain normalized z scores for each raw score point given by referring to the Table of Areas under the Normal Curve in Appendix A of this guide.

Raw Scores:	60	50	40	30	20	10
Cumulative %:	95%	75%	65%	45%	15%	5%

⑩   Assume that 100 students took a test and that the test scores were normally distributed and had a mean of 20 and a standard deviation of 2.

     <u>A</u>.   What are the z scores for the following raw scores?

         16   18   19   20   21   22   24

     <u>B</u>.   Using the Table of Areas under the Normal Curve in Appendix A of this guide, with the z scores you have just obtained, determine the percentage of the scores that fall between the following raw score ranges:

         18 and 22   19 and 21   16 and 24

ANSWERS TO EXERCISES: Review of Basic Statistics and Standard Scores

❶   <u>A</u>.   Table 3 — Test Results Arranged in Descending Order   (N = 50)

97			72	72	
94			71	71	
93			70	70	
90			69	69	
89	89		68		
86			67		
85			66	66	66
84			65		
83			63	63	
82			62		
81			60		
80	80	80	59		
78	78		57		
77			55		
76			54		
75	75		51		
74	74	74	47		
73			41		

     <u>B</u>.   <u>Range</u> $= 97 - 41 + 1 = 57$

     <u>C</u>.   <u>Interval size</u> $= 57 \div 12 = 4.75$ or   5

❶   D and E.

Table 4 — Grouped Frequency Distribution   (N = 50; i = 5)

X Scores	Tallies	f Frequencies
95–99	I	1
90–94	III	3
85–89	IIII	4
80–84	IHI II	7
75–79	IHI I	6
70–74	IHI IHI	10
65–69	IHI III	8
60–64	IIII	4
55–59	III	3
50–54	II	2
45–49	I	1
40–44	I	1

❷   A, B, and C.

Figure 1 — Frequency Polygon for Test Data

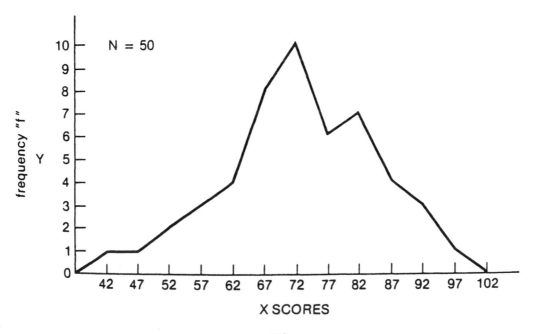

30

❸

Figure 2 — Histogram for Test Data

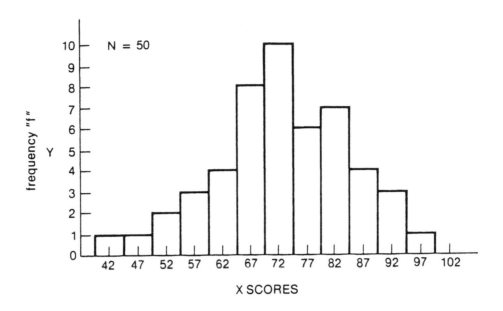

❹   A and B.

Table 5 — Cumulative Frequencies, Proportions, and Percentages

X	f	cf	cp	C%
95–99	1	50	1.00	100
90–94	3	49	.98	98
85–89	4	46	.92	92
80–84	7	42	.84	84
75–79	6	35	.70	70
70–74	10	29	.58	58
65–69	8	19	.38	38
60–64	4	11	.22	22
55–59	3	7	.14	14
50–54	2	4	.08	8
45–49	1	2	.04	4
40–44	1	1	.02	2

● C.

Figure 3 — Cumulative Percentage Distribution

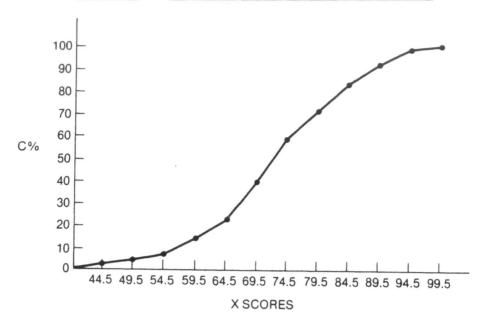

X SCORES

❺ A.   __Mean__ = 60   __Median__ = 60.5   __Mode__ = 61

B.   __Range__ = 17   __SD__ = 4.9   __Variance__ = 24.4

__NOTE:__   All of the variability measures (but none of the measures of central tendency) you have obtained from this exercise coincide exactly with those in the illustration contained in Table 3-2 on p. 53 of the textbook. The reason is, of course, apparent if you examine the data for this exercise and for the one in Table 3-2 of the text. The scores for this exercise were altered only by adding a constant of 20 to each of the scores in Table 3-2. This illustrates an important difference between measures of variability and measures of central tendency.

C.

Raw Scores	z scores
52	− 1.63
54	− 1.22
56	− 0.82
58	− 0.41
60	0.00
61	+0.20
61	+0.20
63	+0.61
67	+1.43
68	+1.63

❻ A. Percentage Scores for Alan, Betty, and Carlos

	Alan	Betty	Carlos
Geography Test	61	96	80
Spelling Test	73	67	93
Math Test	75	83	93

B. Lineraly Derived z Scores for Alan, Betty, and Carlos

	Alan	Betty	Carlos
Geography Test	− 1.4	+1.2	0.0
Spelling Test	+0.5	0.0	+2.0
Math Test	+1.0	+1.6	+2.4

C. Percentile Scores for Alan, Betty, and Carlos

	Alan	Betty	Carlos
Geography Test	8th	88th	50th
Spelling Test	69th	50th	98th
Math Test	84th	95th	99th

D. T Scores for Alan, Betty, and Carlos

	Alan	Betty	Carlos
Geography Test	36	62	50
Spelling Test	55	50	70
Math Test	60	66	74
Average T scores	50	59	65

❼ A. Deviation IQ Scores for Alan, Betty, and Carlos

	Alan	Betty	Carlos
Geography Test	79	118	100
Spelling Test	108	100	130
Math Test	115	124	136

B. <u>CEEB Scores for Alan, Betty, and Carlos</u>

	<u>Alan</u>	<u>Betty</u>	<u>Carlos</u>
Geography Test	360	620	500
Spelling Test	550	500	700
Math Test	600	660	740

NOTE: Although school achievement test scores typically are not reported in terms of deviation IQs or CEEB-type scores, there is no reason, other than custom or convenience, for using certain combinations of means and SDs for standard score transformations. Since these standard scores were all derived linearly, they stand in the same relative positions to one another regardless of the differences in units, a fact that is quite noticeable upon inspection of these results.

<u>Stanines for Alan, Betty, and Carlos</u>

	<u>Alan</u>	<u>Betty</u>	<u>Carlos</u>
Geography Test	2	7	5
Spelling Test	6	5	9
Math Test	7	8	9

<u>Raw Scores</u>	<u>C%</u>	<u>Normalized z Scores</u>
60	95	+1.64
50	75	+0.67
40	65	+0.39
30	45	− 0.13
20	15	− 1.04
10	5	− 1.64

NOTE: These z scores, which were obtained through a nonlinear transformation, could be further transformed into other types of derived scores, as was done in Exercises 7 A and 7 B.

A.

<u>Raw Scores</u>	<u>z Scores</u>
16	− 2.0
18	− 1.0
19	− 0.5
20	0.0
21	+0.5
22	+1.0
24	+2.0

B.   68 percent would fall between 18 and 22;
             38 percent would fall between 19 and 21; and
             95 percent would fall between 16 and 24.

FILL IN THE BLANKS: Key Terms and Concepts

1. When test scores are interpreted in terms of how far along the normal sequence an individual has progressed, the frame of reference is that of _ _ _ _ _ _ _ _ _ _ _ _ _ _ _ _ _.

2. The major types of developmental norms described in the textbook are _ _ _ _ _ _ ages, _ _ _ _ _ equivalents, and _ _ _ _ _ _ scales.

3. A mental age score from a test whose items are grouped into year levels consists of the sum of the _ _ _ _ _ _ _ _, which is the highest age at and below which all tests were passed, and the additional credits earned at higher age levels.

4. _ _ _ _ _ _ _ _ _ _ _ _ _ _ _ _ are a type of developmental norm that is obtained by computing the average raw scores obtained by children in various *grade* levels.

5. The _ _ _ _ _ _ _ _ _ _ _ _ _ _ _ _ _ _ _ Schedules are one example of an ordinal scale which shows the developmental level a child has attained in motor, adaptive, language, and personal-social behavior.

6. _ _ _ _ _ _ _ – _ _ _ _ _ _ norms are a frame of reference for score interpretation based on an evaluation of the individual's performance in terms of the most nearly comparable group.

7. Whereas the 50th percentile corresponds to the _ _ _ _ _ _ _, the 25th and 75th percentiles are known as the first and third _ _ _ _ _ _ _ _ points, respectively.

8. A(n) _ _ _ _ _ _ _ _ _ _ _ _ _ _ chart is a graphic representation of scores that is plotted on paper especially designed to show percentile points spaced in the same way they are in a normal distribution.

9. Comparability of norms can be achieved by using an anchor test to develop equivalency tables for scores on different tests. The _ _ _ _ _ _ _ _ _ _ _ _ _ _ _ _ method, wherein scores on two tests are considered equivalent when they have equal percentiles in a given group, is one way to do this.

10. Until April of 1995, the Scholastic Assessment Test (formerly Scholastic Aptitude Test) used a _ _ _ _ _ _ _ _ _ _ _ _ _ group of 11,000 candidates who took the

test in 1941 to provide comparability and continuity of scores without evaluating performance normatively each year.

11. The approach to test equating known as _ _ _ _ _ _ _ _ _ _ _ _ theory uses a uniform and "sample-free" scale of measurement based on data derived from anchor items or anchor tests representing a wide range of ability and item difficulty.

12. _ _ _ _ _ _ _ _ _ computer interpretations of test results are produced by means of a computer program that associates prepared verbal statements with particular patterns of test responses.

13. _ _ _ _ _ _ _ _ _ _ _ computer systems allow an individual to, in effect, engage in a dialogue with a computer. In the field of assessment, they have been used primarily for educational and career planning.

14. The kind of testing that uses a specified content area as its interpretive frame of reference is called _ _ _ _ _ _ – _ _ _ _ _ _ _ _ _ _ testing. One of the major features of this type of assessment is the procedure of testing for _ _ _ _ _ _ _.

15. _ _ _ _ _ _ _ _ _ _ _ _ _ _ _ _ _ _ and _ _ _ _ _ _ _ _ _ _ _ _ _ _ _ _ _ _ are two of the methods that can be used to express test scores in terms of the probability of different criterion outcomes.

ANSWERS TO FILL-IN-THE-BLANKS: Key Terms and Concepts

1. developmental norms
2. mental (ages) / grade (equivalents) / ordinal (scales)
3. basal age
4. grade equivalents
5. Gesell Developmental (Schedules)
6. within-group (norms)
7. median / quartile
8. normal percentile (chart)
9. equipercentile (method)
10. fixed reference (group)
11. item response (theory) (IRT)
12. narrative (computer interpretations)
13. interactive (computer systems)
14. domain-referenced / mastery
15. expectancy tables / expectancy charts

Multiple Choice: Test Yourself

1. Norms for an educational or psychological test are established by _____.
   a. the opinion of experts in the field covered by the test
   b. testing a representative sample of people
   c. examining the performance of the top and bottom 10% of a population
   d. using item analysis procedures for each item and combining the results for those taking the test

2. The major advantage of converting raw test scores to derived scores is that _____.
   a. derived scores show a test taker's relative standing compared with others taking the test
   b. some derived scores permit the direct comparison of scores made on different tests
   c. derived scores show the test taker's score in relation to perfect performance
   d. a and b

3. The normal curve is _____.
   a. bilaterally symmetrical
   b. more likely to be approximated when small groups are used
   c. one that has a mean value that is less than 10% higher than the median
   d. one that shows only positive standard scores

4. Which of the following is a measure of central tendency? _____.
   a. Standard deviation
   b. Average deviation
   c. Mean
   d. Variance

5. What is the mean for the following set of scores? 10, 8, 7, 2, 1 _____.
   a. 7.0
   b. 28.4
   c. 5.6
   d. 4.0

6. The simplest measure of variability is the _____.
   a. average deviation
   b. mean
   c. variance
   d. range

7.   What is the median for the following set of scores? 64, 53, 50, 57, 61, 56, 58, 59
     _____.
     a.   57
     b.   58
     c.   57.5
     d.   57.25

8.   The mental age units used in revisions of the Stanford-Binet prior to 1986
     _____.
     a.   remain constant with advancing age
     b.   shrink with advancing age
     c.   become larger with advancing age
     d.   bear no real relationship to age

9.   The major problem associated with the use of percentiles is that _____.
     a.   they are difficult to interpret
     b.   they are more difficult to calculate than most other derived scores
     c.   in a normal distribution percentile units are not equal throughout the scale
     d.   they show little relationship to other derived scores

10. Linearly derived standard scores or z scores are based on _____.
     a.   a raw score's distance from the mean in SD units
     b.   derived percentile ranks
     c.   the relation of a raw score to a normalized distribution
     d.   expectancy scores

11. A stanine is an example of a (an) _____.
     a.   ordinal scale value
     b.   standard score
     c.   z score
     d.   norm-equivalent score

12. A person obtains a percentile score of 76. This means that the person_____
     _____.
     a.   answered 76% of the items correctly
     b.   did not score as well as 76% of those taking the test
     c.   has a z score of − 0.76
     d.   outperformed 76% of those who also took the test

13. Systematic variations among the scores obtained by a single individual on different
     tests might be due to_____.
     a.   differences in test content
     b.   differences in scale units among the tests

38

c. the composition of the standardization samples of the different tests

d. any or all of the above

14. The main focus of domain-referenced testing is on _____.

a. score comparisons with a known group

b. what individuals know within a specified field of knowledge

c. how students compare with their classmates

d. expectancies of how a person will do in the future

15. An expectancy table _____.

a. gives the probabilities of different criterion outcomes for persons who obtain each test score

b. shows the relationship between raw scores and expected standard scores

c. is presented in terms of z scores

d. is an important feature in mastery testing

Miniprojects/Suggested Homework Activities:

A thorough understanding of the concepts presented in Chapter 3 is crucial to an effective grasp of most of the material in the rest of the textbook. Therefore, instead of going beyond the subject matter covered in this chapter, your follow-up should consist of deepening your knowledge of what is covered. To this end it may be helpful for you to pinpoint the topics or concepts you may need to study further. For example, a review of your performance in the statistical exercises may reveal a need for you to upgrade your knowledge of some aspects of statistics. If so:

☞ Find a good basic textbook in statistics, preferably one geared to the behavioral and social sciences, such as *Statistical Methods for Psychology*, 4th edition, by D. C. Howell (Belmont, CA: Duxbury Press, 1997). A review of such a text is likely to strengthen both your grasp of this area and your self-confidence.

☞ Take the time to study the nature and characteristics of the normal distribution in as much detail as possible. Review carefully the Table of Areas under the Normal Curve presented in Appendix A of this guide as well as the relationships among various types of scores presented in Figure 3-6 of the text. An expanded version of the figure can be found in Test Service Notebook #148, a pamphlet available from Harcourt Brace Educational Measurement (see Appendix B of the text for the address).

☞ Investigate how distributions can differ from the normal curve in terms of their shape. Review concepts such as the "skewness" and "kurtosis" of distributions and what these terms mean with regard to data.

☞ See the video programs on "Normal Distributions" and "Normal Calculations" which are part of the Corporation for Public Broadcasting series *Against All Odds*. They provide excellent visual illustrations and basic explanations of the normal curve and how it is used in psychometrics. The whole series, narrated by Dr. Teresa Amabile, consists of 26 half-hour programs on elementary statistics, and is well worth watching in its entirety. If it is not available in your college library or media resource center, you might suggest that they consider purchasing it from The Annenberg/CPB Project at 901 E Street NW, Washington, DC 20004-2006 (1-800-LEARNER).

☞ Replicate, or expand on, some of the exercises in this chapter of the guide, especially any that were troublesome for you, with a different set of data. You could, for example, ask an instructor to provide you with the raw scores for an examination from a class with a large enrollment. With this "data bank" you could proceed to calculate measures of central tendency and variability, compute percentiles, z scores, T scores or stanines for each student and draw a frequency polygon or a histogram to represent the performance of the class.

☞ Study Table 3-5 of the textbook and, using the Table of Areas under the Normal Curve, see if you can find the percentage data for the standard deviation values given in Table 3-5, or for different SD values (e.g., 10 or 20), within the IQ intervals listed. This will allow you to practice standard score transformations and will increase your understanding of the impact that the value chosen for the SD has on the meaning of deviation IQs.

ANSWERS TO MULTIPLE CHOICE/TEST YOURSELF ITEMS:

1.	b	6.	d	11.	b
2.	d	7.	c	12.	d
3.	a	8.	b	13.	d
4.	c	9.	c	14.	b
5.	c	10.	a	15.	a

RELIABILITY

Chapter Outline

The Correlation Coefficient
      Meaning of Correlation
      Statistical Significance
      The Reliability Coefficient

Types of Reliability
      Test-Retest Reliability
      Alternate-Form Reliability
      Split-Half Reliability
      Kuder-Richardson Reliability and Coefficient Alpha
      Scorer Reliability
      Overview

Reliability of Speeded Tests

Dependence of Reliability Coefficients on the Sample Tested
      Variability
      Ability Level

Standard Error of Measurement
      Interpretation of Individual Scores
      Interpretation of Score Differences

Reliability Applied to Mastery Testing and Cutoff Scores

Chapter Summary

      Measures of the reliability or consistency of test scores allow us to estimate the proportions of total variance attributable to error variance and to true variance. Reliability is gauged by the degree of relationship between two independently derived sets of scores from the same test. The degree of relationship between two sets of scores can be graphically represented by a scatter diagram and/or expressed numerically by a correlation coefficient which can range from $+1.00$ to -1.00. The most common type of correlation coefficient is the Pearson Product-Moment Correlation Coefficient or Pearson r, which is actually the mean of the cross-products of two sets of standard scores. Although the degree of correlation desirable for reliability coefficients is in the .80s or higher, a correlation coefficient can be statistically significant at a much lower value.

The types of reliability that are applicable for a given test depend on the nature of the sources of error or irrelevant fluctuations that are likely to enter into test scores. Methods of gauging reliability include some that assess a single source of error variance, such as split-half reliability which estimates variance due to content sampling, and some that assess two sources of error variance, such as delayed alternate-form reliability which estimates variance due to time and content sampling. Methods of gauging reliability also vary with regard to whether they utilize a single administration of a single test form or whether they use two administrations of a single test form separated by an interval. Kuder-Richardson reliability and coefficient alpha—both measures of interitem consistency influenced by content sampling and content heterogeneity—are examples of the former. Test-retest reliability, which assesses time sampling error, exemplifies the latter. Yet another method, immediate alternate-form reliability, utilizes contiguous administrations of two test forms and results in an estimate of content sampling error only. In addition, for tests in which scorer differences may be a potential source of error, scorer reliability coefficients can be used to gauge the extent of those differences.

Another issue that needs to be considered in the process of investigating the reliability of tests is the extent to which speed plays a role in determining test scores. If a significant proportion of the total variance of test scores is attributable to speed, single-trial reliability coefficients are not applicable unless procedures used in obtaining them are modified to take time into account.

Correlation coefficients are affected by the variability of the samples in which they are found as well as by the composition of those samples. Therefore, every reliability coefficient should be accompanied by a description of the type of group on which it was obtained to allow for a determination of whether such a coefficient applies to the groups with which a test will be used. In situations wherein the variability of scores is likely to be reduced, such as in criterion-referenced or mastery testing, the procedures used to evaluate reliability need to be suitably modified.

The standard error of measurement is an alternative way of expressing test reliability and can be used to interpret individual scores in terms of the reasonable limits within which they are likely to fluctuate as a function of measurement error. When a comparison of the significance of the differences between scores on different tests is needed, the standard error of the difference is a useful statistic that takes into account the combined errors of measurement of the two tests.

Domain-referenced tests typically are designed to assess the extent to which individuals have mastered certain skills and knowledge after training. Due to this circumstance, the variability of scores among persons is often greatly reduced in this type of testing and the usual methods of assessing reliability are not appropriate. Various techniques have been specifically devised to gauge the reliability of domain-referenced tests.

Comprehensive Review

STUDY QUESTIONS:

1.   Define reliability and relate it to the concept of error of measurement.

2.   Describe the meaning of correlation and of correlation coefficients.

3.   Discuss the notion of statistical significance as it applies to the evaluation of correlation coefficients used as measures of reliability.

4.   Describe the procedures involved in gathering test-retest, alternate-form, split-half, and Kuder-Richardson estimates of reliability.

5.   Describe the procedure involved in estimating scorer reliability and explain how this type of reliability differs from the other types.

6.   Discuss the considerations that are pertinent to the selection of each method of estimating reliability.

7.   Describe the difference between a pure speed test and a pure power test and the impact of the role of speed on the procedures used to gauge the reliability of a test.

8.   Discuss two sample characteristics that can affect the size of a reliability coefficient.

9.   Compare and contrast the standard error of measurement with the reliability coefficient in terms of their derivation and applicability.

10. Explain why the standard error of the difference between two scores is always larger than the standard error of measurement of either one of the scores.

EXERCISES: Statistical Aspects of Reliability

❶   Prepare a scatter diagram for the following set of bivariate data:

Person	Variable X	Variable Y
A	10	3
B	2	7
C	9	1
D	7	5
E	3	8
F	5	5
G	1	7
H	3	7

②   For the bivariate data presented in Exercise 1, calculate the Pearson product-moment correlation coefficient, using the formula given in the textbook.

③   A test of 100 items has a reliability of .88. What would be the estimated reliability if the length of the test were:

        <u>A</u>. doubled;
        <u>B</u>. cut to only 25 items?

④   The following set of data represents the raw scores of students A through F on the odd and even halves of a 40-item multiple choice test from a course in Psychological Testing. Calculate the split-half (odd-even) reliability and use the Spearman-Brown formula to estimate the reliability of the entire test.

RAW SCORES

<u>Student</u>	<u>Odd Half</u>	<u>Even Half</u>	<u>Total Score</u>
A	20	18	38
B	19	17	36
C	19	17	36
D	15	17	32
E	15	16	31
F	13	13	26

⑤   As a follow-up to the previous exercise, calculate the Kuder-Richardson Formula 20 (K-R 20) reliability coefficient for the same 40-item multiple choice test. Use the data that follow, and the K-R 20 formula. You will also need to refer back to the total test scores for the students (given in the last column in the previous item) in order to compute the variance (SD_t^2) term for the K-R 20. After you have calculated the K-R 20 reliability coefficient, compare it to the odd-even coefficient you obtained in the previous item and explain the difference between the two coefficients.

$$\underline{\text{K-R 20 Formula:}}\quad r_{tt} \;=\; \left(\frac{n}{n\,-\,1} \right) \frac{SD_t^2 \,-\, \Sigma pq}{SD_t^2}$$

where n = the number of items in the test
                SD_t = the standard deviation of total test scores
                p = the proportion of students who passed each item
                q = the proportion of students who failed each item

Table 6 — Item Statistics

Item #	p	q	Item #	p	q
1	1.00	0.00	21	0.83	0.17
2	0.50	0.50	22	0.83	0.17
3	1.00	0.00	23	0.50	0.50
4	0.83	0.17	24	1.00	0.00
5	0.83	0.17	25	1.00	0.00
6	1.00	0.00	26	0.67	0.33
7	0.83	0.17	27	0.83	0.17
8	0.83	0.17	28	0.67	0.33
9	0.83	0.17	29	0.83	0.17
10	1.00	0.00	30	0.67	0.33
11	1.00	0.00	31	1.00	0.00
12	1.00	0.00	32	1.00	0.00
13	1.00	0.00	33	0.50	0.50
14	0.83	0.17	34	0.50	0.50
15	0.67	0.33	35	0.83	0.17
16	1.00	0.00	36	1.00	0.00
17	0.67	0.33	37	0.67	0.33
18	0.33	0.67	38	0.67	0.33
19	1.00	0.00	39	1.00	0.00
20	1.00	0.00	40	1.00	0.00

Note: Consult p. 97-99 of the textbook for a more complete explanation of Kuder-Richardson reliability and the K-R 20 Formula.

❻ A test has a standard deviation of 9 and a reliability of .88. What is the standard error (SE) of measurement for the test?

❼ Calculate the standard errors of measurement for each of the following reliability coefficients:

.90   .75   .50   .25

with each of the following standard deviation values:

10   15   20   25

(For a total of 4 x 4 = 16 standard errors of measurement)

8   A student obtains a Verbal IQ (VIQ) of 90 and a Performance IQ (PIQ) of 101 on an intelligence test. The standard errors of measurement are 3 for the VIQ and 4 for the PIQ. Using the Table of Areas under the Normal Curve in Appendix A of this guide, determine the level of significance for the difference between the two IQ scores and explain the meaning of the level of significance you find.

9   Using the Table of Areas Under the Normal Curve (again), determine how far apart a Verbal IQ (VIQ) and a Performance IQ (PIQ) must be in order for the difference between them to be significant at the .01 level, given that the standard errors of measurement are 4 for the VIQs and 6 for the PIQs.

ANSWERS TO EXERCISES: Statistical Aspects of Reliability

1

Figure 4 — Scatter diagram of bivariate data

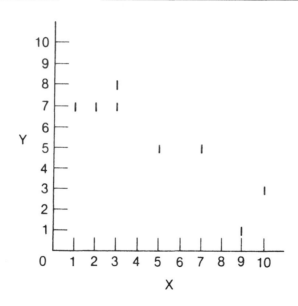

2   Pearson r = − 0.898 or − 0.90

3   **A.**   r = 0.936 or 0.94   **B.**   r = 0.647 or 0.65

4   Odd-even reliability = 0.81
Spearman-Brown estimate for the whole test = 0.895

5   The K-R 20 reliability is 0.75, which is somewhat lower than the odd-even reliability coefficient obtained in the previous exercise. The difference is due to the fact that the K-R 20 takes into account content heterogeneity as well as content sampling error whereas the odd-even reliability only takes into account content sampling error.

❻   Standard error (SE) of measurement = 3.12

❼   Table 7 — Standard Errors of Measurement

Reliability	SD = 10	SD = 15	SD = 20	SD = 25
.90	3.16	4.74	6.32	7.91
.75	5.00	7.50	10.00	12.50
.50	7.07	10.61	14.14	17.68
.25	8.66	12.99	17.32	21.65

Note that the standard errors of measurement for a given reliability coefficient are a constant proportion of the standard deviation values. Study this table and extend it to other reliability coefficients and SD values, if possible. Consider, for example, what the SE of measurement would be if reliability were perfect (+ 1.00) or zero.

❽   Standard error (SE) of the difference between scores = 5

Absolute difference between the scores = 11

$$z = \frac{\text{Difference between scores}}{\text{SE of the difference}} = \frac{11}{5} = 2.2$$

The Table of Areas under the Normal Curve indicates that the probability of obtaining a difference of 11 points between the scores (in either direction) if there were no difference at all between the two "true" scores is less than 3 out of 100 (p is exactly 0.0139 x 2 or 0.0278).

❾   The Table of Areas under the Normal Curve indicates that the z value necessary for a significance level of .01 is 2.58. Since the SE of the difference between VIQs and PIQs is 7.21, the difference between IQs would have to be at least 19 points for it to be significant at that level (7.21 x 2.58 = 18.60 or 19).

FILL IN THE BLANKS: Key Terms and Concepts

1.   The concept of _ _ _ _ _ _ _ _ _ _ _ or consistency of scores underlies the computation of the _ _ _ _ _ of _ _ _ _ _ _ _ _ _ _ _ which, in turn, allows us to predict the range of fluctuation likely to occur in a score as a result of irrelevant or chance factors.

2.   The total variance of test scores is made up of differences in the characteristic being measured by a test or "_ _ _ _" variance and chance factors or _ _ _ _ _ variance.

3. A _____ _____ or _____ diagram is a graphic representation of the relationship between two variables wherein each person's scores on both variables are simultaneously represented by a single tally mark.

4. The probable fluctuation to be expected from sample to sample in the size of correlations, means, and any other group measures can be estimated by determining a _____ of _____ for the value of those statistics.

5. ____ – _____ reliability is found by administering the identical test on two occasions and correlating the scores obtained on each occasion. This method estimates the amount of error variance attributable to ____ sampling.

6. The _____ formula is an alternate method for finding split-half reliability that is based on the variance of differences between scores on the two half-tests as a proportion of total variance.

7. A major difference between the usual split-half methods of investigating reliability and measures of interitem consistency, such as _____ – _____ reliability, is that the former assess error variance due to _____ sampling whereas the latter assess error variance due to _____ _____ as well as to content sampling.

8. Estimates of _____ _____ need to be included in the manual for tests in which the judgment of a person enters into the scoring process.

9. A major problem inherent in two-trial methods of establishing reliability, such as test-retest and alternate forms, is that the correlation between the two trials may be spuriously high due to _____ or _____.

10. Sorting out the sources of error variance in test scores is the essence of a theory of reliability that is known as _____ theory.

11. In a pure power test the proportion of total test variance attributable to individual differences in speed would be _____, whereas in a pure speed test that proportion would be _._.

12. The standard error of measurement (SEM) and the reliability coefficient are alternative ways of expressing test reliability. The SEM is used in interpreting _____ _____ whereas the reliability coefficient serves in comparing _____ _____ to one another.

13. Measures of correlation, such as reliability coefficients, are affected by the range of individual differences or_____ in the groups used to calculate them.

48

The main effect of a restriction in the range of one or both of the correlated variables is that the _ _ _ _ _ _ _ _ _ _ _ between them will be lowered.

ANSWERS TO FILL-IN-THE-BLANKS: Key Terms and Concepts

1. reliability / error (of) measurement
2. "true" (variance) / error (variance)
3. bivariate distribution (or) scatter (diagram)
4. level (of) significance
5. test-retest (reliability) / time (sampling)
6. Rulon (formula)
7. Kuder-Richardson (reliability) / content (sampling) / content heterogeneity
8. scorer reliability
9. recall (or) practice
10. generalizability (theory)
11. zero / 1.00
12. individual scores / different tests
13. variability / correlation

TRUE/FALSE and WHY?

1. A correlation coefficient of $+0.30$ indicates a stronger relationship between the correlated variables than a correlation coefficient of -0.67. (T/F) Why? _____

   _____

2. The .01 and the .05 levels of significance traditionally have been applied in most psychological research because they indicate 99% and 95% levels of confidence, respectively, that the data support the hypothesis being tested. (T/F) Why? _____

   _____

3. When retest reliability and/or delayed alternate-form reliability are reported it is desirable to give some indication of relevant intervening experiences that might have occurred between the two administrations of the test. (T/F) Why? _____

   _____

4. The technique of retesting with the identical test is appropriate for finding the reliability coefficient of most psychological tests. (T/F) Why? _____

   _____

5. All other things being equal, the longer a test is, the more reliable it will be in terms of content sampling. (T/F) Why? _____

   _____

6. If the criterion one is trying to predict with a test is highly heterogeneous, the content heterogeneity of test items is not necessarily a source of error variance. (T/F) Why?

    _____

    _____

7. Most aptitude and intelligence tests, whether speeded or not, are designed to prevent the achievement of perfect scores. (T/F) Why? _____

    _____

8. If the reliability coefficient reported in a test manual was calculated for a group ranging across all high school years, it can be safely assumed that the reliability would be at least as high if recomputed within a single year level. (T/F) Why? _____

    _____

ANSWERS TO TRUE/FALSE:

1.	False	5.	True
2.	True	6.	True
3.	True	7.	True
4.	False	8.	False

Multiple Choice: Test Yourself

1. The best definition of reliability is _____.
    a. consistency
    b. exactness of measurement
    c. correlational coefficient
    d. validity of measurement

2. A correlation of −1.24 means _____.
    a. an inverse relationship between two variables
    b. a direct negative correlation
    c. a moderate negative correlation
    d. an error has been made

3. A correlation of +0.32 is found to be significant at the .01 level. This means that

    _____.
    a. the correlation is definitely real
    b. the correlation is significant at the 99% level
    c. there is a 1% chance or less that the true r is zero
    d. the minimum real value for r is greater than zero

4. The most basic method of determining reliability involves the administration of a test on more than one occasion and is known as _____ .
   a. coefficient alpha
   b. test-retest reliability
   c. Kuder-Richardson 21
   d. the Rulon method

5. If a test shows high split-half reliability, it probably means that _____ _____ .
   a. the test is valid
   b. the correlation is negative
   c. variation due to content sampling is not a large problem
   d. the proportion of error variance to true variance is high

6. The time interval between the first and second administrations for test-retest reliability should be _____ .
   a. one hour or less
   b. between one hour and two days
   c. reported along with the obtained coefficient
   d. determined by the validity coefficient

7. When reliability is determined by the delayed alternate-form method, error variance is contributed by each of the following except _____ .
   a. test takers' differences in what is being measured
   b. content sampling
   c. time between form 1 and form 2
   d. differences in the test takers' emotional state

8. The Spearman-Brown formula is used to estimate changes in the reliability of a test when _____ .
   a. more persons are added to or taken from the sample
   b. alternate forms are used to determine reliability
   c. the test has undergone revision
   d. the length of the test is varied

9. A test with 30 items and a reliability of .60 is lengthened to 60 items. What is its expected reliability? _____ .
   a. 0.75
   b. − 0.75
   c. 0.69
   d. 0.84

10. The coefficient alpha is used to determine the interitem consistency of tests with items
_____.
   a.   that are extremely heterogeneous
   b.   of varying levels of difficulty
   c.   that can receive different numerical scores
   d.   that are scored simply as right or wrong, pass or fail

11. A test has a reliability coefficient of .91. This means that approximately
_____.
   a.   9% of the variance is real
   b.   83% of the variance is real
   c.   91% of the variance is true
   d.   91% of the questions were answered correctly

12. The reliability for a speeded test _____.
   a.   can be calculated in the same way as for an unspeeded test
   b.   will be lower than for an unspeeded test
   c.   is found by the split-half method
   d.   will be spuriously high if found by the usual single-trial methods

13. A test writer wishes to ensure that his test will show the highest reliability possible. He should _____.
   a.   increase the number of items on the test
   b.   try to maintain item homogeneity
   c.   administer the test to a very heterogeneous standardization sample
   d.   all of the above will increase reliability

14. A test has a standard deviation of 5 and a reliability of .91. What is the standard error of measurement? _____.
   a.   15.0
   b.   1.5
   c.   2.5
   d.   6.0

15. The standard error of measurement for Test I is 2.5. The standard error of measurement for Test II is 3.1. The standard error of the difference between the two tests will be _____.
   a.   less than 3.1
   b.   between 2.5 and 3.1
   c.   less than 2.5
   d.   greater than 3.1

Miniprojects/Suggested Homework Activities:

1. As was the case in Chapter 3, the present chapter presupposes familiarity with the basic statistical techniques that underlie reliability. Once again, a review of pertinent areas in a basic statistics textbook is *highly recommended*. Use your performance in the statistical exercises for this chapter to find the areas in which you need to expand your knowledge. In particular, the notion of correlation and the specific techniques used to measure it, such as the Pearson r, should be thoroughly understood in order to achieve a good grasp of the material on reliability, as well as validity, and related topics. The concept of statistical significance—part of the larger topics of probability and statistical estimation using the normal curve as the underlying distribution—should be well understood for a meaningful grasp of the material on "standard errors" in this and later chapters.

2. Locate a table of the critical values of the Pearson r (discussed on pp. 89-90 of the textbook) in a statistics textbook. Study the table and notice the impact that sample size and the different levels of significance have on the critical values listed in the table. Try to explain the meaning of the table to someone else in your own words or write a short essay describing the table.

3. Although the traditional methods of inferential statistics are still widely used, the case against relying principally on these methods in psychological research has been building up for many years. Analyses of the problems with tests of statistical significance now abound in the psychological literature. For examples of such critiques, and information on alternative methods of data analysis, see the following articles:

    ☞   Falk, R., & Greenbaum, C.W. (1995). Significance tests die hard: The amazing persistence of a probabilistic misconception. *Theory and Psychology, 5*, 75-98.

    ☞   Schmidt, F. L. (1996). Statistical significance testing and cumulative knowledge in psychology: Implications for training of researchers. *Psychological Methods, 1*, 115-129.

ANSWERS TO MULTIPLE CHOICE/TEST YOURSELF ITEMS:

1.	a	4.	b	7.	a	10.	c	13.	d
2.	d	5.	c	8.	d	11.	c	14.	b
3.	c	6.	c	9.	a	12.	d	15.	d

5

VALIDITY: BASIC CONCEPTS

Chapter Outline

Evolving Concepts of Test Validity

Content-Description Procedures
  Nature
  Specific Procedures
  Applications
  Face Validity

Criterion-Prediction Procedures
  Concurrent and Predictive Validation
  Criterion Contamination
  Criterion Measures
  Validity Generalization
  Meta-Analysis

Construct-Identification Procedures
  Developmental Changes
  Correlations with Other Tests
  Factor Analysis
  Internal Consistency
  Convergent and Discriminant Validation
  Experimental Interventions
  Structural Equation Modeling
  Contributions from Cognitive Psychology

Overview and Integration
  Comparison of Validation Procedures
  Inclusiveness of Construct Validation
  Validation in the Test Construction Process
  Individual and Social Consequences of Testing

Chapter Summary

The process of validating a test consists of ascertaining what the test actually measures, and how well it does so, through both logical and empirical methods that illuminate the relationship between performance on the test and independently observable facts about the behavior in question. The validity of a test is not established in the abstract; rather, it must be established with reference to the particular use for which the test is being considered. The specific techniques used in validating a test are numerous and as diverse as the various applications of testing. Nevertheless, from a conceptual perspective, test validation procedures can be grouped into three major types: content-description procedures, criterion-prediction procedures, and the all-inclusive category of construct-identification procedures.

Content-description procedures are most commonly applied in educational and occupational testing. They involve a determination of the adequacy of coverage of the relevant behavior domain by means of a systematic examination of test content. Content validity is built into a test through selection of items that sample the specified domain of skills and knowledge to be tested in an appropriate and representative fashion. Content validity differs from "face validity" in that the former is established through objective and empirical procedures whereas the latter refers to what the test superficially appears to measure.

Criterion-prediction procedures are relevant whenever a test is used to forecast an individual's performance in specified activities. A major distinction among criterion-prediction procedures concerns the temporal aspects of the relationship between the test and the criterion. Concurrent validation takes place when criterion information is available at the time of testing or when the purpose of testing is the diagnosis of existing status. Predictive validation procedures, on the other hand, involve a time interval between the gathering of test and criterion data or pertain to the prediction of a future outcome from test data. The criteria used in test validation can encompass various indices of performance in educational, vocational, or employment settings, membership in contrasted groups, including psychiatric diagnostic categories, ratings developed for the purpose of defining a criterion, and correlations with available tests. Regardless of their source, criterion measures must be gathered independently and guarded against contamination which could take place if test scores were to influence standing on the criterion. Moreover, the analysis of criterion measures themselves—in terms of their adequacy as indices of various aspects of job performance—has recently become the focus of attention. The application of meta-analytic procedures to investigate validity generalization across settings and occupations has also been on the rise since the early 1980s and has proved to be of value in integrating findings from many different studies.

Construct-identification is a complex and comprehensive process that involves the accumulation of diverse data which shed light on the extent to which a test measures a theoretical construct or trait. In this sense, construct validity encompasses the previous categories of test validation procedures as well as all of the uses and interpretations of tests which expand, enhance or corroborate the meaning of test scores. Data that contribute to construct validation range from the internal consistency of the test itself to the relationship between test performance and a wide network of variables external to the test. Such variables may include: age differentiation, experimental effects, empirically derived factors, and other tests with which the one in question should or should not correlate. The techniques of structural equation modeling and path analysis also can be used to investigate the relationships between constructs, including possible avenues of reciprocal influence among them. Cognitive psychologists have expanded the range of construct validation techniques further by exploring cognitive constructs themselves through a detailed breakdown, analysis, and manipulation of the information-processing components and knowledge stores necessary to perform the tasks presented by test items.

Regardless of the preferred terminology adopted to describe various validation procedures, it is clear that the use of constructs of appropriate breadth is more effective than the use of isolated criterion measures or test scores. The investigation of causal relations among constructs can contribute mightily to the understanding of how and why tests work.

As our recognition of the scope of construct validity has expanded, it has been argued that the term validity should be reserved for construct validity alone. If this were done, the concepts presently subsumed under content validity might be labeled "content relevance" and "content coverage" instead. Predictive and concurrent criterion validity could be viewed, respectively, as the predictive and diagnostic utility of a test. Some experts have also recommended that the consequences of testing for individuals and for society be included in the concept of validity. Although such considerations are clearly of utmost importance, they more properly belong in the realm of ethics and social policy than in the technical areas of statistics and empirical methodology.

Comprehensive Review

STUDY QUESTIONS:

1. Describe how the conceptualization of validity has evolved from the earliest uses of tests through the current historical period.

2. Define content validation and explain the specific procedures that are used to determine the content validity of a test.

3. Describe when content validation is an appropriate technique for evaluating tests and explain why this is so.

4. Define face validity and contrast it with other types of validity.

5. Define and compare concurrent and predictive validation.

6. Define criterion contamination and explain its effects on validation studies.

7. List and describe several types of criteria commonly used in concurrent and predictive validation.

8. Discuss the notions of validity generalization and situational specificity as they are currently understood.

9. Explain how meta-analysis can be applied in the fields of occupational selection and classification research.

10. Define construct validity and describe three methods whereby it can be studied.

11. Describe the multitrait-multimethod matrix design and how the concepts of convergent and discriminant validation fit into that method.

12. Discuss structural equation modeling, from the point of view of its origins and its potential contributions to the understanding of constructs.

13. Discuss the contributions of cognitive psychology to the area of construct validation.

14. Contrast the psychometric and cognitive approaches in terms of their contributions to the understanding of psychological constructs.

15. Describe the relationship between content-description, criterion-prediction, and construct-identification procedures in the test construction process.

16. Discuss the role that the individual and social consequences of testing should play in validity, according to Messick.

FILL IN THE BLANKS: Key Terms and Concepts

1. In psychological testing, the concept of _ _ _ _ _ _ _ _ refers to a determination of what the test measures and how well it does so.

2. The type of validation procedures that are concerned with whether a test covers a representative sample of the knowledge domain to be measured are _ _ _ _ _ _ _ – _ _ _ _ _ _ _ _ _ _ _ procedures.

3. _ _ _ _ _ _ _ validity is built into a test from the outset through the choice of appropriate items. For educational tests, the items are designed to meet the _ _ _ _ _ _ _ _ _ _ _ _ _ _ _ _ drawn-up by subject matter experts.

4. _ _ _ _ validity pertains to whether a test looks valid to the people who take it and is not a type of validity in the technical sense.

5. Concurrent and predictive validation are two aspects of _ _ _ _ _ _ _ _ validation that differ in terms of the time relation between criterion and test. In addition, a distinction between these two aspects of validation—based on their objectives—is that _ _ _ _ _ _ _ _ _ _ validation is relevant to tests used to diagnose existing status whereas in _ _ _ _ _ _ _ _ _ validation interest is centered on a future outcome.

6. When a person who is involved in the assignment of criterion ratings knows the examinees' test scores, the criterion has undergone _ _ _ _ _ _ _ _ _ _ _ _ _ _.

7. Whereas the most common criteria used in validating intelligence tests are indices of _ _ _ _ _ _ _ _ _ _ _ _ _ _ _ _ _ _, special aptitude tests are most frequently validated with criteria based on performance in specialized _ _ _ _ _ _ _ _ or actual _ _ _ performance.

8. The many practical reasons why predictive validation utilizes_ _ _ _ _ _ _ _ _ _ _ _ _ rather than ultimate criteria, include the possible unavailability and multidetermined nature of the latter.

9. Validation by the method of _ _ _ _ _ _ _ _ _ _ _ _ _ _ _ involves a composite criterion that reflects the cumulative and uncontrolled selective factors operating in daily life that bring about survival in, versus elimination from, a certain group.

10. One criterion that may be used in validating certain personality tests, provided it is based on prolonged observation and detailed case history data rather than on a cursory interview or examination, is _ _ _ _ _ _ _ _ _ _ _ _ _ _ _ _ _ _.

11. _ _ _ _ _ _ _ _ can be used as the core of the criterion measure themselves or they can also be used as a subsidiary technique to derive criterion data on, for example, academic achievement and job success.

12. Since the 1980s, attention has been focused on _ _ _ _ _ _ _ _ _ _ _ _ _ _ _ _ _ _ _, a previously neglected aspect of test development research aimed at identifying the major constructs relevant to the performance of a given job.

13. The work of Schmidt, Hunter, and their coworkers in the realm of industrial validation studies suggests that, as far as certain aptitude tests are concerned, _ can occur far more widely across occupations than previously recognized.

14. One of the advantages of meta-analyses is that they permit the computation of the estimated magnitude of findings or _ _ _ _ _ _ _ _ _ _ _.

15. The _ _ _ _ _ _ _ _ _ validity of a test is the extent to which the test can be

shown to measure a certain trait.

16. The _ _ _ _ _ _ _ _ _ validity of a test is essentially the correlation of the test with whatever is common to a group of tests or other indices of behavior that have been subjected to _ _ _ _ _ _ analysis.

17. When a test is validated by the method of _ _ _ _ _ _ _ _ _ _ _ _ _ _ _ _ _, the criterion is the total score on the test itself.

18. The process whereby construct validity is demonstrated by a test's high correlation with variables with which it should correlate is called _ _ _ _ _ _ _ _ _ _ validation. On the other hand, a demonstration that a test does not correlate significantly with variables from which it should differ is called _ _ _ _ _ _ _ _ _ _ _ _ _ validation.

19. The work of cognitive psychologist Susan Embretson has expanded the concept of construct validation by separating two of the aspects it encompasses. The first aspect, _ _ _ _ _ _ _ _ _ _ _ _ _ _ is the same as traditional construct-related validation in that it is concerned with the relations between test performance and a network of other variables. The second aspect, or _ _ _ _ _ _ _ _ _ _ _ _ _ _ _ _ _ _ _, on the other hand, is concerned with identifying the specific information-processing components and knowledge required to perform test tasks.

20. Messick is one of the main exponents of the notion that the concept of validity should be broadened to include the _ _ _ _ _ _ _ _ _ _ _ _ of testing on individuals and on society.

ANSWERS TO FILL-IN-THE-BLANKS: Key Terms and Concepts

1.   validity
2.   content-description (procedures)
3.   content (validity) / test specifications
4.   face (validity)
5.   criterion (validation) / concurrent (validation) / predictive (validation)
6.   (criterion) contamination
7.   academic achievement / (specialized) training / job (performance)
8.   intermediate (criteria)
9.   contrasted groups
10. psychiatric diagnosis
11. ratings
12. criterion analysis
13. validity generalization
14. effect sizes
15. construct (validity)

16. factorial (validity) / factor (analysis)
17. internal consistency
18. convergent (validation) / discriminant (validation)
19. nomothetic span / construct representation
20. consequences

TRUE/FALSE and WHY?

1. In general, the names of tests are quite helpful in providing meaningful clues to the areas of behavior that tests cover. (T/F) Why? _____
   _____

2. The task of validating a test is complete once the test has been shown to have high validity. (T/F) Why? _____
   _____

3. Content validation is an appropriate technique for educational and occupational achievement tests but not for aptitude or personality tests. (T/F) Why? _____
   _____
   _____

4. The correlation between a new test and a previously available one may be used as evidence of criterion validity only when the former is a shorter or simpler form of the latter. (T/F) Why? _____
   _____

5. Since the mid-1970s, the situational specificity of job requirements has been regarded as a more serious limitation in the use of selection tests than was previously thought. (T/F) Why? _____
   _____

6. The major advantage of using age differentiation as a criterion of validity is the fact that developmental changes can be assumed to be universal. (T/F) Why? _____
   _____
   _____

7. In validation studies, when correlations between a new test and similar earlier tests are obtained, it is desirable for those correlations to the highest possible. (T/F) Why?
   _____
   _____

8. The procedures known as structural equation modeling are designed to test for hypothesized causal relations among variables. (T/F) Why? _____

9. The process of validating a test should normally be linked to the last stages of test development. (T/F) Why? _____

_____

10. As far as applied research and practice are concerned, the relationship between the psychometric and cognitive approaches to construct validation can be characterized as complementary. (T/F) Why? _____

_____

_____

ANSWERS TO TRUE/FALSE:

1.	False	3.	True	5.	False	7.	False	9.	False
2.	False	4.	True	6.	False	8.	True	10.	True

Multiple Choice: Test Yourself

1. By definition, validity deals most directly with _____

_____.

   a. what a test measures
   b. criterion reliability
   c. the economic utility of a test
   d. the accuracy of test scores

2. Which of the following activities would be especially suitable for investigating the content validity of an achievement test? _____.
   a. Reading the manual
   b. Looking up the test in the Mental Measurements Yearbook
   c. Studying the test items
   d. Looking at the norms

3. The test specifications drawn up for the purpose of preparing an achievement test should _____.
   a. list all the content areas to be included
   b. reflect the importance of each topic
   c. indicate the important instructional objectives
   d. all of the above

4. Content validation is most appropriate for _____.
   a. aptitude tests
   b. achievement tests
   c. personality tests
   d. all of the above

5. Face validity is especially important when testing _____.
   a. children
   b. adults
   c. for aptitude
   d. to assess content validity

6. Criterion validation procedures include _____.
   a. content validation
   b. concurrent, predictive, and construct validation
   c. construct validation
   d. predictive and concurrent validation

7. Test A has been in use for many years. It is highly respected as a test of intelligence. Test B is a new intelligence test which is much shorter and easier to administer than Test A. The use of Test A to validate Test B would constitute _____ validation.
   a. content
   b. concurrent
   c. predictive
   d. discriminant

8. Criterion contamination occurs when _____.
   a. a test is lacking in construct validity
   b. the criterion measure is found to be invalid
   c. knowledge of test scores influences decision-making
   d. errors are made in predicting criterion performance

9. Academic achievement is most often used to validate _____.
   a. intelligence tests
   b. personality tests
   c. interest tests
   d. comprehensive testing programs

10. The ultimate criterion for most tests would be _____.
    a. academic achievement
    b. personality as assessed by other tests
    c. actual performance in real life or on the job
    d. convergent validation with moderator tests

11. A musical aptitude test is given, at the same time, to a number of music majors and to a group of college students in other majors. This method of validating the musical aptitude test is known as _____.
   a. concurrent validation
   b. contrasted groups method
   c. both of the above
   d. neither a nor b

12. Analyses of developmental changes, age differentiation, factor analysis, and internal consistency data are all especially important to _____ validity.
   a. predictive
   b. construct
   c. synthetic
   d. content

13. A new reading test is found to correlate very highly with an intelligence test, but near zero with a personality test. This information is important for _____.
   a. convergent and discriminant validation
   b. predictive validity
   c. establishing normative standards
   d. internal consistency analysis

14. Correlating each item on a test with overall test performance is an example of_____
   _____.
   a. factorial validity
   b. content validation
   c. internal consistency validation
   d. factor analysis

15. If two or more traits are measured by two or more different techniques, all of which claim to measure the traits, validity is established through _____.
   a. the predictive approach
   b. the factorial approach
   c. the multitrait-multimethod approach
   d. none of the above

16. A multitrait-multimethod matrix design would contain all of the following except
   _____.
   a. reliability coefficients
   b. factorial validities
   c. convergent validities
   d. discriminant validities

17. Protocol analysis is a widely used procedure for cognitive task decomposition wherein individuals _____.
    a. solve a problem within certain specified time limits
    b. are able to inspect their own responses to previously taken tests
    c. can experiment with novel problem-solving approaches
    d. think aloud as they solve a problem

18. _____ validity has come to be recognized as the fundamental and all-encompassing validity concept.
    a. construct
    b. criterion
    c. content
    d. face

Miniprojects/Suggested Homework Activities:

1. One of the most enlightening activities you could undertake in order to gain a better understanding of content validation is to prepare a short achievement test covering a specific segment of this course, such as the section on Statistical Concepts in Chapter 3, for example. To guide you in this activity, use a short book by Norman Gronlund entitled *Constructing Achievement Tests*, 3rd edition (Englewood Cliffs, N.J.: Prentice Hall, 1982) or any other similar publication (several are cited in Chapter 17 of the textbook). Construct items of several types—e.g., multiple choice, matching, true/false—on each of several topics. After you have completed writing your test, give it to one or more of your classmates and then score it and discuss it with them.

2. Criterion-prediction is particularly relevant to tests, such as the SAT and GRE, used for admission into colleges and graduate schools. To investigate this concept further, read the sections on Tests for the College Level and Graduate School Admission, on pp. 485-487 of the textbook, for information on validity data available about those tests. The most recent information on the SATs and GREs is available from the College Entrance Examination Board and the Graduate Record Examinations Board respectively (their addresses are in Appendix B of the textbook).

3. The Strong Interest Inventory (SII) is an example of a test in the area of personality which, because of its longevity and widespread use, has been thoroughly investigated in terms of concurrent and predictive, as well as contruct, validity. A review of the 1994 *Applications and Technical Guide* for the SII (prepared by L. W. Harmon, J. C. Hansen, F. H. Borgen, and A. L. Hammer and published by Consulting Psychologists Press of Palo Alto, California) should provide you with a clearer understanding of several validation techniques, including the method of contrasted groups, internal

consistency, and convergent and discriminant validation, among others. If you are able to take this test, perhaps at the Counseling Center in your school, you should do so before reading the guide. The process of reviewing the SII materials will become more meaningful and relevant if you can apply what you learn to your own scores.

4. Samuel Messick has had a great deal of influence in the conceptualization of validity. Several of his publications are cited in Chapters 5 and 6, and elsewhere in the textbook. For a brief introduction to Messick's recent thinking on the subject, see his article on "Validity in psychological assessment: Validation of inferences from persons' responses and performances as scientific inquiry into score meaning," in the September 1995 issue of *American Psychologist* (*50*, 741-749).

5. Additional information on the technique of structural equation modeling is available in the following basic references:

   ☛ Baldwin, B. (1989). A primer in the use and interpretation of structural equation models. *Measurement and Evaluation in Counseling and Development, 22,* 100-112.

   ☛ Francis, D. J. (1988). An introduction to structural equation models. *Journal of Clinical and Experimental Neuropsychology, 10,* 623-639.

   ☛ Martin, J. A. (1987). Structural equation modeling: A guide for the perplexed. *Child Development, 58,* 33-37.

ANSWERS TO MULTIPLE CHOICE/TEST YOURSELF ITEMS:

1.	a	7.	b	13.	a
2.	c	8.	c	14.	c
3.	d	9.	a	15.	c
4.	b	10.	c	16.	b
5.	b	11.	c	17.	d
6.	d	12.	b	18.	a

∞ 6 ∞

VALIDITY: MEASUREMENT AND INTERPRETATION

Chapter Outline

Chapter Summary

The use of psychological tests requires a consideration of validity in two different stages. The first consists of ascertaining, from test manuals and published data, whether the construct or trait that a test seems to be measuring is compatible with the purposes for which the test will be used. The second stage consists of determining the validity of the test against specific local criteria. The quantitative techniques for expressing and interpreting validity discussed in this chapter pertain to both stages but are especially relevant for the latter.

The relationship between test scores and criteria can be expressed in terms of validity coefficients, bivariate distributions, expectancy tables, or expectancy charts. The kind of correlation coefficient used to express the relationship between test scores and criterion measures depends on how the data are expressed. The Pearson r, which is one of the most frequently used coefficients of correlation, for example, assumes that both the test and the criterion are continuous variables. In addition, the Pearson r assumes that the relationship between the correlated variables is linear and uniform throughout the range.

Validity coefficients can vary in magnitude depending on the nature and heterogeneity of the group on which they are found, but they should be high enough to be statistically significant at least at the .05 or .01 levels. The accuracy of prediction of a test with a given validity can also be interpreted through the standard error of estimate, which shows the margin of error to be expected in a predicted criterion score as a result of the imperfect validity of the test.

Decision theory can be useful in evaluating the contribution of a test of known validity to the decision-making process. Essentially, decision theory uses quantitative information about the context in which decisions are made—such as base rates and selection ratios—along with validity measures to project the gains in accuracy and productivity that can be realized by using a test. In addition, to the extent that the value of expected outcomes can be quantified—e.g., in terms of dollars—decision theory can be used to calculate the expected utilities of various outcomes. If more parameters are taken into account, more complex decision strategies can be instituted to increase the effectiveness of a test. Examples of strategies include sequential decision-making and the use of treatments adapted to individual characteristics, such as alternative training procedures.

Information from several tests can be combined in a test battery to predict a single criterion. The two main strategies for combining test data are multiple regression equations and profile analysis in terms of cutoff scores. Multiple regression equations are derived from the correlation of each test in the battery with the criterion and with each of the other tests; they aim to predict criterion standing by weighting the score of each test in direct proportion to its validity and to the uniqueness of its contribution to the battery. The cutoff scores strategy, on the other hand, simply determines the minimum score level needed on each test for a prediction of acceptable performance on the criterion; only those people who score above the cutoff on all tests are selected. Which of the two strategies to use, or whether to combine the strategies, depends on the type of relations found between tests and criteria and on the question of critical skills and compensatory qualifications.

Not all of the decisions made on the basis of tests are as simple as whether to accept or reject an individual. In placement decisions, for example, individuals are not rejected but assigned to appropriate "treatments" on the basis of a single score. Classification decisions are even more complex—but also hold greater potential benefits. They involve the assignment of individuals to "treatments" based on multiple predictors whose validities are determined separately against more than one criterion. The aim of occupational or educational classification decisions is to maximize the utilization of talent by an a priori, battery-based determination of the best match between individuals' abilities and the requirements of the fields to which they are assigned.

In the past two to three decades there has been a great deal of concern about the possibility that test scores may have a different predictive meaning for people of various subgroups, especially ethnic minorities in the United States. This concern has prompted a good deal of research on whether tests show a bias, or systematic error, in prediction when applied to African-Americans in particular. The main questions in this research have been whether tests have differential validities (slope bias) for different groups and whether test scores overpredict or underpredict criterion performance for various groups (intercept bias). Comprehensive surveys done to date have not supported the hypothesis that ability tests are less valid for Blacks than for Whites and have shown no significant tendencies for tests to underpredict the criterion scores of Blacks either. One conclusion that can be drawn from this research is that classification strategies based on multiple aptitude testing and adaptive treatments, such as individualized training, are likely to be more useful in correcting social inequities than statistical manipulations of test scores, cutoffs, or regression formulas.

Comprehensive Review

STUDY QUESTIONS:

1. List and describe the factors that should be considered when evaluating a published validity coefficient.

2. Explain the meaning of the standard error of estimate and discuss its role in the evaluation of the validity of a test.

3. Describe the basic approach of decision theory in the evaluation of the usefulness of a selection procedure.

4. Define incremental validity and explain how it is gauged.

5. Explain how the validity of a test can be used to estimate changes in productivity.

6. Discuss the role of values in determining the relative utility of a selection procedure.

7. Describe how the expected utility (EU) of a selection strategy can be calculated.

8. Describe and contrast sequential versus terminal decision-making strategies.

9. Define the concept of moderator variables and cite an example of one.

10. Compare and contrast the use of multiple regression equations versus cutoff scores in combining information from a test battery.

11. Define and differentiate selection, placement, and classification decisions.

12. Explain slope and intercept biases and cite examples of how each of them might be manifested.

13. List three constructive approaches that can be used, instead of statistical score manipulations, to try to correct the results of past social inequities.

EXERCISES: Statistical Aspects of Validity

❶ Calculate the term $\sqrt{1 - r^2_{xy}}$ for the following validity coefficients and explain the meaning of the resulting values.

Validity Coefficients: .10   .30   .50   .70   .90

❷ The standard deviation for the criterion measure to be predicted by a test with a validity coefficient of .60 is 8. What is the standard error of estimate for the predicted criterion scores?

❸ If you wished to calculate the predicted criterion score (Y') for a specific individual who took the test mentioned in the previous exercise, you would need to know the individual's score on the test and the coefficients of the regression equation, which would be calculated from the bivariate data on test and criterion scores. However, without any further information, you can find the limits within which any given obtained criterion score (Y) is likely to deviate from the criterion score (Y') that is predicted with the use of the test. Using the Table of Areas under the Normal Curve in Appendix A of this guide and the standard error (SE) of estimate obtained in Exercise 2, calculate those limits for the 95% and 99% levels of confidence.

❹ Sixty percent of the applicants hired for a particular job in a large factory are usually successful on the job. Use of a predictive test with a validity of .60 is instituted. The top 30% of the applicants who take the test are hired. What would be the new expected percentage of successful employees selected by using the test? (See Table 6-1 on p. 147 of the textbook.)

⑤ Determine the expected increase in productivity for the example in Exercise 4, with the use of Table 6-2 on p. 150 of the textbook.

⑥ The following multiple regression equation was developed for the purpose of predicting performance in Calculus, based on the Numerical (N) and Reasoning (R) portions of an aptitude test:

$$Calculus\ score = Y' = .31N + .20R + 1.50$$

Assume that a student has a stanine score of 7 on Numerical Aptitude and a stanine score of 5 on Reasoning Aptitude. What is the student's predicted stanine score in Calculus (Y')?

⑦ The four scatter diagrams in Figure 5 represent four sets of bivariate data. In each case, as is customary, the scores on the test or predictor are on the X axis and the scores on the criterion are on the Y axis. Inspect each of the diagrams to determine which one of the distributions is homoscedastic. Then, for the remaining distributions, explain the relationship that exists between test scores and the criteria.

Figure 5 — Scatter Diagrams of Different Degrees of Variability

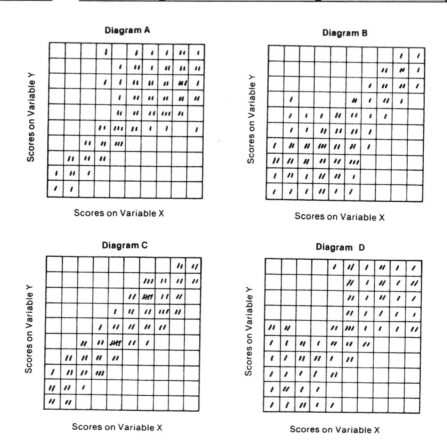

⑧ Look at Figure 6-1 on page 145 of the textbook and recompute the number of valid and false acceptances as well as valid and false rejections that would result if the cutoff score on the test were lowered by one of the units represented in the graph. Then, look at the computations on pp. 152–153 of the textbook and calculate the expected utility (EU) for the modified decision strategy, assuming that the cost of testing remains at .10 on the utility scale.

⑨ Each of the schematic drawings in Figure 6 represents a hypothetical scatter diagram of the bivariate distributions of data on a predictor, Test X, and a criterion (Y) for samples of Whites and Blacks. For each of the diagrams, determine whether the test appears to be a valid predictor for each of the racial groups and what would happen if each test were used as a selection device.

Figure 6 — Hypothetical Scatter Diagrams[1]

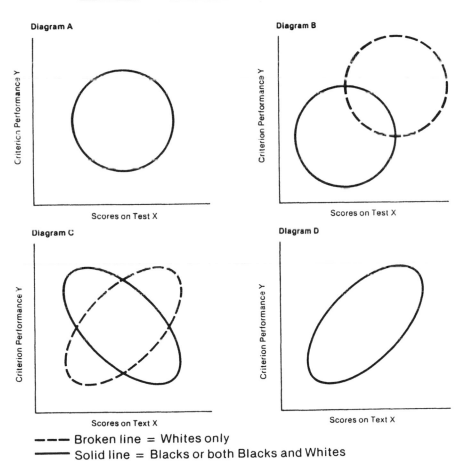

---‒‒‒ Broken line = Whites only
——— Solid line = Blacks or both Blacks and Whites

[1]Adapted from R. S. Barrett's "How to Improve Selection While Hiring Minorities and Women." Paper presented at the 1976 American Psychological Association convention.

❶   *Validity Coefficients* $\sqrt{1 - r^2_{xy}}$

                .10   .99
                .30   .95
                .50   .87
                .70   .71
                .90   .44

        <u>Explanation:</u>   By using a test with a validity coefficient of .50, for example, the error in prediction would be 87% as large as the error that would result by chance. The use of such a test would allow us to predict criterion performance with a 13% smaller margin of error than what would result from a mere guess.

❷   <u>Standard error of estimate</u> = 6.4

❸   Chances are 95 out of 100 that any obtained criterion score would fall between ± (1.96) (6.4) or ± 12.54 of the criterion score predicted by the test in question. Chances are 99 out of 100 that any obtained criterion score would fall between ± (2.58) (6.4) or ± 16.51 of the predicted criterion score.

❹   <u>Base rate</u> = .60   <u>Validity</u> = .60   <u>Selection ratio</u> = .30

        The new percentage of successful employees would be 87%; the incremental validity would be the difference between a success rate of 60% and a success rate of 87%.

❺   The mean criterion performance of the group selected with the use of the test would be .69 standard deviation units above the expected base performance mean of applicants selected without the use of the test.

❻   Y' = .31 (7) + .20 (5) + 1.50 = 4.67 or Stanine 5

❼   The data in Diagram C are homoscedastic. Diagram A shows greater variability at the top of the range. Diagram B shows greater variability at the bottom of the range. Diagram D shows greater variability at the top *and* bottom of the range than in the middle.

❽   Valid acceptances   =   38 + 10 = 48
        False acceptances   =   7 + 11 = 18

Valid rejections $= 33 - 11 = 22$
False rejections $= 22 - 10 = 12$

EU $= (.48)(1.00) + (.18)(-1.00) + (.22)(0) + (.12)(-0.50) -.10$

EU $= +.14$

⑨ *Diagram A*: There is no relationship between X and Y for either group; therefore the test, although technically "culture fair," would be useless as a selection device.

Diagram B: There is no relationship between X and Y for either group, but Whites—as a group—perform better than Blacks on both. If the results had not been separated by race, the test might appear to be valid for the combined racial groups. This test, if used, would be unfair in that even though it is not valid, the vast majority of individuals selected by it would be White.

Diagram C: This diagram suggests that the test is an equally valid predictor of Y for both groups (same slope) but in opposite directions. Use of this test would require a different strategy for each racial group, i.e., the selection of high-scoring Whites and low-scoring Blacks, a practice that would be difficult—if not impossible—to justify.

Diagram D: The test appears to be a fairly good and equally valid predictor of Y for both Blacks and Whites and could, therefore, be used properly as a selection device.

FILL IN THE BLANKS: Key Terms and Concepts

1. The effect of greater sample _ _ _ _ _ _ _ _ _ _ _ _ _ or variability on correlation coefficients is to increase the magnitude of the obtained correlation.

2. The use of the _ _ _ _ _ _ _ _ _ _ _ _ _ _ of _ _ _ _ _ _ _ _ to evaluate the predictive efficiency of a test is unrealistically stringent, unless one needs to predict an individual's exact position on the criterion distribution.

3. The Pearson product-moment correlation coefficient is only applicable when both variables are _ _ _ _ _ _ _ _ _ _ _. In addition, the Pearson r assumes that the relationship between the two variables is _ _ _ _ _ _ and _ _ _ _ _ _ _ throughout the range.

4. In personnel selection, the term used to designate the category of persons who score below the cutoff point on a selection test, but above the criterion cutoff is _ _ _ _ _
 _ _ _ _ _ _ _ _ _.

5. In decision theory terminology the _ _ _ _ _ _ _ _ _ _ _ _ _ _ _ refers to the proportion of applicants who must be accepted.

6. Decision-making might be improved if _ _ _ _ _ _ _ _ _ _ strategies were used as an alternative to terminal decisions.

7. The collective name for several especially selected tests that are used together to predict a single criterion is _ _ _ _ _ _ _ _ _ _ _.

8. The multiple correlation (R) between a criterion and a test battery can be expected to show some _ _ _ _ _ _ _ _ _ when the battery of tests is cross-validated on a second sample.

9. The strongest argument in favor of using multiple cutoffs rather than a regression equation centers around the issue of _ _ _ _ _ _ _ _ _ _ _ _ _ qualifications.

10. A(n) _ _ _ _ _ _ _ _ _ _ _ variable is one that appears in the regression equation with a negative weight for the purpose of eliminating the irrelevant variance introduced by another test in the battery.

11. _ _ _ _ _ _ _ _ _ is a term that refers either to the earlier stages of selection or to any rough or rapid selection process.

12. When individuals are assigned to two or more specific jobs or treatments on the basis of multiple predictors, the decision process is one of _ _ _ _ _ _ _ _ _ _ _ _ _ _ _. When the assignment to a specific treatment is based on a single score, the decision involved is one of _ _ _ _ _ _ _ _ _.

13. The _ function is a mathematical procedure for determining how closely a person's scores on a set of predictors approximate the scores typical of the members of a certain group.

14. In the statistical sense, the term _ _ _ _ _ _ _ _ refers to a constant or systematic error, as opposed to chance error, inherent in the use of the test with certain groups.

15. In the context of test bias, the term "differential validity" is used to designate differences in the _ _ _ _ _ of the regression lines obtained from two groups.

16. When the point at which the regression line intersects the vertical or Y axis is different for two groups, the resulting problem is called _ _ _ _ _ _ _ _ _ bias.

1. (sample) heterogeneity
2. standard error (of) estimate
3. continuous / linear / uniform
4. false rejections
5. selection ratio
6. sequential (strategies)
7. test battery
8. shrinkage
9. compensatory (qualifications)
10. suppressor (variable)
11. screening
12. classification / placement
13. multiple discriminant (function)
14. test bias
15. slope
16. intercept (bias)

Multiple Choice: Test Yourself

1. Tests designed to predict success in college show a moderate correlation with actual success as measured by academic grades. It has been argued that many students who would not have succeeded in college anyway choose not to take those tests or attempt college-level work, thus engaging in a form of self-selection. What would be the effect on validity coefficients if every high school senior took a predictor test and attempted one year of college?_____.
    a. Validity coefficients would increase markedly
    b. Validity coefficients would decrease
    c. There would be no effect on validity coefficients
    d. It is impossible to tell what would happen

2. A situation wherein low-scoring and high-scoring applicants who take a selection test show more variability than middle-scoring applicants in terms of job performance would produce an example of_____.
    a. an invalid test
    b. an unfair test
    c. homoscedasticity
    d. heteroscedasticity

3. When the predictive validity coefficient for a test is recomputed on a new sample that is more homogeneous than the sample on which it was originally found, the coefficient will be_____but the predictions based on the test_____.

a. lower / will be more accurate
b. higher / will be less accurate
c. lower / may be just as accurate
d. higher / may be just as accurate

4. The purpose of a regression equation is to_____.
a. establish validity for a test
b. adjust test validity for criterion factors
c. predict criterion performance
d. determine test reliability

5. The standard deviation of a criterion measure to be predicted by a test is 2. The validity coefficient of the test is .60. What is the standard error of estimate for the criterion scores?_____.
a. 0.36
b. 16.00
c. 1.6
d. none of the above

6. When a test has a validity of zero for a particular use, the standard error of estimate will be_____.
a. zero
b. the same as the standard deviation of the criterion
c. infinity
d. indefinite

7. All other things being equal, the incremental validity resulting from the use of a selection test would be highest with a selection ratio of_____.
a. .05
b. .50
c. .90
d. 1.00

8. All other things being equal, the incremental validity resulting from the use of a test would be highest with a base rate of_____.
a. zero
b. 5%
c. 50%
d. 95%

9. Moderator variables_____.
a. if present, would result in slope bias
b. can be assumed to affect validity in most cases

c.   are limited to sex and socioeconomic level

d.   have been shown to improve prediction substantially

10.   A test that is uncorrelated with the criterion but has a high correlation with another test in the battery may improve prediction when it is incorporated into a multiple regression equation. Such a test would be called a_____.

a.   suppressor variable

b.   moderator variable

c.   cutoff factor

d.   regression weight

11.   The multiple cutoff procedure would be more appropriate than the use of multiple regression equations for_____.

a.   counseling an individual who has no clear occupational pattern or plans

b.   selecting sonar operators, for whom auditory discrimination is of critical importance

c.   assigning clinical patients to particular types of therapy

d.   planning a remedial program for a child with a reading disability

12.   A general intelligence test correlates .45 with success in a particular college. To improve the predictive accuracy, the applicants are also given three other intelligence tests, all of which correlate very highly with each other and the first test. What will be the effect of adding scores from the three additional tests to the regression equation?_____.

a.   Predictive accuracy will improve dramatically

b.   Only a very small improvement will occur

c.   Predictive accuracy will decrease

d.   One cannot tell from the information provided

13.   Assume the military drafts 1000 people. They are all tested to determine their best roles in the service. Which of the following types of decisions are being made?_____.

a.   Selection

b.   Placement

c.   Classification

d.   Positioning

14.   Multiple discriminant functions are a statistical technique for_____.

a.   predicting job success

b.   classifiying examinees in the group whose scores they most closely resemble

c.   organizing test scores into multiple regression equations

d.   establishing a formula for determining multiple cutoff scores

15. Critical analyses of studies reporting validity coefficients for Black and White employment samples have found that_____.
    a. discrepancies in the validities for Blacks and Whites are large and significant
    b. intercept bias in favor of Whites is quite common
    c. there is no significant evidence of slope or intercept bias that penalizes Blacks
    d. there is significant evidence of both slope and intercept bias that penalizes Blacks

16. After a many years of intensive research into test bias with minorities, the current movement is toward_____.
    a. virtual elimination of any test shown to have any bias
    b. the design of culture-free tests
    c. better selection strategies for fair test usage with minorities
    d. development of special tests for minorities

Miniprojects/Suggested Homework Activities:

1. The concept of statistical prediction and its accuracy is at the heart of the material in Chapter 6. Correlation and regression are, in turn, central to that topic. Therefore, once again, a review of a good textbook in statistics is strongly recommended especially, at this point, with reference to regression equations, regression coefficients, regression lines, and how each of these is used in prediction.

2. Miniproject 2 for the previous chapter suggested a review of the evidence concerning the validity of academic admission tests. An appropriate follow-up to that project would be to obtain some local validity data by correlating the admission test scores and final grade point averages (GPAs) for at least 20 students who have already graduated from your school. You might be able to obtain the test scores and GPAs from the office of Student Records, provided that no names are attached to the data. Otherwise, you could gather the data directly by asking alumni for it or even by asking students who are nearing graduation for their test scores and latest GPAs. In any event, you should be aware that you will be dealing with a preselected sample and that the correlation you obtain would be affected by this factor as well as by the size of the sample of data that you gather.

3. Select an "intermediate" and an "ultimate" criterion of success in the field which you are currently preparing to enter. The intermediate criterion might consist of some index of academic success, such as graduation with honors. The ultimate criterion should be an index of success appropriate to the profession or field you have chosen. Describe how you would proceed if you had to predict your eventual standing and that of your classmates on each of these two criteria. What data would you select to predict each criterion? How would you combine the data?

4. The "Principles for the Validation and Use of Personnel Selection Procedures" (published by the Society for Industrial and Organizational Psychology, whose address is listed in Appendix B of the textbook) are of major importance in the realm of employee selection practices. A review of this document is certain to increase your understanding of many of the practical issues of test validation and fairness.

ANSWERS TO MULTIPLE CHOICE/TEST YOURSELF ITEMS:

1. a
2. d
3. c
4. c
5. c
6. b
7. a
8. c
9. a
10. a
11. b
12. b
13. c
14. b
15. c
16. c

ITEM ANALYSIS

Chapter Outline

Item Difficulty
> Percentage Passing
> Interval Scales
> Thurstone Absolute Scaling
> Distribution of Test Scores
> Relating Item Difficulty to Testing Purpose

Item Discrimination
> Choice of Criterion
> Statistical Indices of Item Discrimination
> Use of Extreme Groups
> Simple Analysis with Small Groups
> The Index of Discrimination
> Phi Coefficient
> Biserial Correlation

Item Response Theory
> Item-Test Regression
> Item Response Theory (IRT): Basic Features
> Other IRT Models
> Current Status

Item Analysis of Speeded Tests

Cross-Validation
> Meaning of Cross-Validation
> An Empirical Example
> An Example with Chance Data
> Conditions Affecting Validity Shrinkage

Differential Item Functioning
> Statistical Procedures
> Judgmental Procedures
> A Notorious Case of Misuse of DIF

Explorations in Item Development

Chapter Summary

The validity and reliability of a test depend on the characteristics of its items. Test items, therefore, need to be analyzed both qualitatively and quantitatively throughout the process of test development. The two main aspects of quantitative item analysis are the measurement of item difficulty and item discrimination.

A determination of the difficulty of items is essential to the development and evaluation of ability tests. The most basic measure of item difficulty is the percentage (P) or proportion (p) of persons who answer it correctly. This ordinal measure can be expressed directly or it can be transformed into an equal-unit interval scale by reference to a table of normal curve frequencies. Item difficulty can also be translated into a uniform scale, applicable to two or more groups, by means of the absolute scaling procedure developed by Thurstone. In any event, measures of item difficulty allow the test developer to select those items that will produce, most efficiently and appropriately, the type of discrimination sought, whether that consists of differentiating maximally among individuals or identifying a certain segment of test takers.

Item discrimination indices evaluate the degree to which each item differentiates correctly among test takers with regard to the behavior that the test is designed to measure. Depending on the nature and purpose of the test, item discrimination can be evaluated (a) on the basis of a criterion external to the test; (b) by using the total score on the test itself as the criterion; or (c) by a combination of both procedures. Item discrimination procedures typically involve the use of contrasting criterion groups and the computation of the difference between them, such as in the D index. Alternatively, correlational techniques, such as the phi coefficient, can also be used to assess the relationship between item responses and standing on the criterion.

Item-test regression graphs allow for the simultaneous representation of item difficulty and item discrimination. They provide a picture of the relationship between item performance and total score. Item-score regression techniques have served as the basis for the development of a sophisticated form of item analysis, variously designated as item response theory (IRT), latent trait theory, or item characteristic curve (ICC) theory. This approach uses mathematically derived functions to plot curves that represent various item parameters, including difficulty, discrimination, and the probability of guessing the correct responses. Item response theory also allows for the computation of item information functions that can serve to select the most reliable items for a test. IRT parameters, computed on groups of varying abilities, are sample-free or invariant and can thus provide a uniform scale of measurement for use with different groups. Although the relative merits of various IRT procedures are still being debated, the use of these techniques is accelerating, especially in the realm of computerized adaptive testing for which they are particularly appropriate.

The item analysis of speeded tests poses a number of problems due to the fact that both item difficulty and item discrimination measures are significantly affected when only a portion of the people taking a test attempt a given item. Some empirical and statistical procedures have been developed to deal with those difficulties but item analysis data from speeded tests still need to be carefully scrutinized from the technical and logical standpoints.

Another critical issue in test development concerns the need for cross-validation, i.e., the determination of test validity on a sample of people different from that used to select the items. The validity coefficient of a test, as established through an initial sample, can shrink dramatically and even approach zero when the test is cross-validated. This is most likely to occur when (a) the initial pool of items is large and assembled without a preestablished rationale, and (b) the validation sample and the proportion of items retained are small.

Differential item functioning (DIF) is an area of item analysis that seeks to identify items that may be culturally biased. The analysis of test items with regard to their potential cultural bias requires a combination of statistical and judgmental procedures. Statistical analyses attempt to establish whether individuals of equal ability from different cultural groups have different probabilities of success on an item. This can be accomplished by a variety of methods. One of the most promising is based on item response theory (IRT). It consists of comparing the item characteristic curves for the same item, relative to overall test performance, in two different groups. Judgmental analysis of cultural biases in item content can be useful at the initial stage of test construction and, more so, in the final stage when it can aid in the evaluation and interpretation of statistically deviant items.

The greatly expanded use of computers in recent years has stimulated interest in new and much more sophisticated approaches to item construction. In addition, the techniques of cognitive psychology offer test developers the possibility of incorporating item specifications that are far more refined than those of the past. Both of these developments, together, hold a great deal of potential to improve and facilitate test construction techniques.

Comprehensive Review

STUDY QUESTIONS:

1. Explain how the process of item analysis can result in a shortened test that is more valid and reliable than the original longer test.

2. Describe how the difficulty of an item is determined and explain the relationship between the difficulty level of an item and the differentiations it makes.

3. Explain how item difficulty can be expressed on an equal-unit interval scale.

4. Describe the procedure for absolute scaling of item difficulty developed by Thurstone and explain its uses.

5. Describe the cumulative effect of inappropriate levels of difficulty of test items on test scores, conceptually and graphically.

6. Relate item difficulty to selection ratio and to other testing goals.

7. Define item discrimination and explain how it relates to test homogeneity.

8. Discuss the roles of external validation and internal consistency in test construction.

9. Explain the use of extreme groups in the analysis of item discrimination through an example dealing with a teacher-made classroom test.

10. Define the index of discrimination and explain its purpose.

11. Describe and compare the phi coefficient and the biserial correlation.

12. Describe the item response theory (IRT) approach to the analysis of items and contrast it with other approaches.

13. Discuss the problems inherent in the item analysis of speeded tests.

14. Explain the use of cross-validation in test construction, as well as its importance to that process.

15. Define the concept of differential item functioning (DIF) and describe the ways in which it can be assessed.

EXERCISES: Item Analysis Statistics

❶ Out of 35 students, 26 got item number 20 correct on an exam. Calculate the percentage (P) and the proportion (p) passing for that item.

❷ Exactly 16 percent of the students got item number 10 correct. If we assume that the trait measured by the item is normally distributed, what is the z value for item 10? (You may need to look at the Table of Areas under the Normal Curve in Appendix A of this guide to solve this problem.)

❸ Figure 7 represents a hypothetical distribution of total scores for a standardized test of ability. Describe the problem that this score distribution suggests, as far as the difficulty level of the test is concerned, and how the test might be modified in order to correct the problem.

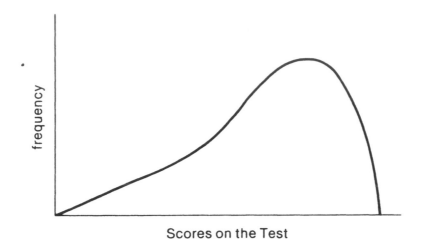

Scores on the Test

❹ For the following item analysis data, which are given in terms of frequencies, compute the item difficulty and discriminative values, in frequencies, for each item; identify the items that appear questionable and explain why they do.

Item	U (N = 25)	M (N = 25)	L (N = 25)
1	22	17	8
2	5	10	15
3	4	0	1
4	15	14	15
5	24	12	0

❺ With the same data used in the preceding exercise, compute the index of discrimination (D) for each of the five items.

❻ What are the minimum values that a phi coefficient computed on a sample of 64 cases must have in order for it to be significant at the .05 and .01 levels? (See p. 187 of the text.)

❼ Plot an item-test regression graph for the hypothetical data, shown below, on two items from a ten-item test. Use Figure 7-5 on p. 189 of the text as a model. Identify which of the two items is more difficult, which one discriminates better, and why.

	Proportion Correct	
Total Score	**Item 1**	**Item 2**
10	1.00	.95
9	.55	.90
8	.80	.70
7	.65	.50
6	.70	.45
5	.85	.30
4	.60	.00
3	.50	.00
2	.20	.00
1	.25	.00

ANSWERS TO EXERCISES: Item Analysis Statistics

❶ $P = 74\%$ and $p = .74$

❷   According to the Table of Areas under the Normal Curve, the z value for $p = .16$ is $+1.00$.

❸   The score distribution is skewed in such a way as to suggest an insufficient test ceiling, meaning that for the group that was tested many items were "too easy" and therefore there is a piling of scores at the upper end of the scale. One way to correct the problem would be to add more difficult items to the test; another way, which could lower reliability—among other things—would be to eliminate a good portion of the easiest items.

❹

Item	**Difficulty** U + M + L	**Discrimination** U − L
1	47	14
2	30	−10*
3	5	3*
4	44	0*
5	36	24

*These items appear to be problematic: Item 2 has a negative discriminative value which means that the highest scoring students are failing it more frequently than the lowest scoring students. Item 3 was passed by a very small number of students and, thus, may be too difficult. Item 4 does not discriminate among the extreme groups at all and, thus, may be "dead weight" on the test, depending on its purpose.

❺

Item	Percentage Passing		D
	Upper Group	Lower Group	
1	88	32	56
2	20	60	− 40
3	16	4	12
4	60	60	0
5	96	0	96

❻ In order for the phi coefficient to be significant at the .05 level, it has to have a value of:

$$\Phi_{.05} \quad = \quad \frac{1.96}{\sqrt{64}} \quad = \quad \frac{1.96}{8} = \quad .245$$

To reach the .01 level of significance, the phi coefficient has to have a value of:

$$\Phi_{.01} \quad = \quad \frac{2.58}{\sqrt{64}} \quad = \quad \frac{2.58}{8} = \quad .323$$

<u>Note</u>: This time, maybe you did not even have to look up the z values corresponding to p = .05 and p = .01 in the Table of Areas under the Normal Curve, as they are given in the textbook and they have been used before. However, if you *are* puzzled by those values, inspection of the Table will prove helpful.

❼

<u>Figure 8</u> — <u>Item–Test Regression for Items 1 and 2</u>

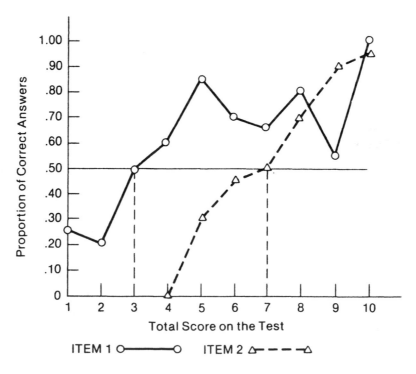

ITEM 1 o——o   ITEM 2 △– – – –△

NOTE: Item 2 is more difficult than Item 1 because its 50% threshold is higher. Item 2 also discriminates better than Item 1, which can be deduced from the fact that its curve is steeper than that of Item 1, among other things.

TRUE/FALSE and WHY?

1. When a test is shortened by the elimination of items that are shown—through item analysis—to be least satisfactory, the shorter version of the test may be more valid and reliable than the original. (T/F) Why?_____

   _____

2. A test item that is passed by everyone would always have to be considered as excess baggage on the test. (T/F) Why? _____

   _____

3. A piling of test scores at the low end of the score distribution would suggest that the test has too many easy items for the group that was tested. (T/F) Why? _____

   _____

4. When test items are selected on the basis of their correlation with a complex external criterion, the internal consistency of the test will most likely be lowered. (T/F) Why?

   _____

5. Item discrimination indices for items which occur late in a speeded test are likely to overestimate the discriminative power of those items. (T/F) Why? _____

   _____

6. If persons from different cultural groups have different probabilities of success on certain test items, those items fit the psychometric definition of bias. (T/F) Why?

   _____

7. The analysis of differential item functioning, based on item response theory, is becoming the method of choice for such analyses. (T/F) Why? _____

   _____

8. The "Golden Rule" case exemplifies a legal decision that was made after adequate consideration of the validity of the items involved. (T/F) Why? _____

   _____

ANSWERS TO TRUE/FALSE:

1.	True	3.	False	5.	True	7.	True
2.	False	4.	True	6.	False	8.	False

LIST OF KEY TERMS AND CONCEPTS:

Use the following list of key terms and concepts from Chapter 7 as a review tool to make sure you can define/identify each of them in your own words. The textbook page or pages given after each term are those which contain the definition or explanation of the term.

1. item analysis (p. 172)
2. item difficulty (p. 173)
3. percentage passing (p. 173)
4. difficulty value (p. 174)
5. Thurstone absolute scaling (pp. 174–176)
6. skewness (p. 177)
7. item discrimination (p. 179)
8. index of discrimination (D) (p. 185)
9. phi coefficient (p. 186)
10. biserial correlation (p. 187)
11. item-test regression (pp. 187–188)
12. item response theory (IRT) / latent trait theory / item characteristic curve (ICC) theory (pp. 189–190)
13. theta (θ) (p. 189)
14. item information function (p. 191)
15. unidimensionality (p. 192)
16. cross-validation (p. 194)
17. validity shrinkage (p. 195–196)
18. differential item functioning (DIF) (pp. 196–197)

Multiple Choice: Test Yourself

1. The principal function of item analysis is to_____.
   a. identify test items that may be faulty or superfluous
   b. determine the discrimination index for a test
   c. shorten a test
   d. calculate the validity coefficient for each item on the test

2. Item difficulty is customarily defined as the _____.
   a. percentage of examinees who fail an item
   b. percentage of examinees who pass an item
   c. biserial correlation for an item
   d. correlation of the item with the criterion

3. The ideal value for item difficulty is _____.
   a. less than 50%
   b. about 50%

c.   greater than 70%
d.   dependent on many factors

4.   An item is passed by 84% of the students who take it. The z value for the item is
     _____.
     a.   − 1.0
     b.   + 1.0
     c.   + 1.5
     d.   − 1.5

5.   A test item with a difficulty z value of − 3.0 may be improved by _____
     _____.
     a.   adding more distractors
     b.   changing the distractors no one chooses into more plausible distractors
     c.   removing possible cues for the correct answer
     d.   all of the above

6.   A test is given to a fifth grade class primarily to identify the bottom third of the class
     for special instruction. The average difficulty (p) for the test items should be
     approximately _____.
     a.   .30
     b.   .50
     c.   .70
     d.   the same as for any other test

7.   Item discrimination means _____
     _____.
     a.   the extent to which an item correctly discriminates against some examinees
     b.   the extent to which an item correctly differentiates among examinees on the
              appropriate behavior
     c.   the amount of reliability in an item
     d.   none of the above

8.   If all items for a test are chosen on the basis of their correlation with a total test score,
     the result will yield _____.
     a.   maximum test homogeneity
     b.   a reduction of test-retest reliability
     c.   an increase in validity against external criteria
     d.   unpredictable changes

9.   In determining item discrimination, it is customary to look at the upper and lower
     27% of the examinees as the extreme groups. This percentage was chosen to_____
     _____.

a. simplify the calculations
b. obtain reliable results and sufficient differentiation
c. maintain tradition
d. increase discrimination to a maximum value

10. The D value in item analysis represents _____
    _____.

a. the reliability of the item
b. the biserial correlation coefficient
c. the difference in p between the upper and lower groups
d. absolute item quality

11. The biserial correlation is applied when _____
    _____.

a. the item response and the criterion are genuine dichotomies
b. the item response and the criterion are continuous variables
c. a continuous and normally distributed trait underlies the dichotomous item response and the criterion
d. the item-criterion relationship is not independent of item difficulty

12. Item response theory models are _____
    _____.

a. no longer the subject of debate
b. less accurate than item discrimination indices
c. being increasingly applied in test development
d. increasing test unidimensionality

13. Indices of item difficulty and item discrimination from a speeded test typically _____.

a. are just as meaningful as those from unspeeded tests
b. reflect the item's position in the test
c. will be artificially high
d. cannot be computed

14. If validity is figured on a test without cross-validation, the coefficient is likely to be _____.

a. too high
b. too low
c. unpredictable
d. too low by as much as the standard deviation of the test

15. In order to keep shrinkage of a test's validity to a minimum upon cross-validation, it would be best to _____.

a. use small samples
b. start with a relatively large initial pool of items
c. make sure there is no rationale for the items
d. none of the above

16. Differential item functioning is an aspect of item analysis that seeks to identify _____
_____.
    a. items that discriminate between groups
    b. items on which different cultural groups have different probabilities of success
    c. items on which equally able persons from different groups have different probabilities of success
    d. the ability level needed to answer an item correctly

Miniprojects/Suggested Homework Activities:

1. A review of the statistical techniques traditionally used in item analysis is strongly recommended at this point. In particular, it would be desirable to investigate the special correlational methods used in item analysis, such as the point-biserial and the tetrachoric correlation coefficients, in addition to the phi coefficient and the biserial correlation discussed in the textbook. Any good basic textbook in statistics for psychology would cover these. See, for example, Chapter 10 of *Statistical Methods for Psychology* (4th ed.) by D.C. Howell (Belmont, CA: Duxbury Press, 1997). J. P. Guilford and B. Fruchter's *Fundamental Statistics in Psychology and Education* (6th ed, New York: McGraw-Hill, 1978) also has a fine presentation of various alternative correlational procedures (pp. 304-318) as well as further information on traditional item analytic procedures in general (pp. 457-469).

2. The material presented in Chapters 3 through 7 has undoubtedly given you a greater understanding of the process of test development than you ever had before. Chapter 7, in particular, points out in some detail the laboriousness of the process of generating suitable test items. In light of this information, your attitudes toward standardized testing, as well as teacher-made tests, might well have changed. Identify and list any such attitudinal changes you may have had and discuss them with your classmates. One of the areas you might consider would be your perception of the desirability of legislatively mandating the release of items from tests such as the SAT and GRE and their answers. Another relevant area about which your attitudes and perceptions might have changed concerns the need for and role of item analysis in classroom testing.

3. Prepare and, if possible, carry out a plan for replicating a demonstration of the need for cross-validation similar to the one conducted by Cureton and described in page

195 of the textbook. You will need to select a criterion and a way of generating item responses randomly, in order to obtain "test" scores. You will also need to decide on an index of item discrimination—suitable to the criterion and item responses—for use in your item analysis (see Miniproject #1). Finally, you should be able to establish the "validity" of your entire "test" by correlating the original criterion measures with the scores obtained on the test. In planning this replication, keep in mind the factors that affect validity shrinkage.

4. Miniproject #1 for Chapter 5 consisted of constructing a short achievement test covering a specific segment of this course. If you did that, you now have an opportunity to do an item analysis of that instrument, provided you give it to a few more people in order to generate data for your analysis. The best model to follow for a simple analysis is the one described in the textbook (pp. 183-186). If you did not do the first miniproject in Chapter 5, this would be a good time to try it and follow up with the analysis suggested here.

5. A short but excellent overview of the basics of item response theory (IRT) can be found in Appendix D of the *Differential Ability Scales: Introductory and Technical Handbook* by C. D. Elliott (San Antonio, TX: The Psychological Corporation, 1990). This source also contains a clear explanation of how the Rasch model of IRT was applied in the development of the Differential Ability Scales (DAS).

ANSWERS TO MULTIPLE CHOICE/TEST YOURSELF ITEMS:

1.	a	5.	d	9.	b	13.	b
2.	b	6.	c	10.	c	14.	a
3.	d	7.	b	11.	c	15.	d
4.	a	8.	a	12.	c	16.	c

PART III   Ability Testing

∘∘ **8** ∘∘

INDIVIDUAL TESTS

Chapter Outline

Stanford-Binet Intelligence Scale
    Evolution of the Scales
    The Fourth Edition Stanford-Binet (SB-IV): General Description
    Administration and Scoring
    Standardization and Norms
    Reliability
    Validity

The Wechsler Scales
    Antecedents and Evolution of the Wechsler Intelligence Scales
    Description of the Scales
    Abbreviated Scales
    Norms and Scoring
    Reliability
    Validity
  Concluding Remarks on the Wechsler Scales

The Kaufman Scales
  Kaufman Assessment Battery for Children
    Nature and Development
    General Evaluation
  Kaufman Adolescent and Adult Intelligence Test
    Nature and Development
    General Evaluation
  Kaufman Brief Intelligence Test

Differential Ability Scales
    Description
    Scaling and Norming
    Reliability and Validity
    General Evaluation

Das-Naglieri Cognitive Assessment System

93

Chapter Summary

The Fourth Edition of the Stanford-Binet Intelligence Scale (SB-IV) is the current version of the scale published in 1916 by Terman and his associates which, in turn, was a revision of the original Binet-Simon scales published in France between 1905 and 1911. The SB-IV is an individually administered instrument that retains the adaptive testing procedure and many of the item types from earlier forms but goes beyond them in content coverage. It reflects recent developments in the conceptualization of intellectual functioning and in test construction methodology. The current SB expands on the verbal focus of earlier editions to include more coverage of quantitative, spatial, and short-term memory tasks. Unlike earlier editions, in which items were grouped into age levels, the items of the SB-IV are grouped according to type. They provide separate scores for up to 15 tests and four major cognitive areas in addition to the composite score for performance on the entire scale. The current scale, which was standardized on a larger sample than ever before, has been subjected to a greater variety of validation procedures from the outset. While keeping the same numerical units as the traditional deviation IQs of earlier editions, the SB-IV uses the term "Standard Age Scores" (SAS) rather than "IQ" to designate its scores.

The Wechsler intelligence scales encompass a series of instruments designed for three age levels, from adults to preschool children. The original scale—known as the Wechsler-Bellevue Intelligence Scale—was devised by David Wechsler, and published in 1939, with the purpose of providing an intelligence test suitable for adults both in content and normative procedures. The current version of the adult scale, which covers the age range of 16 to 74 years, is the Wechsler Adult Intelligence Scale-Revised (WAIS-R); a third edition of the WAIS is scheduled for publication in the second half of 1997. The Wechsler Intelligence Scale for Children was first published in 1949 and is now in its Third Edition (WISC-III). It is aimed at children aged 6 to 16 years, whereas the Wechsler Preschool and Primary Scale of Intelligence-Revised (WPPSI-R) covers the span from 3 to 7 years. Each one of the scales provides separate Verbal, Performance, and Full Scale deviation IQs based, respectively, on the scores from the verbal subtests, the performance subtests, and the entire scale. The format allows for a number of intertest comparisons and probably accounts for much of the popularity of the WAIS and the other Weschler scales, which have followed the same pattern, with some variations to accommodate the needs of younger test takers.

Periodic revisions of the Wechsler scales of intelligence are carried out in order to update norms, content, and other aspects of the tests. The WISC-III, for example, now provides four additional index scores derived from subtests that assess Verbal Comprehension, Perceptual Organization, Freedom from Distractibility, and Processing Speed factors. The standardization samples of the three scales are typically large and representative of the population of the United States. The manuals of the Wechsler scales address the issue of reliability and error of measurement rather well and provide information that is needed for evaluating the significance of the differences obtained between the various scores. Furthemore, in contrast with past practice, the most recent manuals also provide abundant data on validity, especially from the point of view of the factorial composition of the scales and their correlations with similar instruments. However, critics of the Wechsler tests point to their atheoretical basis and their failure to take into account developmental changes in the nature of intelligence both of which, in turn, limit the interpretive usefulness of the scales.

The tests developed by Alan and Nadine Kaufman in the 1980s and 1990s have been expressly designed to be both developmentally appropriate and anchored in contemporary theories of intelligence. The Kaufman Assessment Battery for Children (K-ABC) attempts to assess the intellectual functioning of children (aged 2.5 to 12.5) from an information processing viewpoint. The K-ABC incorporates some of the advances that occurred in cognitive psychology in the 1960s and 1970s. It also has a more comprehensive approach to validation than the older Stanford-Binet and Wechsler scales. The design of the K-ABC and its global scores for Sequential Processing, Simultaneous Processing, and Achievement represent an attempt to focus on the tasks of hypothesis generation and hypothesis testing and to get away from the simple labelling that has become associated with traditional tests of intelligence. Although empirical corroboration for the theoretical basis of the K-ABC has failed to materialize, its global scores are generally considered to be similar to those obtained from the comparable Wechsler scales. The Kaufman Adolescent and Adult Intelligence Test (KAIT) uses as its bases the theory of fluid and crystallized intelligence proposed by Horn and Cattell, as well as other theoretical postulates about adult intelligence. The KAIT's items were carefully developed and selected to appeal to adult test takers and are more unusual and interesting that those of the more traditional individual intelligence scales. However, the overall success of this new instrument will, as usual, depend on whether a database sufficient to justify its research and applied uses develops over time.

The Differential Ability Scales (DAS) is one of the newest tools for individual intellectual assessment and embodies a number of significant advances in psychometrics. The DAS was designed as an eclectic and flexible tool for differential diagnosis and treatment planning for children and adolescents. Its theoretically based, hierarchical approach to mental abilities results in an overall summary score which represents an individual's level of General Conceptual Ability (GCA), as well as several other indices of performance at different levels of generality and specificity. The developers of the DAS used item response theory procedures to calibrate the difficulty of items. These procedures allow for the implementation of an unusually flexible testing strategy and permit the comparison of results based on the administration of different subsets of items. Such comparisons are ideally suited for gauging both intra- and interindividual variability. The DAS is rather complex in terms of its administration and scoring and is suitable for a relatively restricted age range (2.5 years to 17 years and 11 months). Nevertheless, it represents the "state of the art" in instruments of its type in that it meets or exceeds previous standards of test construction.

Comprehensive Review

STUDY QUESTIONS:

1. Describe the major landmarks in the history of the Binet scales in terms of their content and standardization.

2. Describe the main administration and scoring features of the Fourth Edition of the Stanford-Binet (SB-IV).

3. Discuss the role of individual intelligence tests, such as the SB-IV, in clinical assessment from the point of view of their usefulness versus their cost.

4. Describe the validation procedures that have been applied to the SB-IV.

5. Discuss the history of the development of the Wechsler intelligence scales.

6. Describe the salient features of the current versions of Wechsler's intelligence scales and compare them to each other in terms of their range of applicability.

7. Discuss the positive and negative characteristics of the Wechsler scales.

8. Describe the major features of the Kaufman Assessment Battery for Children (K-ABC) as well as its strengths and weaknesses.

9. Discuss the unique features of the Kaufman Adolescent and Adult Intelligence Test (KAIT).

10. Enumerate the advantages and disadvantages of abbreviated versions of the Wechsler scales and similar instruments such as the Kaufman Brief Intelligence Test (K-BIT).

11. Explain the major improvements made in the development of the Differential Ability Scales and contrast this with other individual tests described in Chapter 8.

12. Describe the types of tasks that are used in the Das-Naglieri Cognitive Assessment System (CAS).

EXERCISES: Statistics in Individual Intelligence Testing

❶ The Standard Age Scores (SAS) for the 15 separate tests of the SB-IV have a mean of 50 and a standard deviation of 8. Using the Table of Areas under the Normal

Curve in Appendix A, find the z scores and percentile rank equivalents for the following SAS values for SB-IV tests:

74   64   54   48   38   28

❷ Express each of the percentile ranks you obtained in the previous item in terms of their equivalent SB-IV area or composite SAS values.

❸ The test-retest reliability coefficient for the composite SAS for five-year-olds tested with the SB-IV after intervals of between two and eight months is .91. Suppose that you had tested Sally on her fifth birthday and retested her after six months and that her SB-IV composite SAS values were 95 and 110, respectively.

    A.   Would the difference between Sally's scores on the two occasions be statistically significant and, if so, at what level of significance?

    B.   What other factors, if any, would you need to consider in interpreting the obtained difference?

❹ Locate the manuals for the WISC-III and WPPSI-R and study the information each of them provides on stability coefficients. This information can be found in Tables 5.3 to 5.5 (pp. 170–172) of the WISC-III manual and Table 10 (p. 131) of the WPPSI-R manual. In light of what you have learned about reliability, what are some of the relevant pieces of information you should notice in evaluating these data?

❺ Following the example displayed in Figure 8-4 on p. 226 of the textbook, develop a "vocabulary" of 20 simple rebuses.

☞ HINTS: (a) Be sure to include several nouns and verbs, as well as a few articles, conjunctions, prepositions, and maybe an adjective or two; (b) Rebuses are easier to learn if they have some graphic resemblance to the words they represent; (c) Make sure your vocabulary includes at least 5 or 6 concrete objects, such as "house" or "car," which are easy to represent schematically; (d) Words that can double as a noun and a verb (e.g., heat, handle, drink, toy) are particularly useful.

☞ Make up 4 or 5 short sentences using only the words from your rebus vocabulary and draw each sentence on a separate blank index card. Develop a system for teaching your rebuses, on a one-to-one basis, to a few willing classmates or friends. Test them by asking them to "read" the sentences on the cards. Note individual differences in the performance of your "subjects." What major abilities will you have "assessed" with your Rebus Learning minitest? What factors do you think may have affected the performance of your subjects? How could you improve your procedures?

❶ and ❷

SAS Tests	z scores	Percentiles	SAS Area or Composites
74	+3.00	99.87th	148
64	+1.75	96th	128
54	+0.50	69th	108
48	−0.25	40th	96
38	−1.50	7th	76
28	−2.75	0.30th	56

Note that, because of the numerical relationship between the test and the area or composite SAS units, the latter are exactly twice the value of the former. If you have access to the *Technical Manual* for the SB-IV, you can look up these and other SAS values—and their corresponding percentile ranks—directly in Table D.1 (p. 129).

❸ **A.**   The 15-point difference between Sally's scores on the two occasions would be significant at $p = .0018$. The SE of measurement $= 16 \sqrt{1- .91} = 4.8$ and the z value for that difference would be 3.13 (15 divided by 4.8).

B.   The interpretation of the difference between Sally's scores on the two occasions should take into account the fact that the scores obtained by preschool children are typically less reliable than those of older children. This has, to some extent, been accomplished through the use of a reliability coefficient specific to that age group. Of greater significance would be the possible influence of practice effects. In addition, because of the rather large difference, one would want to learn more about any specific situational factors that might have been at play during the two administrations, e.g., Sally's health at both times, examiner influences, setting in which each testing was conducted, etc. Finally, an examination of the extent and pattern of the differences between Sally's scores on the separate tests of the SB-IV on each administration would probably be helpful in interpreting her score gains.

❹   One should note the size and age of the samples used in each case, the intervals between test and retest, the differences between means and standard deviations from the first and the second testing, as well as the patterns of the stability coefficients across subtests and across age groups.

⑤ According to the manual for the Kaufman Adolescent and Adult Intelligence Test (KAIT), the Rebus Learning subtest is one of the tasks in the "Fluid Scale." This, in contrast to the "Crystallized Scale," is meant to assess the ability to solve new problems involving stimuli or concepts available to nearly anyone in a culture. The specific tasks involved in the Rebus Learning subtest require visual memory, efficiency in learning novel material, and visual sequencing—among other skills. Performance on this test may be affected by factors such as attention span, concentration, and frustration tolerance; these, in turn, will be influenced by the test takers' level of cooperation and motivation, as much as by their abilities. In addition, the procedures you use for teaching and testing your "subjects," undoubtedly will play a role in their perfomance. If you carry out this exercise conscientiously, the need for standardization of procedures, advance preparation of the examiner, and a suitable testing environment (see Chapter 1) will become abundantly clear to you.

Details of administration, scoring, and interpretation of the Rebus Learning subtest, can be found in Kaufman, A. S., & Kaufman, N. L. (1993). *Kaufman Adolescent and Adult Intelligence Test: Manual.* Circle Pines, MN: American Guidance Service. For more information about the notions of "fluid" and "crystallized" intelligence, see Horn, J. L., & Cattell, R. B. (1966). Refinement and test of the theory of fluid and crystallized general intelligences. *Journal of Educational Psychology, 57,* 253 270 as well as Miniproject #3 later in this chapter.

FILL IN THE BLANKS: Individual Intelligence Tests

1. _ _ _ _ _ _ _ _ _ _ _ _ _ tests are the direct descendants of the original Binet scales, are designed for use in a wide variety of situations, and are validated against relatively broad criteria.

2. The chronological series 1905, 1908, and 1911 would, for the person who is well-versed in individual intelligence testing, immediately recall the sequence of revisions of the _ _ _ _ _ – _ _ _ _ _ scales.

3. The Fourth Edition of the _ _ _ _ _ _ _ _ – _ _ _ _ _ Intelligence Scale is the current version of the scale published by Terman in 1916.

4. In contrast with earlier editions, the Stanford-Binet-IV uses _ _ _ _ _ _ _ _ _ _ _ _ _ _ _ _ _ (SAS) for separate tests, for areas, as well as for the entire scale, and has largely discarded the concept of mental ages and the use of IQs.

5. The first form of the Wechsler scales, published in 1939 specifically as an intelligence test for adults, was the _ _ _ _ _ _ _ _ – _.

6. The current version of the scale cited in the preceding item is the _ _ _ _ _ _ _ _ _
   _ _ _ _ _ _ _ _ _ _ _ _ _ _ _ _ _ _ _ – _ _ _ _ _ _ _ (WAIS-R), which itself
   is due to be replaced by a new edition.

7. The current downward extension of the WAIS, published in 1991 and appropriate for
   individuals between the ages of 6 years and 16 years and 11 months, is known as the
   _ for _ _ _ _ _ _ _ _ –Third Edition
   (WISC-III).

8. The _ _ _ _ _ _ _ _ _ _ _ _ _ _ _ _ _ _ and _ _ _ _ _ _ _ _ _ _ _ _ _ of
   Intelligence–Revised (WPPSI-R) is the formal title of the "baby" of the Wechsler series
   of intelligence scales, which now covers the age range of 3 years to 7 years and 3
   months.

9. The _ for _ _ _ _ _ _ _ (K-ABC) is
   an individually administered clinical instrument, developed in the 1980s and suitable
   for the ages of 2.5 to 12.5 years, whose focus is on the assessment of information
   processing.

10. The _ (DAS) is a revision and
    extension of a British test, noteworthy–among other things–because of its author's
    assertion that the terms "intelligence" and "IQ" are *not* part of its vocabulary.

ANSWERS TO FILL-IN-THE-BLANKS: Individual Intelligence Tests

1. Intelligence (tests)
2. Binet-Simon (scales)
3. Stanford-Binet (Intelligence Scale)
4. Standard Age Scores (SAS)
5. Wechsler-Bellevue Intelligence Scale
6. Wechsler Adult Intelligence Scale-Revised (WAIS-R)
7. Wechsler Intelligence Scale (for) Children-(Third Edition) (WISC-III)
8. Wechsler Preschool (and) Primary Scale (of Intelligence–Revised) (WPPSI-R)
9. Kaufman Assessment Battery (for) Children (K-ABC)
10. Differential Ability Scales (DAS)

MATCHING: Key Terms and Concepts   (One letter per number)

_____ 1. Starting point for the SB-IV tests, determined on the basis of the examinee's
         chronological age and Vocabulary test score.
_____ 2. On the SB-IV, the point at which four items on two consecutive levels are
         passed.

_____ 3. On the SB-IV, the point at which three out of four or all four items on two consecutive levels are failed.

_____ 4. Shorter versions of a test battery, such as the Wechsler scales, used for screening or special purposes.

_____ 5. K-ABC scale for subtests that require synthesis and organization of spatial and visuo-perceptual content that can be surveyed as a whole.

_____ 6. K-ABC scale for subtests that require serial or temporal arrangements of verbal, numerical, and visuo-perceptual content.

_____ 7. K-ABC scale that assesses ability in reading, arithmetic, word knowledge, and general information.

_____ 8. Component of the KAIT that measures concepts acquired from schooling and acculturation.

_____ 9. Component of the KAIT that taps the ability to solve new problems.

_____ 10. Name for the overall summary score of the DAS that encompasses the sum of the scores on the "core" subtests of the cognitive battery.

A. Entry level
B. Achievement Scale
C. Crystallized Scale
D. Sequential Processing Scale
E. Abbreviated scales
F. Ceiling level
G. Simultaneous Processing Scale
H. Fluid Scale
I. General Conceptual Ability (GCA) score
J. Basal level

ANSWERS TO MATCHING ITEMS:

1-A   2-J   3-F   4-E   5-G   6-D   7-B   8-C   9-H   10-I

Multiple Choice: Test Yourself

1. Intelligence tests are usually validated against_____.
   a. personality tests
   b. tests of problem-solving skills
   c. individual success in life
   d. scholastic success

2. The 1960 revision of the Stanford-Binet_____.
   a. combined Forms L and M
   b. utilized totally new norms
   c. introduced no new content

d.   both a and c

3. Compared with the norms of the 1930s and 1940s, the 1970's norms for the Binet and other intelligence tests were _____.
    a.   about the same
    b.   higher
    c.   lower
    d.   going up until a reversal began in 1970

4. The administration of the Stanford-Binet requires a highly trained examiner because_____.
    a.   scoring is difficult
    b.   rapport must be established
    c.   clinical information should also be gathered
    d.   all of the above

5. The basal level of the SB-IV is_____.
    a.   reached when four items on two consecutive levels are passed
    b.   the minimal performance level for passing
    c.   reached at the first level when all items are failed
    d.   a minimum score required for one's mental level

6. The major innovation in the 1972 edition of the Stanford-Binet was_____
    _____.
    a.   new norms
    b.   extensive content revision
    c.   a change in the scoring
    d.   all of the above

7. In the SB-IV, normative tables are used to convert raw scores to_____.
    a.   an improved ratio IQ
    b.   standard age scores
    c.   mental age over chronological age
    d.   scores with a mean of 500 and a standard deviation of 50

8. A person obtains an overall composite SAS score of 118 on the SB-IV. Considering the standard error of measurement of the scale, which is approximately 2.5, there is a 95% chance that the person's true score differs by approximately _____ points from her or his obtained score.
    a. $\pm$ 2.5
    b. $\pm$ 5.0
    c. $\pm$ 7.5
    d. $\pm$ 10.0

9. As an examinee becomes older, the scores on the Stanford-Binet become_____.
   a. more reliable
   b. less reliable
   c. less valid
   d. cannot say without more information

10. The major scores provided by the Wechsler scales are_____.
   a. ratio IQs
   b. a global IQ and general factor scores
   c. verbal, performance and full scale deviation IQs
   d. standard age scores

11. Norms for the WPPSI-R extend over which of the following age ranges?_____.
   a. 2.5 to 12.5 years
   b. 3 years to 7 years and 3 months
   c. 6 years to 16 years and 11 months
   d. 16 to 74 years

12. Which of the following factors is incorporated into the standard scoring of the WISC-III but *not* usually found in factor analyses of the WAIS-R across different samples?
   _____
   a. Verbal Comprehension
   b. Perceptual Organization
   c. Freedom from Distractibility
   d. Processing Speed

13. The primary focus of the Kaufman Assessment Battery for Children is on _____.
   a. information processing
   b. factual knowledge acquired in school
   c. information derived from an interview with the subject's parents
   d. determining IQ level

14. The Kaufman Brief Intelligence Test (K-BIT) is a shortened version of _____.
   a. the K-ABC
   b. the KAIT
   c. neither of the above
   d. both a and b

15. The Differential Ability Scales (DAS) _____.
   a. has an inadequate standardization sample for its age range coverage
   b. results in a global IQ that summarizes performance on the entire test
   c. allows for interscore comparisons across different occasions
   d. has relatively simple administration and scoring procedures

Miniprojects/Suggested Homework Activities:

1. The relationship between scores on intelligence tests and educational attainment is strong. In fact, several people have suggested that when IQs are needed for comparative purposes, but are not available, one way to estimate them is to use the years of education completed by a subject as the basis for a regression formula. Although this practice is not unanimously endorsed, it is interesting to examine its empirical bases. To do that, and to review some of the issues discussed in Chapter 8, read some of the studies on the subject, such as J.D. Matarazzo and D.O. Herman's "Relationship of education and IQ in the WAIS-R standardization sample" (*Journal of Consulting and Clinical Psychology*, 1984, *52*, 631–634).

2. A careful selection of readings from some of the references mentioned in the textbook would be extremely helpful in rounding out your knowledge about a number of testing issues and procedures discussed in the text. The following are three specific recommendations, selected from sources cited in Chapter 8:

    ☞ A.S. Kaufman's *Intelligent Testing with the WISC-III* (New York: Wiley, 1994) presents an exceptionally thorough approach to the use of the WISC-III in the process of clinical assessment (see especially Chapter 3 for a detailed description of Kaufman's method for interpreting WISC-III profiles).

    ☞ *Clinical and Research Applications of the K-ABC* by Randy W. Kamphaus and Cecil R. Reynolds (Circle Pines, MN: American Guidance Service, 1987) is an excellent source of information on the "intelligent" use of the Kaufman Assessment Battery for Children.

    ☞ An exemplary volume, already mentioned in connection with Miniproject # 5 for Chapter 7, is the *Introductory and Technical Handbook* for the Differential Ability Scales by Colin D. Elliott (San Antonio, TX: The Psychological Corporation, 1990). This handbook—aimed at prospective and actual users of the DAS—has clear explanations of theoretical and technical issues in cognitive assessment.

    Further discussion of the application of intelligence tests in the context of individual assessment, as well as additional references, can be found on pp. 512–514 of the textbook.

3. For anyone interested in the newest approaches to intelligence testing, or in the major current theoretical perspectives and controversies in the field, the volume on *Contemporary Intellectual Assessment: Theories, Tests, and Issues*, edited by D. P. Flanagan, J. L. Genshaft, and P. L. Harrison (New York: Guilford Press, 1997) will provide a

great deal of valuable information. This book includes chapters—written by the authors of the respective tests—on some of the newest instruments discussed in Chapter 8 of your textbook (e.g., the DAS, the KAIT, and the CAS), as well as chapters on alternative techniques for the assessment of intelligence, including dynamic assessment. In addition, the major contemporary perspectives on the nature of intelligence and on the organization of cognitive abilities are presented by their main proponents. These theoretical perspectives include: Howard Gardner's Theory of Multiple Intelligences, the Three-Stratum Theory of Cognitive Abilities proposed by John B. Carroll, and Robert J. Sternberg's Triarchic Theory of Intelligence, among others. Several new procedural directions in intellectual assessment are also discussed in various chapters. One example is a "cross-battery" approach proposed by Dawn P. Flanagan and Kevin S. McGrew, who recommend using whichever tests are proven indicators of the abilities to be assessed, even if the tests belong in different batteries. This approach relies on McGrew's integration and synthesis of Carroll's theory with the Horn-Cattell taxonomy of cognitive abilities, also presented in the book. Because of the breadth of its coverage, *Contemporary Intellectual Assessment* can serve as a source of further information for many of the topics in Part III of your textbook.

4. To learn more about how individual intelligence testing is actually conducted, see the short (33-minute) film entitled "K-ABC: An Administration Videotape," available from American Guidance Service (AGS). If your college or university Media Center does not have it, you may want to suggest it for possible acquisition (see Appendix B of the textbook for the address of AGS). A longer (70-minute) and more recent film, the "KAIT: Training Video," is also available from AGS and would serve a similar purpose.

ANSWERS TO MULTIPLE CHOICE/TEST YOURSELF ITEMS:

1.	d	6.	a	11.	b
2.	d	7.	b	12.	d
3.	b	8.	b	13.	a
4.	d	9.	a	14.	c
5.	a	10.	c	15.	c

oo **9** oo

TESTS FOR SPECIAL POPULATIONS

<u>Chapter Outline</u>

Infant and Preschool Testing
    Historical Background of Infant and Preschool Testing

  Standardized Tests of Early Childhood Development
    Bayley Scales of Infant Development
    McCarthy Scales of Children's Abilities

  Piagetian Scales
    Evaluation of the Piagetian Approach

  Current Trends in Infant and Early Childhood Assessment

Comprehensive Assessment of Mentally Retarded Persons

Testing Persons with Physical Disabilities
    Hearing Impairments
    Visual Impairments
    Motor Impairments

Multicultural Testing
    The Problem
    Typical Traditional Instruments
    Approaches to Cross-Cultural Testing
    The Assessment of Environment

<u>Chapter Summary</u>

    Individuals who cannot be properly examined with traditional instruments, due to disabling conditions, inadequate oral or written language skills, or some other reason, are usually tested with measures especially designed or modified to accommodate their needs. Such instruments may consist of: (a) performance tests, which involve manipulation of objects and minimal use of paper and pencil; (b) nonlanguage tests, which can be administered and taken without the use of oral or written language; or (c) nonverbal tests, which do not require reading. This chapter deals with specialized tests for infants and preschool children, for mentally retarded persons, for people with physical disabilities, and for persons from culturally diverse groups, as well as with some of the problems involved in testing those populations.

Tests designed for infants and preschool children are individually administered and are mostly performance tests or oral tests that either do not require use of paper and pencil or involve their use only minimally. The testing of infants places a heavy emphasis on sensorimotor development. It consists mainly of standardized procedures for observing and evaluating the behavioral development of infants. Such testing usually is aimed at assessing current status rather than at predicting future ability levels.

Arnold Gesell led the first efforts to refine, elaborate, and systematize the qualitative observations of pediatricians. His longitudinal studies of the normal course of development in young children resulted in the Gesell Developmental Schedules, a pioneering instrument in the field. More recently, the Bayley Scales of Infant Development and the McCarthy Scales of Children's Abilities provide two outstanding examples of tests especially designed, respectively, for infants and for the preschool level. In addition to these prototypical instruments, the assessment of children has been enriched by several experimental scales especially designed to investigate the stages of cognitive development postulated by Jean Piaget. These instruments are typically more flexible and open to qualitative interpretation than others; they exemplify the ordinal approach to norms and the use of age differentiation as a validating criterion. The Ordinal Scales of Psychological Development and the Concept Assessment Kit—Conservation are among the best known Piagetian instruments.

The current emphasis on early identification and remediation of cognitive deficits has generated renewed attempts to develop the best possible tools for the assessment of infants and young children. If they are to be of practical value, these tools need to demonstrate some predictive power. Moreover, it is clear that the assessment of infants and young children must be comprehensive, involving professionals from all the pertinent disciplines, taking into account the child's environment, and providing explicit links to remedial intervention.

The comprehensive assessment of mentally retarded persons has undergone a spurt of growth as a result of legislation aimed at assuring that their special educational needs will be recognized and met. Assessment programs for mentally retarded persons use traditional intelligence tests to identify the extent of retardation from the normative viewpoint. In addition, they typically include a measure of adaptive behavior in everday-life situations, such as the Vineland Adaptive Behavior Scales, and an examination of motor development, with instruments such as the Bruininks-Oseretsky Test of Motor Proficiency. A major challenge in the assessment of mental retardation lies in distinguishing it from developmental delays that arise from such factors as sensory and motor disabilities or adverse environments.

The problems of testing persons with disabilities have also received special attention as a result of legislative mandates that extend the rights and opportunities of these individuals. The testing of physically disabled persons poses special problems in terms of both test administration and interpretation. Often, these difficulties are handled by modifying existing tests or by including nontest information, such as life history data, in an attempt to individualize the assessment process. However, some efforts also have been made to establish separate norms on various instruments, and to develop specialized instruments, for people with specific disabilities. The WISC-R Performance Scale, for example, was standardized separately for persons with hearing impairments, and the Hiskey-Nebraska Test of Learning Aptitude was developed and standardized on deaf and hard-of-hearing children. Tests for persons with visual impairments, which usually have to rely on oral presentation, include modifications of the Binet and Wechsler scales, adaptations of some group tests, and a few specialized instruments, such as the Blind Learning Aptitude Test.

Testing people with motor disabilities poses yet another set of problems in that, depending on the severity of the disorder, such individuals may be unable to respond either orally or in writing. Efforts to accommodate the needs of this population include special adaptations of the Leiter International Performance Scale and the Porteus Mazes, as well as the use of picture vocabulary tests or pictorial classification tests. In the latter, examinees can respond to the presentation of stimuli by pointing, nodding, or otherwise indicating their choices through whatever communication means they have available.

Multicultural, or cross-cultural, testing is a rapidly expanding field. It encompasses problems such as developing instruments for educational and occupational selection and placement in different nations, as well as assessing culturally diverse populations within a single nation, such as the United States. Traditional cross-cultural tests have attempted to rule out the parameters along which cultures differ, e.g., language, reading skills, and emphasis on speed. "Culture-free" tests—aimed at ruling out test content that is tied to the experiential background specific to certain cultures—have also been tried, without success.

Typical instruments in the cross-cultural field include the Leiter International Performance Scale-Revised, Raven's Progressive Matrices, and the Goodenough-Harris Drawing Test. Although cross-cultural tests are needed for research on many important issues, their validation in different cultures has often been neglected or poorly executed and their results have not always been shown to have the same meaning and/or significance in different cultures. Nevertheless, attempts to develop instruments suitable to certain specific cultures or applicable across cultures continue. Furthermore, since several of these instruments have also proved to be applicable in counseling and clinical settings, a new generation of nonverbal measures has been developing rapidly in recent years.

Awareness of the significant contributions of one's surroundings to the particular ways in which intelligence evolves has led to increased activity in the area of assessment of environments. Global indices of socioeconomic status, empirically based techniques for the description and classification of behavior settings, as well as measures for the assessment of families and the home environment are among the principal tools available in this field.

Comprehensive Review

STUDY QUESTIONS:

1. Define and contrast performance, nonlanguage, and nonverbal tests and cite an example of each.

2. Discuss the characteristics of tests designed for infants and describe the Bayley Scales of Infant Development, Second Edition (Bayley-II), as an example of those tests.

3. Describe the characteristics of the McCarthy Scales of Children's Abilities as an example of tests for preschool children and summarize its unique contributions.

4. Explain the basic approach that underlies the development of Piagetian scales and describe one example of such a scale.

5. Discuss the results of comparative studies using Piagetian scales and list some of the obstacles and advantages that go along with that approach.

6. Describe the current trends in the assessment of infants and young children and explain the rationale for these developments.

7. Describe the procedures involved in the identification and classification of mentally retarded individuals.

8. Explain the role of adaptive behavior scales in the assessment of mentally retarded persons and describe the elements involved in one such scale.

9. Discuss the problems involved in the assessment of physically disabled individuals and the major approaches that have been used in that area.

10. Name and describe two examples of tests used to assess individuals with hearing, visual, or motor impairments.

11. Discuss the problems involved in cross-cultural testing and outline the three major approaches that may be used to develop tests for persons from diverse cultural backgrounds.

12. List and describe in detail two examples of instruments typical of existing tests that are applicable across cultures.

13. Describe the role environmental measures in the assessment of individuals and cite two examples of the approaches taken in that field.

FILL IN THE BLANKS: Key Terms and Concepts

1. In general, _ _ _ _ _ _ _ _ _ _ _ tests are those that involve the manipulation of objects with minimal, if any, use of paper and pencil.

2. The Army Beta Examination was a prototype of _ _ _ _ _ _ _ _ _ _ _ tests, which are those that can be given and taken without the use of spoken or written words.

3. Although they frequently measure verbal comprehension, _ _ _ _ _ _ _ _ _ tests are especially suitable for preschool children and illiterates because they require no reading or writing.

4. The increasing recognition of the need to take the environment into account while in the process of assessing children is known as the _ _ _ _ _ _ _ _ _ _ orientation.

5. The _ (GCI) of the McCarthy Scales of Children's Abilities (MSCA) is a standard score—with a mean of 100 and a standard deviation of 16—that resembles traditional global measures of intellectual development and is based on 15 out of the 18 tests in the battery.

6. Piaget outlined four stages of cognitive development spanning the period from infancy to adolescence and beyond. They are designated as the _ _ _ _ _ _ _ _ _ _ _ _ stage, the _ _ _ _ _ _ _ _ _ _ _ _ _ _ stage, the _ _ _ _ _ _ _ _ _ _ _ _ _ _ _ _ _ stage, and the _ _ _ _ _ _ _ _ _ _ _ _ _ _ _ _ stage.

7. In Piagetian terminology, the concept of _ _ _ _ _ _ _ _ _ _ _ _ refers to the child's realization that properties of objects—such as weight, volume, or number—remain unchanged when objects undergo transformations in shape, position, or form.

8. The term _ _ _ _ _ _ _ _ is used by Piagetian researchers to describe the phenomenon of inconsistencies between empirical findings and the theoretically postulated sequencing of response patterns.

9. The experimental techniques that combine aspects of Piaget's theory with dynamic assessment, and with the perspective of information processing theory, have been labelled collectively as "_ _ _ – _ _ _ _ _ _ _ _ _" approaches.

10. Since the passage of the 1975 _ _ _ _ _ _ _ _ _ for _ _ _ _ _ _ _ _ _ _ _ _ _ _ _ _ _ _ _ Act (P.L. 94-142), presently known as the _ _ _ _ _ _ _ _ _ _ _ with _ _ _ _ _ _ _ _ _ _ _ _ Education Act (IDEA), the testing of children with mental or physical disabilities has undergone conspicuous growth in the United States.

11. The _____ _____ on ____ __ _____
    (AAMR) characterizes _____ _____ as "significantly subaverage
    general intellectual functioning existing concurrently with related limitations in two or
    more ... adaptive skill areas."

12. Many civil rights provisions mandated for other minorities were extended to cover
    physically disabled persons through Section 504 of the _____
    Act of 1973 and through the _____ ____ _____ Act
    (ADA) of 1990.

13. The Raven's Progressive Matrices (RPM) test is currently available in three forms which
    differ in level of difficulty. The names of those forms, in ascending order of difficulty,
    are the _____ Progressive Matrices (CPM), the _____ Progressive
    Matrices (SPM), and the _____ Progressive Matrices (APM).

14. The basic approach of the tests designated as _____ – ____ is to choose
    items common to many different cultures and validate the resulting test against local
    criteria in the respective cultures.

15. Instruments such as the footprint recognition test standardized on aboriginal
    Australians are really meant to highlight the extent to which the cultural milieu affects
    the cognitive skills and knowledge acquired by an individual; an additional example of
    this type of cross-cultural test is the ____ – – _____ Test.

ANSWERS TO FILL-IN-THE-BLANKS: Key Terms and Concepts

1. performance (tests)
2. nonlanguage (tests)
3. nonverbal (tests)
4. ecological (orientation)
5. General Cognitive Index (GCI)
6. sensorimotor (stage) / preoperational (stage) / concrete operational (stage) / formal
   operational (stage)
7. conservation
8. *décalage*
9. "neo–Piagetian" (approaches)
10. Education (for) All Handicapped Children (Act) / Individuals (with) Disabilities
    (Education Act) (IDEA)
11. American Association (on) Mental Retardation (AAMR) / mental retardation
12. Rehabilitation (Act of 1973) / Americans with Disabilities (Act) (ADA) (of 1990)
13. Coloured / Standard / Advanced (Progressive Matrices) (CPM / SPM / APM)
14. culture–fair
15. Draw–a–Horse

MATCHING: Tests for Special Populations   (One letter per number)

_____ 1.   Multidisciplinary procedure which exemplifies the trend toward comprehensive assessment and is used to identify children, from birth to the age of 3 years, who are at risk for developmental delays.

_____ 2.   Published test, based on one of Piaget's best known formulations, which can serve as an indicator of a child's transition from the preoperational to the concrete operational stage of thinking.

_____ 3.   Current revision of a test series, originally published in Russia, which is the prototype of measures of muscle performance and is useful in testing mentally retarded persons.

_____ 4.   Current title of a prototypical instrument designed to assess developmental level through one's ability to look after one's own practical needs and take responsibility in daily living.

_____ 5.   Individual test, developed and standardized on deaf and hard-of-hearing children, which differs from most performance tests in that it eliminates speed and samples a wider variety of intellectual function.

_____ 6.   Instrument designed to assess variables such as provision of appropriate play materials and other parental behaviors that foster cognitive development in children.

_____ 7.   Measure that assesses selective attention to novel versus familiar visual stimuli in infants from 3 to 12 months of age.

_____ 8.   Adaptation of one of the best known individual intelligence scales that was prepared for use with blind and partially sighted persons.

_____ 9.   Instrument, useful in the assessment of people with motor disabilities, wherein the test taker responds by designating one picture—out of four—that best illustrates the meaning of an orally presented stimulus word.

_____ 10. Test, originally developed for use with children with cerebral palsy, which illustrates the use of pictorial classification in intellectual assessment.

_____ 11. Individually administered scale which features the almost complete elimination of verbal instructions and was originally developed for use with different ethnic groups.

_____ 12. Nonverbal test, used widely in clinics as well as with different cultural and ethnic groups, wherein credit is given for the inclusion of body parts, clothing details, proportion, perspective, and such.

A.   Vineland Adaptive Behavior Scales
B.   Perkins–Binet Tests of Intelligence
C.   Bruininks–Oseretsky Test of Motor Proficiency
D.   Fagan Test of Infant Intelligence
E.   Leiter International Performance Scale–Revised
F.   Concept Assessment Kit–Conservation
G.   Columbia Mental Maturity Scale (CMMS)

112

H. Goodenough–Harris Drawing Test
I. Hiskey–Nebraska Test of Learning Aptitude
J. Peabody Picture Vocabulary Test–Revised (PPVT–R)
K. Home Observation for Measurement of the Environment (HOME)
L. Infant–Toddler Developmental Assessment (IDA)

ANSWERS TO MATCHING ITEMS:

1-L   2-F   3-C   4-A   5-I   6-K   7-D   8-B   9-J   10-G   11-E   12-H.

TRUE/FALSE and WHY?

1. In light of their current psychometric characteristics, infant tests should be used mainly to assess current developmental status rather than to predict subsequent ability levels. (T/F) Why? _____

2. Piagetian scales are characterized by a rigid framework that is devoid of theory and focuses on quantitative interpretation. (T/F) Why?_____

3. Research findings suggest that there is substantial overlap between Piagetian scales, standardized intelligence tests, and school achievement in the overall assessment of children that their indices provide. (T/F) Why? _____

4. The current system of classification of mental retardation has shifted away from a view of this condition as a trait inherent in the individual. (T/F) Why? _____

5. The AAMR and most experts in the field of mental retardation agree that an IQ of 70 constitutes the clear dividing line between normal intelligence and mental retardation. (T/F) Why? _____

6. Testing children who are physically disabled at an early age is not likely to mitigate the effects of their disabilities on their intellectual development. (T/F) Why?_____

7. Psychometric studies of procedural adaptations of tests such as the College Board's SAT and the GRE General Test suggest that they can provide valid measures for disabled test takers. (T/F) Why? _____

8. A cultural difference is not likely to become a cultural disadvantage, or advantage, unless individuals have to adjust to and compete in cultures unlike those in which they were reared. (T/F) Why? _____

_____

9. Factor analytic studies of Raven's Progressive Matrices indicate that performance on this test depends exclusively on the general factor common to most intelligence measures. (T/F) Why? _____

_____

10. The Leiter International Performance Scale–Revised is no longer scored in terms of mental age and ratio IQ. (T/F) Why? _____

_____

11. Investigations that have used the Goodenough Draw-a-Man Test on different cultures and ethnic groups indicate that performance on that test is independent of cultural background. (T/F) Why? _____

_____

12. The desirability of classifying environments along a continuum of better-or-worse is widely recognized in the field of environmental assessment. (T/F) Why? _____

_____

ANSWERS TO TRUE/FALSE:

1.	True	4.	True	7.	True	10.	True
2.	False	5.	False	8.	True	11.	False
3.	True	6.	False	9.	False	12.	False

Multiple Choice: Test Yourself

1. Performance tests can normally be distinguished by their_____

_____.

    a.   total nonreliance on language
    b.   emphasis on object manipulation
    c.   nonverbal characteristics
    d.   unbiased nature

2. Tests for infants and preschool children usually must be_____

_____.

    a.   nonlanguage
    b.   performance

c. individually administered

d. none of the above

3. The Gesell Developmental Schedules, a pioneering technique for the assessment of young children, consist mostly of _____.

a. behavioral data gathered through observation

b. a series of performance tests for children

c. nonverbal interpretation of pictures

d. testing infants' aptitudes

4. The Bayley Scales of Infant Development include _____
_____.

a. a Mental Scale

b. a Motor Scale

c. an Infant Behavior Record

d. all of the above

5. Piagetian scales assume _____.

a. minimum language development

b. uniform developmental sequences

c. motor coordination

d. operational causality

6. The assessment of mentally retarded persons in the United States has _____
_____.

a. improved very little in the past 25 years

b. received increased attention, especially since 1975

c. been replaced by subjective evaluation

d. turned to nonlanguage performance tests

7. The Bruininks–Oseretsky test is employed to assess mental retardation through
_____.

a. an evaluation of social skills

b. Piaget's developmental schedules

c. verbal facility

d. an evaluation of motor development

8. The ability to take responsibility for one's behavior and to take care of one's own needs can be evaluated by the _____.

a. Gesell scale

b. Hiskey–Nebraska test

c. Vineland scale

d. Interim Hayes-Binet

9. Tests used in the evaluation of individuals with disabilities_____
   _____.
   a.   always require special procedural alterations
   b.   cannot involve manipulation of objects
   c.   usually require reconsideration of reliability, validity, and norms
   d.   should not be altered in any way that will affect the established norms

10. The testing of children with hearing impairments is complicated by the fact that_____
    _____.
    a.   these children are usually handicapped by verbal tests
    b.   one cannot assume that the norms of standard tests apply
    c.   the idea of speed is hard to convey to them
    d.   all of the above

11. In preparing tests specifically for blind or visually-impaired individuals, it seems
    advisable to emphasize _____.
    a.   performance items
    b.   numerical items
    c.   the learning process
    d.   the products of past learning

12. Tests for persons with severe motor disabilities should be_____
    _____.
    a.   individually modified in whatever way is necessary to meet the needs of the test
         taker, without regard to norms
    b.   administered in sessions that are as long as possible, so that all the testing is
         done at once
    c.   presented only through visual means
    d.   presented so the test taker only has to point or nod at the correct answer

13. Tests that are designed to minimize cultural influences emphasize_____
    _____.
    a.   speed of response rather than content
    b.   questions that are not specific to any given culture
    c.   performance-type responses
    d.   questions relating to minority subcultures

14. Research on the Goodenough Draw-a-Man Test shows that it_____
    _____.
    a.   provides an accurate measure of intelligence in all cultures
    b.   serves as an excellent personality test
    c.   depends heavily on artistic skills
    d.   is also culturally dependent, as are other tests

15. The current general consensus among experts in multicultural testing is that_____
_____.
    a. soon we will see dramatic improvements in specialized tests in this area
    b. the role of the examiner is of even more importance than the test itself
    c. current cross-cultural tests are quite adequate for most purposes
    d. a truly culture-free intelligence test is not only desirable, but is now feasible

Miniprojects/Suggested Homework Activities:

1. Each of the special groups discussed in Chapter 9 presents unique problems in assessment. These require familiarity with the instruments available as well as with the characteristics of the populations involved. With this in mind, you may wish to become better informed about the area(s) of greatest interest to you by reading one or more of the sources mentioned below:

   - *The Psychoeducational Assessment of Preschool Children*, 2nd ed., edited by Bruce A. Bracken (Boston: Allyn & Bacon, 1991), provides a comprehensive compendium of information on issues, techniques, and specialized subfields pertaining to the assessment of young children within the context of education and remediation. In addition, Jerome M. Sattler's classic volume on the *Assesment of Children*, 3rd ed., is still an outstanding resource on the general subject of testing children and has been updated with a Supplement on the WISC–III and the WPPSI–R (San Diego: Author, 1988, 1992).

   - Implications and ramifications of the revised AAMR definition and classification of mental retardation have been analyzed and debated since the revisions were promulgated in 1992. An informative series of articles on this topic appeared in the Spring 1995 issue of *School Psychology Quarterly* (see p. 249 of the textbook for reference citations of this and other sources). A thorough overview of the scientific findings and practical considerations in the area of mental retardation, is available in the *Manual of Diagnosis and Professional Practice in Mental Retardation*, edited by John W. Jacobson and James A. Mulick (Washington, DC: American Psychological Association, 1996).

   - Part III (Standards for Particular Applications) of the 1985 *Standards for Educational and Psychological Testing* contains brief but informative chapters on "Testing Linguistic Minorities" and "Testing People Who Have Handicapping Conditions." The upcoming revision of the *Testing Standards* will also include chapters on these topics, albeit under different titles (see pp. 29-31 of the textbook for further information).

✏ Among the many sourcebooks and handbooks cited on pp. 253 to 259 of the text in reference to the assessment of individuals with various disabilities, one work that stands out is Jeffery P. Braden's recent volume, entitled *Deafness, Deprivation, and IQ* (New York: Plenum Press, 1994). This book contains a distillation of the findings accumulated from research on deafness and raises many new questions about the subject.

✏ Richard H. Dana's (1993) volume on *Multicultural Assessment Perspectives for Professional Psychology* (Boston: Allyn & Bacon) and the *Handbook of Multicultural Assessment: Clinical, Psychological, and Educational Applications*, edited by Lisa A. Suzuki, Paul J. Meller, and Joseph G. Ponterotto (San Francisco: Jossey-Bass, 1996) are two of the best recently published works in the burgeoning area of multicultural assessment. Further insight into the problems involved in cross-cultural testing can be gleaned from "Translating tests: Some practical guidelines," an article by Fons Van de Vijver and Ronald K. Hambleton (1996) that appeared in the *European Psychologist*, *1*, pp. 89-99.

2. To learn more about testing and its various fields, there is no substitute for a direct examination of the tests themselves. Depending on your interests and what is available to you, examine books, manuals, and test kits of some of the instruments discussed in Chapter 9. For example, review and compare the manuals and kits for the Bayley Scales of Infant Development, Second Edition, and for the McCarthy Scales of Children's Abilities (MSCA). Note especially the directions for administration of these two scales. Such a review would highlight the difference between testing infants and testing older children, as the range of applicability of the MSCA starts at 2.5 years—exactly one year before the age where the Bayley-II ends. You could thus notice the overlap between the easiest items of the MSCA and the most difficult ones of the Bayley-II, as well as the large differences in the range of behaviors that can be sampled in the age groups covered by each of the scales.

3. For additional ways to augment your knowledge of the tests discussed in Chapter 9, and in the rest of the chapters in the book, you might:

☞ Prepare a Test Evaluation according to the suggested outline in Appendix B of this *Study Guide*. The proposed format requires you to evaluate the test materials directly, to read the appropriate sections of the *Standards for Educational and Psychological Testing,* and to look up reviews on the test you choose in the *Mental Measurements Yearbook* series. You could also locate reviews in other sources as well as studies that have been done using the test in question.

☞ Conduct a survey in your community to find out: (a) who is using the test(s) that interest you and (b) their reasons for selecting those instruments. You could contact counselors or psychologists at elementary schools and high schools, mental health agencies, personnel departments, college counseling and/or testing centers, and state or local agencies involved in rehabilitation, among others. Before contacting the individuals concerned, decide exactly what you will ask, on the basis of a review of the specific area of testing in question.

ANSWERS TO MULTIPLE CHOICE/TEST YOURSELF ITEMS:

1.	b	4.	d	7.	d	10.	d	13.	b
2.	c	5.	b	8.	c	11.	c	14.	d
3.	a	6.	b	9.	c	12.	d	15.	b

10

GROUP TESTING

Chapter Outline

Group Tests versus Individual Tests
    Typical Differences in Test Design
    Advantages of Group Testing
    Disadvantages of Group Testing

Adaptive Testing and Computer-Based Administration
    Individually Tailored Tests
    Computerized Adaptive Testing (CAT)

Multilevel Batteries
    Overview
    Representative Batteries
    Typical Test Content at Different Levels
    Recognition of Multiple Aptitudes

Measuring Multiple Aptitudes
    Differential Aptitude Tests
    Multidimensional Aptitude Battery

Chapter Summary

Group testing began during World War I, with the development of the Army Alpha and Army Beta examinations, and has grown enormously since then because of its usefulness to the educational system, industry, and government services, as well as to the armed forces. Group tests, which are suitable for mass testing programs of many sorts, differ from individual tests in the form of their items and in how items are arranged. The typical group test uses multiple-choice items, as opposed to open-ended questions, and presents items of similar content in increasing order of difficulty within separately timed subtests so that each test taker may be exposed to each type of item and have a chance to complete the easier ones first. Some tests utilize special arrangements of items, such as the spiral omnibus format, to ensure that items of each type are attempted within each successive level of difficulty.

Group tests have not only made it possible to conduct large-scale testing programs economically but, because they minimize the roles of the examiner and the scorer, they can be given under more uniform conditions and scored more objectively than individual tests. In addition, the relative ease and speed with which group test data can be gathered have made it possible to accumulate far larger and more representative standardization samples than those obtained for even the best individual tests. On the other hand, group tests provide less opportunity for establishing rapport—or for detecting unusual conditions in the test taker that could influence test performance—than do individual tests. Group tests have also been criticized because of the restrictions they impose on responses, which may occasionally penalize creative test takers, and because their utilization of testing time is not as effective as it can be in individual testing.

Adaptive testing procedures tailored individually to the responses of test takers are being explored increasingly in an effort to combine the flexibility of individual tests with the advantages of group tests. Adaptive techniques, which lend themselves best to computerized test administration, may use a two-stage testing process to route the test taker to the most appropriate one of a set of measures of different levels of difficulty. Another alternative is to start with an item of intermediate difficulty and route the examinee upward or downward after each response, depending on its correctness. More complex sequential testing models, which use ability estimates for each item as the basis for scoring, and item information functions for deciding when to stop testing, are feasible only with computerized adaptive testing. Research findings with these methods indicate that they can be as reliable and valid as conventional tests in spite of their smaller number of items and shorter testing times. Computerized adaptive testing (CAT) strategies offer great potential not only in circumventing the limitations of traditional group tests, but also in expanding the range of item types and response options available to test takers and providing better linkage between testing and remedial interventions. The correlations between well constructed CAT instruments and their paper-and-pencil counterparts suggest that both modalities can measure the same constructs; however, there are some testing situations for which CAT is not suitable.

Multilevel batteries, designed to measure intellectual development over a broad range of age groups in a manner that will produce comparable scores over several years, constitute a traditional type of group test and one that is especially appropriate for use in schools. The main function of these batteries is to assess readiness for school learning at each stage in the educational process. Therefore, the batteries typically consist of separate combinations of tests for the primary, elementary school, and high school levels. Item response theory (IRT) procedures are being used increasingly in the development of these instruments, to attain continuity and comparability of scores throughout the range of school grades they cover. The Otis-Lennon School Ability Test (OLSAT), the Cognitive Abilities Test (CogAT), and the Test of Cognitive Skills (TCS) are three prime examples of multilevel batteries selected for discussion in the textbook because of their generally high quality and the recency of their latest revisions. All of these batteries have gradually evolved into providing narrower measures of specific cognitive traits or aptitudes—in addition to their global composite scores of general scholastic aptitude.

Within other testing fields, the impetus to develop multiple aptitude batteries had already arisen earlier due to the recognition that—because of the way they were designed—

intelligence tests could not measure intraindividual variations in performance reliably, except in the broad categories of verbal and nonverbal skills. In particular, the growing involvement of psychologists in career counseling, and in the selection and placement of personnel, required the construction of specialized measures of performance in vocational areas, such as clerical and mechanical abilities, that would supplement the information derived from intelligence tests. The application of factor analytic techniques provided the theoretical and procedural bases needed to identify, sort, and define different abilities and, thus, to develop multiple aptitude batteries.

The Differential Aptitude Tests (DAT) is one of the most widely used multiple aptitude batteries developed for general use in educational testing, counseling, and personnel classification. In spite of its longevity, and exemplary norms and method of reporting scores, the DAT, like other such batteries, is disappointing with regard to differential prediction, which is precisely the area in which it—and other classification instruments—should excel. On the other hand, increasing evidence of the validity of traditional "general intelligence" and "scholastic aptitude" measures against educational and occupational criteria has led the DAT to emphasize its combined "Verbal Reasoning + Numerical Reasoning" score, which also correlates highly with composite criteria of academic success.

The Multidimensional Aptitude Battery (MAB) is an example of another approach to combining the features of individual and group tests. The MAB is designed to assess the same skills as the Wechsler Adult Intelligence Scale-Revised (WAIS-R) through a group-administered, paper-and-pencil format that dispenses with the use of a highly trained examiner. The scores on the battery, which was standardized in a fashion designed to make it directly comparable to the WAIS-R, correlate very highly with those of the WAIS-R and show consistently high reliabilities as well. In addition, the hierarchical nature of the MAB scores typify the trend toward flexibility currently discernible in the field of ability testing.

Comprehensive Review

STUDY QUESTIONS:

1. Describe the major differences in the design of group versus individual tests.

2. List and explain the advantages of group testing over individual testing.

3. List and explain the disadvantages of group testing compared to individual testing.

4. Discuss the aims of individually tailored tests and describe two examples of strategies that can be used in devising such tests.

5. Discuss the uses and advantages of computerized adaptive testing in individualizing tests and increasing their versatility.

6. Describe the results of research comparing paper-and-pencil with computerized adaptive tests.

7. Discuss the role of multilevel batteries and describe their major features in terms of content coverage and organization.

8. List and briefly describe three examples of representative multilevel batteries.

9. Explain the current thinking, within the field of ability testing, about the measurement of general ability versus the measurement of multiple independent aptitudes.

10. Discuss the reasons for the development of multiple (differential) aptitude testing.

11. Describe the strengths and weaknesses of the Differential Aptitude Tests (DAT) as an example of a multiple aptitude battery for general use.

12. Describe the Multidimensional Aptitude Battery (MAB) and the approach to group testing that it represents.

FILL IN THE BLANKS: Key Terms and Concepts

1. _ _ _ _ _ tests are instruments designed primarily for mass testing, whose chief advantages usually include objectivity, low cost, and large norms and whose main limitations center on their impersonal nature and lack of flexibility.

2. In the _ _ _ _ _ _ _ _ _ _ _ _ format of testing, the easiest items of each type are presented first, followed by the next easiest of each type, and so on, until the most difficult items in the test are presented.

3. Individually tailored tests, also designated as _ _ _ _ _ _ _ _, _ _ _ _ _ _ _ _ _ _, _ _ _ _ _ _ _ _ _ _, _ _ _ _ _ _ _, or _ _ _ _ _ _ _ – _ _ _ _ _ _ _ _ _ _ testing, are techniques that aim to combine some of the advantages of individual and group testing. They are particularly suited to computerized administration.

4. In the _ _ _ _ _ _ _ _ _ testing model, all test takers start with an item of intermediate difficulty and are routed upward or downward depending on the correctness of their responses to that item and to subsequent ones.

5. _ _ _ _ _ _ _ _ _ _ _ _ _ _ _ _ _ _ _ testing (CAT) procedures can utilize items drawn from a pool assembled through item response theory (IRT) techniques in

flexible sequences that are individualized so as to maximize the efficiency of measurement.

6. In CAT, each item in the pool has a(n) _ _ _ _ _ _ _ _ _ _ _ _ _ _ which is used for scoring the responses of individuals and which reflects the difficulty level, discriminative value, and probability of guessing the correct response that are associated with the item.

7. In CAT, the _ _ _ _ _ _ _ _ _ _ _ _ _ _ _ function indicates the precision of measurement and, summed across all of the items attempted, constitutes the _ _ _ _ _ _ _ _ _ _ _ _ _ function which serves the same purpose as the traditional standard error of measurement.

8. _ _ _ _ _ _ _ _ _ _ _ _ _ _ _ _ _ _ have been devised in order to provide comparable measures of intellectual development over a broad range of age groups and/or grade levels.

9. In recently developed or revised multilevel batteries the term _ _ _ _ _ _ _ _ _ _ _ _ has been replaced by more specific designations that reflect their function in assessing readiness for school learning.

10. _ _ _ _ _ _ _ _ _ _ _ _ _ _ batteries were developed primarily as a result of the need to assess intraindividual variations in performance on separate abilities for counseling and placement purposes.

11. The theoretical basis for constructing multiple aptitude batteries was provided by the study of trait organization through the techniques of _ _ _ _ _ _ _ _ _ _ _ _ _ _.

12. Evidence of a large general factor underlying performance in all academic work led to the combination of the verbal plus the numerical reasoning (VR + NR) scores of the DAT, as an index of _ _ _ _ _ _ _ _ _ _ aptitude.

ANSWERS TO FILL-IN-THE-BLANKS: Key Terms and Concepts

1. group (tests)
2. spiral omnibus (format)
3. adaptive / sequential / programmed / dynamic / response-contingent (testing)
4. pyramidal (testing model)
5. computerized adaptive (testing) (CAT)
6. ability estimate
7. item information (function) / test information (function)
8. multilevel batteries
9. intelligence

10. multiple aptitude
11. factor analysis
12. scholastic (aptitude)

MATCHING: Group Tests (One letter per number)

_____ 1. Screening instrument, developed in the armed services, that provided a single score based on an equal number of vocabulary, arithmetic, spatial relations, and mechanical ability items.

_____ 2. Composite instrument used for the purposes of selection and classification in all the armed services.

_____ 3. Paper-and-pencil measure that has shown very high correlations with, and was designed to assess the same functions as, the WAIS-R.

_____ 4. Multilevel battery, for grades K to 12, that was normed jointly with the Stanford Achievement Test series.

_____ 5. Multilevel battery, for grades K through 12, that was normed jointly with the Iowa Tests of Basic Skills and the Tests of Achievement and Proficiency.

_____ 6. Multilevel battery, for grades 2 to 12, that was normed jointly with the California Achievement Tests and the Comprehensive Tests of Basic Skills.

_____ 7. Multiple aptitude battery, first published in 1947, that was designed mainly for educational and career counseling of students in Grades 8 to 12.

A. Test of Cognitive Skills (TCS)
B. Differential Aptitude Tests (DAT)
C. Armed Services Vocational Aptitude Battery (ASVAB)
D. Otis-Lennon School Ability Test (OLSAT)
E. Armed Forces Qualification Test (AFQT)
F. Cognitive Abilities Test (CogAT)
G. Multidimensional Aptitude Battery (MAB)

ANSWERS TO MATCHING ITEMS:

1-E   2-C   3-G   4-D   5-F   6-A   7-B

Multiple Choice: Test Yourself

1. The trend toward a merger of intelligence tests with multiple aptitude batteries is discernible_____.
   a. in both group and individual tests
   b. in group tests only
   c. in individual tests only
   d. neither in group nor in individual tests

2. Compared to individual tests, group tests, on the whole, have the following advantage(s): _____.
    a. more narrowly based norms
    b. more objective scoring procedures
    c. an expanded role for the examiner
    d. all of the above

3. Most group tests use the _____ type of test items.
    a. completion
    b. multiple choice
    c. free-response
    d. omnibus

4. The "spiral-omnibus" format, used in some group tests, is one in which _____
    _____.
    a. the tests include a built-in key for easy scoring
    b. examinees take only the most difficult items for their level of performance
    c. items of each type are presented successively at increasing levels of difficulty
    d. multilevel items of the same type are presented all at once

5. Group tests are often correctly criticized because_____
    _____.
    a. they are not long enough
    b. their norms are based on inadequate samples
    c. examiners often give incorrect instructions
    d. little attention can be given to rapport with the test taker

6. Some people have claimed that group tests do not allow the test taker enough room for original thinking. In view of the item analysis and validity data available on such tests, it appears that_____.
    a. restrictions caused by multiple-choice items do result in serious problems in evaluation
    b. the multiple-choice format is totally inappropriate
    c. restrictions of original thinking in responding to group test items are rare
    d. no investigations have been done on response restrictions

7. The use of a computer to alter the sequencing of item presentation as a result of performance on previous items is called _____ testing.
    a. computer
    b. adaptive
    c. alternative-response
    d. CRT

8. Response-contingent or sequential testing is most appropriate in_____
   _____.
   a. large college lecture courses
   b. private schools
   c. individualized educational programs
   d. elementary school social studies

9. The principal purpose of multilevel batteries is _____.
   a. to identify the underachiever
   b. to indicate students' readiness for learning at each stage
   c. to serve as a basis for advancing students to the next grade
   d. all of the above

10. Group tests that presuppose functional literacy are typically not administered to
    children below the _____ level.
    a. third or fourth grade
    b. fifth or sixth grade
    c. seventh or eighth grade
    d. high school

11. The Kuder-Richardson reliabilities for well-prepared multilevel batteries, such as the
    ones illustrated in the textbook, are usually _____
    _____.
    a. .80 or above
    b. .70 to .79
    c. .60 to .69
    d. under .60

12. The multilevel test—consisting of nine subtests grouped into verbal, quantitative, and
    nonverbal batteries—which was described in the textbook as an example of instruments
    available for the elementary school level is the_____.
    a. Differential Aptitude Tests
    b. Test of Cognitive Skills
    c. Cognitive Abilities Test
    d. Multidimensional Aptitude Battery

13. Multiple aptitude batteries were created primarily to_____
    _____.
    a. minimize intraindividual variation
    b. classify preschool children into mental-age groups
    c. compare the relative abilities of children with different racial backgrounds
    d. gain information about separate abilities

14. Which of the following is best handled by the use of a multiple aptitude test battery? _____.

    a.   Predicting success in medicine for a group of first-year medical students

    b.   Selecting candidates for a school of dentistry

    c.   Placing a group of high school dropouts in specific job-training programs

    d.   Determining the IQ of a group of first-year college students planning to major in science

15. The Differential Aptitude Tests battery _____.

    a.   is now available in CAT form

    b.   is appropriate for use with students from the elementary through the graduate school levels

    c.   was originally published in the 1980s

    d.   has proven to be particularly strong in the area of differential prediction

Miniprojects/Suggested Homework Activities:

1.   Some of the most exciting, and potentially revolutionary, advances in psychological testing stem from the techniques made possible by the use of computers. For a brief overview of some possibilities that technological innovations can bring to testing, read Susan Embretson's 1992 article on "Computerized Adaptive Testing: Its Potential Substantive Contributions to Psychological Research and Assessment," which appeared in *Current Directions in Psychological Science, 1,* 129-131.

2.   During the course of your education you have probably been exposed, as a test taker, to at least one of the tests discussed in Chapter 10 or to other group tests of a similar nature, such as the SATs or the GREs (discussed in Chapter 17). If this is so, chances are that you did not pay much attention to the specific procedures of test administration as you were most likely preoccupied with taking the test. One way to supplement whatever first-hand knowledge you have of group tests is to make your services available as a proctor for an examination session with one of those tests. Although elementary and secondary schools typically use their own personnel for such exams, universities and community colleges usually hire students as proctors or test supervisors for the testing programs they conduct, as long as the students are well recommended and are no longer in the position of having to take the test in question again. In addition, group testing in other institutions, such as military bases, often requires the hiring of personnel to help with test administration. The testing center in your school or your instructor are probably the best sources of information on how to participate in this activity. Its benefits include the fact that you will almost surely go through an informative test orientation session and be paid for your time.

3.   One of the oldest and most versatile of the group tests discussed in Chapter 10 is the Differential Aptitude Tests (DAT) battery. You can learn a great deal about it and about its historical evolution by reading the reviews of its various editions in the *Mental Measurements Yearbook* (MMY) series—starting with the excerpted review of the original DAT, which appeared in the *Third MMY* (1949), through the two reviews of the latest DAT (5th ed.), in the *Twelfth MMY* (1995). In the process, you also are bound to learn more about test development and evaluation.

ANSWERS TO MULTIPLE CHOICE/TEST YOURSELF ITEMS:

 1.   a
 2.   b
 3.   b
 4.   c
 5.   d
 6.   c
 7.   b
 8.   c
 9.   b
10.   a
11.   a
12.   c
13.   d
14.   c
15.   a

NATURE OF INTELLIGENCE

Chapter Outline

Meaning of an IQ

Heritability and Modifiability

Motivation and Intelligence

Factor Analysis of Intelligence
     The Factor Matrix
     The Reference Axes
     Interpretation of Factors
     Factorial Composition of a Test
     Factor Loadings and Correlation
     Oblique Axes and Second-Order Factors

Theories of Trait Organization
     The Two-Factor Theory
     Multiple-Factor Theories
     Structure-of-Intellect Model
     Hierarchical Theories

Nature and Development of Traits
     Experiential History
     Mechanisms of Trait Formation
     Factor Analysis and Cognitive Task Analysis
     General Intelligence

Chapter Summary

Psychological tests are designed to measure behavior. Therefore, their proper interpretation requires knowledge of human behavior. Unless test users possess the psychological information necessary to interpret tests properly, tests are likely to be misused and misinterpreted, regardless of how technically sophisticated the tests themselves may be. Psychological research can contribute to our ability to understand as well as predict intelligent behavior.

Intelligence test scores, such as IQs, should be regarded as descriptive and should be used to help to understand individuals, rather than to label them. These principles need to be followed not only because intelligence tests do not provide an explanation of the reasons why people perform as they do, but also because such tests do not assess "intelligence" in all its various meanings and complexity. An additional source of confusion with regard to intelligence tests has arisen from the practice of computing heritability indexes for intelligence on the basis of questionable empirical data on family resemblance on intelligence test scores. Heritability indexes, in general, have serious limitations in that they apply only to the populations on which they were found and not to individuals or to other populations. In addition, no matter how large the heritability index for a given trait is, it should not be taken to imply that the contribution of the environment to that trait is unimportant. There is, in fact, a large and growing body of evidence that intellectual abilities are quite amenable to environmental interventions. Furthermore, although intelligence test scores are often considered in isolation, it is widely recognized that personality and intellect coexist within the individual and have reciprocal effects on one another that cannot be separated.

Psychological research on the nature and composition of mental traits has relied considerably on the investigation of discernible patterns in the scores obtained by a sample of persons on a wide variety of ability tests. Factor analysis is a statistical technique which serves to explore and understand these behavioral data by reducing the number of dimensions needed to describe them, without sacrificing essential information. Although there are several methods that can be used for analyzing a set of variables into common factors, all of them begin with a complete table of intercorrelations among the variables and all of them end with a factor matrix which shows the weight or loading of each factor in each variable.

When the scores of a sample of individuals on various tests is subjected to factor analysis, the results are factor loadings. These represent the correlation between each test and each factor—also known as the factorial validity of the test. The square of that correlation estimates the proportion of variance common to each test and the factor in question which, along with the variance specific to each test *and* its error variance, add up to the total variance of the test. The nature of a given factor is deduced from an examination of the tests that have high loadings on the factor and from a psychologically informed interpretation of what the tests have in common. When the axes that best fit the graphic representation of test clusters are oblique, rather than orthogonal, it means that the factors emerging from an analysis are themselves correlated. Their intercorrelations can, in turn, be analyzed to arrive at second-order factors. These then account for the variance that is common to the factors and further reduce the number of dimensions needed to describe the original test data.

Over the course of most of the twentieth century, factor analytic techniques have given rise to a variety of different theories about how intellectual traits are organized. Historically, British psychologists tended to begin with a single general factor, to which they attributed the major portion of the common variance, and then turned to group factors to account for the remaining intercorrelations, whereas American factor analysts usually accounted for as much of the common variance as possible through group factors and only postulated a general factor if the data justified it. Spearman's so-called "two-factor theory," with its single "g" factor which accounts for most of the variance in intellectual activities, is a prime example of the original British approach, while Thurstone's multiple-factor theory, with its 7 to 12 "primary mental abilities," exemplifies the American tradition. In addition, there have been alternative designs, such as Guilford's structure-of-intellect (SI) model which organized all intellectual traits along the dimensions of operations, contents, and products for a total of at least 180 distinct possible factors. Still another type of schema that has been used in organizing the multiplicity of factors derived from the analysis of ability test data is the hierarchical approach postulated by Vernon and Humphreys, among others. Because of its theoretical and practical advantages, the hierarchical model—which reconciles the single general factor with multiple-factor patterns—has become increasingly accepted and used to construct a new generation of ability tests.

The proliferation of models of trait organization is understandable when we consider that the traits identified through factor analysis are simply categories that describe the correlation among a set of behavioral measures. Moreover, the factorial composition of a given task may, and frequently does, differ among individuals with diverse experiential backgrounds and can also change within individuals over time, as their cognitive strategies evolve. Thus, the factors extracted from performance on intellectual tasks cannot be viewed as static underlying entities, any more than cognitive skills can be seen as representing fixed or innate properties of the organism.

Research in cognitive psychology has increasingly highlighted the impact of domain specificity on the formation and development of factors. From this perspective, intelligence is seen as the combination of cognitive skills and knowledge that is demanded, fostered, and rewarded by the experiential context in which the individual functions. The view of intelligence as a multifaceted, domain-specific construct has also expanded the variety of contexts in which research is carried out—beyond the schools, into the world of adults and daily living—and has enriched our understanding of intriguing intellectual phenomena such as giftedness and creativity.

Comprehensive Review

STUDY QUESTIONS:

1. Suppose that you took an intelligence test and obtained an extremely high IQ. What, if any, objections should you have to being labeled as a "genius" on the basis of that result?

2. Define what a heritability index is, describe how it is obtained, and discuss the limitations of the concept of heritability estimates in general.

3. Discuss the relationship that exists between personality and cognitive variables and cite two examples of personality traits that have a special impact on cognitive functioning.

4. Explain the purpose of factor analysis and describe the basic elements that are common to all factor analytic techniques.

5. Describe Thurstone's criteria of positive manifold and simple structure and explain why it is useful to rotate reference axes in accordance to those criteria.

6. Discuss how the results of a factor analysis are interpreted.

7. Describe and explain the two basic theorems of factor analysis.

8. Define second-order factors and explain how they are derived.

9. Compare the traditional approaches of British and American psychologists to factor analysis and cite examples of two theories of trait organization that are representative of those approaches.

10. Discuss how general, group, and specific factors are related and explain why factorial research has produced such a multiplicity of factors.

11. Describe Guilford's structure-of-intellect (SI) model.

12. Describe the basic features of hierarchical theories of trait organization and the advantages that hierarchical models possess for testing purposes.

13. Explain the nature of the traits that are identified through factor analysis as well as how and why the factorial composition of a given task may differ across and within individuals.

14. Explain how factor analytic and information-processing procedures can be productively combined to expand our understanding of cognitive trait formation.

15. Discuss the notion of domain specificity and the impact it has had on the psychological study of intelligence.

EXERCISES: Factor Analysis

❶ Reconstruct the original correlation matrix for Tests 1 through 10 from the hypothetical factor matrix presented in Table 11-1 (p. 303) of the textbook. This exercise will require you to go "backwards" from the usual order of steps in factor analysis wherein one starts with a correlation matrix and ends with a factor matrix.

133

However, the calculations you will be doing are actually done in practice as a final step in factor analysis, just to check on the computational accuracy of the analysis. In order to do this exercise you will need to (a) apply the basic factor analytic theorem stating that the correlation between two variables is equal to the sum of the cross-products of their common-factor loadings, and (b) assume that Table 11-1 gives all the common-factor loadings between the tests in question (see pp. 308-309 of the text).

❷ For each of the four tests in Table 8, calculate the proportional contributions of each factor, the error variance, and the specificity of the test. Refer to the textbook (pp. 307-308) for the procedure you will need to follow.

Table 8 — Factor Loadings and Reliabilities for Four Tests

Tests	V	R	N	P	Reliability Coefficient
		Factors*			
Vocabulary	.70	.21	.16	.04	.95
Analogies	.31	.60	.20	.06	.90
Arithmetic	.03	.17	.82	.23	.92
Perceptual Speed	−.02	.00	.10	.65	.88

*V = Verbal   R = Reasoning   N = Numerical   P = Perceptual

ANSWERS TO EXERCISES: Factor Analysis

❶   CORRELATION MATRIX FOR TESTS 1 TO 10

Tests	1	2	3	4	5	6	7	8	9	10
1		.68	.74	.36	.79	−.11	.03	.13	.12	.10
2			.60	.29	.64	−.06	.06	.15	.13	.11
3				.32	.69	−.07	.06	.15	.13	.11
4					.34	−.05	.01	.06	.05	.04
5						−.10	.03	.12	.12	.10
6							.34	.36	.28	.20
7								.45	.36	.25
8									.40	.29
9										.23

134

Note the relatively high and uniformly positive correlations of Tests 1 through 5 (within the solid triangle) with each other and of Tests 6 through 10 (within the broken triangle) with each other. Notice also that the correlations that are outside of the triangles, i.e., those between Tests 1 to 5 and Tests 6 to 10 are either negative or very low. This hypothetical example presents a relatively simple factor analysis that resulted in two distinct and unambiguous factors. Therefore, in this case, an inspection of the original correlation matrix, which you reproduced in this exercise, probably would have led to similar conclusions about the data as the factor matrix does. In practice, however, correlation matrices are not always this clear and factor analysis can reveal patterns that are not obvious in the correlation matrix. In any case, factor analyses do simplify the description of data by reducing the number of dimensions needed to represent them.

❷

SOURCES OF VARIANCE OF TEST SCORES

Proportional Contributions

Tests	V	R	N	P	Specific	Error
Vocabulary	.49	.04	.03	.00	.39	.05
Analogies	.10	.36	.04	.00	.40	.10
Arithmetic	.00	.03	.67	.05	.17	.08
Percept. Speed	.00	.00	.01	.42	.45	.12

FILL IN THE BLANKS: Key Terms and Concepts

1. A _ _ _ _ _ _ _ _ _ _ _ _ _ _ _ _ _ _ _ is a number, calculated on the basis of measures of familial resemblance in a given trait, that shows the proportional contribution of genetic factors to the total variance of the trait in a given population under existing conditions.

2. In the comprehensive schema that Atkinson formulated to represent the interrelationships between abilities, motivation, and environmental variables, the concept of _ _ _ _ – _ _ – _ _ _ _, or time devoted to an activity, is a critical variable which—combined with level of performance—determines final achievement.

3. _ _ _ _ _ _ _ _ _ learning takes place as a result of the fact that even if people are exposed to the same immediate situation, what they attend to—as well as how deeply and for how long they attend to it—plays a pivotal role in learning.

135

4.	The _____ – _____, which may be construed as a sort of private self-fulfilling prophecy, is a pointed example of the interrelationship between aptitude and personality traits in that it can at once be a product of and an influence in a person's achievement history.

5.	The _____ – _____ motive—which can be gauged in infants by the extent and quality of their observation, exploration, and manipulation of their surroundings—is a prime contributor to cognitive development and a good predictor of later intellectual competence.

6.	The technique of _____ _____, whose principal aim is to simplify the description of data by reducing the number of variables, has been instrumental in identifying the common traits shared by various tests of ability.

7.	All factor analyses begin with a table that shows the interrelationships among a set of variables , which is called a(n) _____ _____. They end with a(n) _____ _____, which is a table showing the weight or loading of each factor in each variable.

8.	_____ ____ are the customary way to represent factors geometrically in order to plot each test, in the process of factor analysis.

9.	The rotation of reference axes in factor analysis is customarily carried out in accordance with the criterion of _____ _____, which requires rotation to such a position as to eliminate all significant negative weights, and the criterion of _____ _____, which means that each test should have loadings on as few factors as possible.

10.	When an orthogonal rotation of axes is applied in the factor analysis of test data, the _____ _____ of each test is evaluated by its factor loadings which represent the correlation of the test with each factor.

11.	One of the basic theorems of factor analysis states that the total variance of a test is the sum of the variances contributed by the _____ factors (those shared with other tests), the _____ factors (those occurring in that test alone,) and the _____ variance.

12.	The _____ of a test is that portion of its "true" variance it does not share with any other test with which it was factor analyzed.

13.	Another basic theorem of factor analysis states that the correlation between any two variables is equal to the sum of the _____ – _____ of their _____ – _____ loadings.

14. Reference axes that are at right angles to each other are called _ _ _ _ _ _ _ _ _ _ axes, and represent factors that are uncorrelated, whereas axes that are not at right angles are called _ _ _ _ _ _ _ axes, and represent factors that are correlated to each other.

15. When the factors that result from an analysis are themselves correlated, it is possible to "factorize the factors" and derive _ _ _ _ _ _ _ – _ _ _ _ _ factors.

16. Spearman's two-factor theory maintained that all intellectual activities share a single common factor, called the _ _ _ _ _ _ _ factor or "g." In addition, the theory postulated many _ _ _ _ _ _ _ _ _ or "s" factors, unique to each activity.

17. The extraction of factors such as verbal comprehension, associative memory, and perceptual speed is typical of _ _ _ _ _ _ _ _ _ – _ _ _ _ _ _ theories such as Thurstone's, which included about a dozen _ _ _ _ _ factors.

18. Thurstone referred to the group factors he had identified through research on intellectual measures as _ _ _ _ _ _ _ _ _ _ _ _ _ abilities.

19. On the basis of over two decades of factor analytic research, Guilford postulated a boxlike model he called the _ _ _ _ _ _ _ _ _ –of– _ _ _ _ _ _ _ _ _ _ (SI) model which classifies all intellectual traits along three dimensions and consists of 180 cells.

20. The three dimensions of the SI model are _ _ _ _ _ _ _ _ _ _ , which consist of what the respondent does, _ _ _ _ _ _ _ _ _ , which concern the nature of the information used, and _ _ _ _ _ _ _ _ , or the form in which the information is processed.

21. Spearman's two-factor theory, Thurstone's multiple-factor theory, and Guilford's SI model are examples of three different theories of _ _ _ _ _ _ _ _ _ _ _ _ _ _ _ _ _ _ .

22. Another schema that has been used to organize factors, in addition to the ones mentioned in the previous item, is the _ _ _ _ _ _ _ _ _ _ _ model, proposed by P.E. Vernon, among others, which starts with the "g" factor at the top and progresses downward to increasingly narrower factors.

23. _ _ _ _ _ _ _ _ are descriptive categories that reflect the changing interrelationships of performance in a variety of situations. They are the products of the individual's cumulative experiential history.

24. The _ of the same objective task may differ among individuals with diverse experiential backgrounds and may change within individuals depending on their choice of strategies.

25. The establishment of _ _ _ _ _ _ _ _ _ _ _ _ , which enable a person to learn more

efficiently the "second time around," can mediate the emergence of certain factors. _ _ _ _ _ _ _ _ of _ _ _ _ _ _ _ _, as well, allows a person to apply acquired skills to the solution of new problems.

ANSWERS TO FILL-IN-THE-BLANKS: Key Terms and Concepts

1.   heritability index
2.   time-on-task
3.   selective (learning)
4.   self-concept
5.   environmental-mastery (motive)
6.   factor analysis
7.   correlation matrix / factor matrix
8.   reference axes
9.   (criterion of) positive manifold / (criterion of) simple structure
10. factorial validity
11. common (factors) / specific (factors) / error (variance)
12. specificity (of a test)
13. (sum of the) cross-products / common-factor (loadings)
14. orthogonal (axes) / oblique (axes)
15. second-order (factors)
16. general (factor or "g") / specifics (or "s" factors)
17. multiple-factor (theories) / group (factors)
18. primary mental (abilities)
19. structure-(of)-intellect (SI) (model)
20. operations / contents / products
21. (theories of) trait organization
22. hierarchical (model)
23. factors
24. factorial composition
25. learning sets / transfer (of) training

Multiple Choice: Test Yourself

1.   According to the textbook, the widely publicized book entitled *The Bell Curve* has _____ .

    a.   perpetuated misconceptions about ethnic and gender differences in intelligence test performance

    b.   clarified relevant issues concerning the origins of differences in intelligence test performance among ethnic groups once and for all

    c.   increased the general public's level of understanding about the nature of intelligence

d. explained how individuals may be brought up to their maximum possible levels of intellectual functioning

2. Heritability indexes_____.
   a. are widely applicable once they have been determined
   b. constitute a good way to gauge the modifiability of a trait
   c. have frequently been based on studies of twins
   d. refer to an individual's hereditary make-up

3. In terms of the relationship between personality and aptitudes, there is a growing consensus to the effect that aptitudes_____.
   a. should be investigated independently of affective variables
   b. can no longer be investigated independently of affective variables
   c. may or may not be investigated independently of affective variables
   d. are not significantly related to affective variables

4. The principal object of any factor analysis is to_____.
   a. simplify the description of data
   b. generate new ways to explain interindividual variation
   c. reduce the amount of error in psychological measurements
   d. identify new personality traits

5. A factor matrix _____.
   a. lists the correlation of each variable with every other variable
   b. places the original raw scores in a table for generating factor scores
   c. presents the loadings of each factor in each test
   d. identifies the most valid questions on a test

6. The first step in a factor analysis is_____.
   a. developing a correlation matrix
   b. determining if tests have sufficient validity and reliability
   c. replacing all raw scores with their z score equivalents
   d. identifying the principal factors

7. The interpretation and naming of factors calls for_____.
   a. advanced statistical training
   b. psychological insight
   c. intercorrelations between factors
   d. the loading of individual test items

8. A factor loading is a_____

_____.
   a.   measure of the power of each factor
   b.   measure of the extent to which a test may be used to predict academic success
   c.   correlation between all possible combinations of items found on two or more tables
   d.   none of the above

9. The reason for rotating the reference axes, either orthogonally or obliquely, is to_____.
   a.   obtain the factor structure
   b.   help interpret and name the factors
   c.   determine the specificity of a test
   d.   find the second-order factors

10. Based on the following factor matrix, what is the correlation between tests A and B?

_____.

FACTOR MATRIX		
	Factor I	Factor II
Test A	.90	.05
Test B	.40	.20

   a.   .37
   b.   .20
   c.   .84
   d.   .56

11. Historically, the differences between the British and American views of trait organization have centered on the fact that_____

_____.
   a.   British psychologists place more emphasis on the importance of a general factor
   b.   American psychologists are more likely to seek specific factors
   c.   American psychologists usually work with only one or two "s" factors
   d.   both a and b are true

12. Guilford's structure-of-intellect model classifies intellectual traits into _____.
   a.   146 cells
   b.   3 dimensions
   c.   44 categories
   d.   14 factors

13. The structure-of-intellect model has _____

_____.

a. had a great deal of impact on the development of tests for general use
b. not been used as a blueprint for the design of any test
c. been found to fit Guilford's original data better than any competing models
d. helped focus attention on the distinction between content and operations

14. Currently, the most widely accepted model of intelligence, for both practical and theoretical purposes, is the _____model.
a. two-factor
b. multiple-factor
c. structure-of-intellect
d. hierarchical

15. The technique wherein an individual is instructed to "think aloud" as he or she solves a problem is known as _____.
a. context analysis
b. factor analysis
c. protocol analysis
d. cathartic problem solving

Miniprojects/Suggested Homework Activities:

1. Many psychologists have pointed out that one of the major problems in validating intelligence tests is the difficulty of defining the construct of intelligence. An early definition, proposed by E.G. Boring, is frequently cited as the epitome of that problem. His definition stated that intelligence is what intelligence tests measure, Although the redundancy of it was clear to virtually everyone, in practice, the idea really took hold. For example, the most widely used intelligence tests—such as the Stanford-Binet and the Wechsler scales—have relied heavily on their high correlations with each other and with other similar tests for evidence of validity. An interesting discussion of the history and the problem of defining intelligence can be found in the first chapter of R.J. Sternberg's *Intelligence Applied: Understanding and Increasing Your Intellectual Skills* (San Diego, CA: Harcourt Brace Jovanovich, 1986). Another volume, edited by R.J. Sternberg and D.K. Detterman and entitled *What Is Intelligence? Contemporary Views on Its Nature and Definitions* (Norwood, NJ: Ablex, 1986), contains the opinions of 24 experts—including Anne Anastasi—on the subject.

2. The section on factor analysis (pp. 303-309) in the textbook provides a clear and concise explanation of this important statistical technique. If you study it carefully, you may be able to read and understand much of the psychological literature that is based on factorial research, without delving further into the computational details of factor analysis. Should you wish to learn about such details, read Paul Kline's *An Easy Guide to Factor Analysis* (New York: Routledge, 1993) or the two classic (1978)

monographs by Jae-On Kim and Charles W. Mueller entitled *Introduction to Factor Analysis: What It Is and How to Do It* and *Factor Analysis: Statistical Methods and Practical Issues*, which are part of the Sage University Papers Series on Quantitative Applications in the Social Sciences (Thousand Oaks, CA: Sage Publications).

3. To deepen your knowledge of factor analysis—and expand your understanding of the theories and models discussed in Chapter 11—read John B. Carroll's masterful reanalyses and integration of factor analytic research on cognitive abilities conducted over the past seven decades (*Human Cognitive Abilities: A Survey of Factor-Analytic Studies*, New York: Cambridge University Press, 1993). The survey, which culminates in an exposition of Carroll's "Three-Stratum" hierarchical theory of cognitive abilities, is an indispensable reference for anyone who wants to be familiar with the literature on individual differences in this area.

4. Read the manuals of some of the many tests that have used factor analysis to investigate construct validity or that are based on factorial research, and you will learn more about this technique in the context of psychological testing. The three suggested references barely scratch the surface of possible readings of this kind. They were selected because they exemplify different ways of using factor analysis in test construction and development:

   ✍ The *Guilford-Zimmerman Aptitude Survey* (GZAS), published by Consulting Psychologists Press, is a multiple aptitude battery developed by J.P. Guilford before he devised his SI model. Although it is not nearly as well-normed, nor as widely used, as the Differential Aptitude Tests or some of the other multiple aptitude batteries discussed in Chapters 10 and 17 of the text, the GZAS has a succinct manual. This characteristic, which would be undesirable from other standpoints, makes it ideal for a brief first-hand look at instruments of its kind.

   ✍ The *Sixteen Personality Factor Questionnaire* (16 PF), discussed in Chapter 13 of the text (pp. 363-364), is an example of a *personality* test based on extensive factor analytic research conducted by Raymond B. Cattell over the course of many years. One interesting feature of the 16 PF is that it provides scores on five second-order factors (now designated as "global" factors), besides the 16 "primary" factors it was designed to assess. A review of the 16 PF manual, published by the Institute for Personality and Ability Testing, should expand your understanding of factors and their intercorrelations.

   ✍ The Fourth Edition of the *Stanford-Binet Intelligence Scale* (SB-IV)—discussed in Chapter 8 of the text—uses the intercorrelations between its tests, along with subsequent factor analyses, as a principal source of validation data. Read Chapter 6 of the *Technical Manual* for the SB-IV—published by Riverside

Publishing Company—for a clear and succinct presentation of these data, typical of the factor analyses done on all the major individual intelligence tests.

ANSWERS TO MULTIPLE CHOICE/TEST YOURSELF ITEMS:

1. a
2. c
3. b
4. a
5. c
6. a
7. b
8. d
9. b
10. a
11. a
12. b
13. d
14. d
15. c

PSYCHOLOGICAL ISSUES IN ABILITY TESTING

Chapter Outline

Longitudinal Studies of Children's Intelligence
      Stability of Intelligence Test Performance
      Instability of Intelligence Test Performance

Intelligence in Early Childhood
      Predictive Validity of Infant and Preschool Tests
      Nature of Early Childhood Intelligence
      Implications for Intervention Programs

Problems in the Testing of Adult Intelligence
      Age Decrement
      The Seattle Longitudinal Study (SLS)
      Individual Differences and Age
      Nature of Adult Intelligence

Population Changes in Intelligence Test Performance
      Rising Scores
      Declining Scores
      Overview

Cultural Diversity
      The Field of Cultural Psychology
      Cultural Differences versus Cultural Handicap
      Language in Transcultural Testing
      The Testing Situation

Chapter Summary

Because psychological testing has been somewhat isolated from other fields of psychology, many of the advances in test construction have not been taken into account by people who apply tests in various contexts. As a result, outdated interpretations of test results have survived and some discontent with testing—based largely on past misuses of tests—lingers in the public's mind. Chapter 12 highlights psychological research findings that can enhance the use of ability tests and correct popular misconceptions about intelligence tests and their scores.

An important contribution that psychological research has made to the understanding of the construct of "intelligence" derives from longitudinal studies of the same individuals over long periods of time. These studies have shown that intelligence is both complex and dynamic, rather than unitary and constant. Although research on groups demonstrates that intelligence test performance is quite stable over the elementary, high school, and college periods, studies of individuals reveal that people can undergo large shifts in IQ as a consequence of environmental influences and personality characteristics.

Assessing the intelligence of people who have not yet started, or who have already discontinued, their schooling presents a unique difficulty because of the diversity of their activities, in contrast to the relative uniformity of experience of school-age individuals. For infants, this problem is compounded by the fact that their intelligence appears to be qualitatively different from that of school-age children. Thus, the test results of infants have little, if any, validity for predicting later performance unless they are markedly atypical. For older preschoolers, intelligence test scores do have moderate predictive validity.

Attempts to enhance the academic readiness of children from disadvantaged backgrounds have shown that (a) numerous variables, such as parental involvement, must be taken into account, and (b) remedial interventions and assessment should be aimed at improving specific skills instead of broad developmental indexes such as the IQ. Furthermore, evaluating the effectiveness of intervention programs calls for considerable methodological sophistication in both experimental design and interpretation of test results.

Cross-sectional studies of adult intelligence have typically shown a peak during the early adulthood years followed by a steady decline in older age groups, while longitudinal studies, as a rule, have shown continuing improvement or stability in several abilities. This difference is most likely attributable to methodological artifacts of the two types of research designs. Cross-sectional studies usually compare older and less educated adults with younger and better educated ones. Longitudinal comparisons frequently use intellectually superior individuals or otherwise confound the effects of aging on intelligence test performance. The results of cross-sequential research on adult intelligence—which combines both designs with other time-based comparisons—indicate that, in most functions, age decline starts later and is less pronounced than traditional cross-sectional comparisons would indicate. In addition, declines in ability are not uniform across all intellectual functions and the changes that do occur vary widely among individuals, as a function of health status, lifestyle, and opportunities for intellectual stimulation.

As far as the general population is concerned, there has been a rise in the mean intelligence test performance over the past several decades which *may* be attributable to increasing literacy, higher educational levels, and other cultural changes. Nevertheless, this rise is by no means uniform in all segments of the population or across all time periods. One of the clear exceptions to the secular rise in tested intelligence is the highly publicized decline in Scholastic Aptitude Test (SAT) scores between 1963 and 1977. This decline has been commonly attributed to specific changes in the composition of the college-bound segment of the population and to subsequent curricular adjustments to those changes. However, current explanations for the conflicting trends in ability test performance are far from satisfactory or complete. Proper understanding of the research findings on changes in the test performance of populations requires a consideration of a multiplicity of variables, including the type of instruments and norms involved, the timing of the tests, the kinds of populations sampled, as well as the cultural conditions which might have affected them.

The field of cultural psychology, which deals with behavioral differences among groups living in identifiably diverse cultural contexts, has been rapidly expanding over the past three decades. In essence, this is due to the growing recognition that all human behavior is culture-specific. The same psychological processes may give rise to vastly diverse results for members of different cultures. The pervasiveness of cultural influences on behavior, and the fact that hereditary and environmental factors are inextricably intertwined, make a "culture-free" test impossible. In fact, since each culture encourages certain abilities and ways of behaving, the very notions of what is an asset or what is a handicap may differ across cultures. This makes it difficult to devise a test that will be "fair" to more than one cultural group, especially when cultures differ significantly from one another.

The traditional cross-cultural approach to testing has relied heavily on nonverbal content. This is not an adequate solution to the problem of devising culture-fair instruments because: (a) we cannot assume that nonverbal tests measure the same functions as verbal tests, and (b) nonlanguage tests may, in fact, be even more culturally loaded than verbal tests. From the point of view of the tests themselves, no single solution to this dilemma is totally satisfactory. Translations of tests, for instance, are problematic because they must be comparable not only in terms of their reliability, validity, and norms, but also in terms of the relative difficulty of item content for members of diverse cultures. In addition, removing from a test those parts that may pose special difficulty for test takers from some cultures may also lower its validity and effectiveness. Thus, the solution that has been recently emphasized is to focus on properly trained examiners as the most effective means of ensuring that cross-cultural testing is conducted in an informed and sensitive manner.

Comprehensive Review

STUDY QUESTIONS:

1. Discuss the relationship between psychological testing and psychological science, as well as why and how that relationship needs to change.

2. Describe the major findings of longitudinal studies of children's intelligence.

3. List and discuss three conditions that have been cited as explanations for the stability of IQs during the course of human development.

4. Discuss the major conditions associated with significant increments and decrements in IQ as far as young people are concerned.

5. Describe the differences that exist in the results of tests of intelligence for infants and for older preschoolers and discuss the major reasons for those differences.

6. Discuss the role of psychological research, in general, and of psychological tests, in particular, in the planning and evaluation of intervention programs for preschoolers from disadvantaged backgrounds.

7. Contrast and explain the typical findings of longitudinal versus cross-sectional studies of adult intelligence.

8. Describe the advantages of the cross-sequential design for studying changes that occur over the lifespan; discuss the major findings of research that has used this design in the realm of tested abilities.

9. Cite two major examples of seemingly contradictory findings in the area of population changes in ability test performance and the possible reasons that have been offered to explain each of these findings.

10. Outline and explain the various items of information necessary to properly understand research findings on the changes in the test performance of populations over time.

11. Define the field of cultural psychology and discuss the reasons for the growth spurt it has undergone in recent decades.

12. Describe what is meant by a "culture-free" and a "culture-fair" test; explain the difficulties inherent in trying to devise instruments of this sort.

13. Discuss the use of nonverbal tests in cross-cultural testing and explain why they might be less effective than verbal tests.

14. List three types of cultural differentials and describe the ways in which each one might affect (a) test performance and (b) the broader behavior domain that a test is designed to sample.

15. Suppose that you were an examiner about to undertake some cross-cultural testing. How would you construe your role in the testing process?

FILL IN THE BLANKS: Key Terms and Concepts

1. _____ studies are those which examine the same group of individuals over long periods of time.

2. The growing consistency of intelligence test performance in individuals has been explained partly by the role of _____ _____ skills, which is a concept similar to that of "readiness" within the context of education.

3. The extent to which parents deliberately train a child in skills that are not yet essential has been called a(n) _____ attempt and has been associated with rising IQs.

4. The concept of _____ _____ describes the qualitative changes in competence behavior appropriate at different ages, such as the infant's progression from discovering that he or she can affect the environment to complex, goal-directed activities.

5. In the context of developmental research a same-age _____ is a group of persons born in the same year or other specified period.

6. _____ – _____ comparisons are those in which persons of different ages are examined at the same time.

7. The _____ – _____ design combines data from traditional cross-sectional and longitudinal studies and compares same-age cohorts at different time periods in an attempt to separate the effects of age from those of cultural factors.

8. The _____ _____ _____ (SLS), began in 1956, is an outstanding instance of the use of a cross-sequential design to investigate the effects of age on intellectual performance.

9. The field of _____ _____ is primarily concerned with the behavioral differences that exist among groups reared and functioning in identifiably diverse contexts.

10. When psychologists realized it was futile to try to develop tests free from cultural influences, the goal in cross-cultural testing became to devise tests presupposing only experiences common to different cultures, or "_____ – ____" tests.

11. Cultural _____ become cultural _____ only in cases where individuals move out of the culture or subculture in which they were reared and attempt to function, compete, or succeed in a different milieu.

12. According to Feuerstein, cultural deprivation consists of a lack of experiences which foster the establishment of learning sets, orientations, and other behavior patterns that facilitate subsequent learning, or _ _ _ _ _ _ _ _ _ _ _ _ _ _ _ _ experiences.

13. _ _ _ _ _ _ _ _ _ _ _ _ _ _ _ _ _ _ _ _ _ _ is a reaction of some test-takers who, through an awareness of existing stereotypes, may be negatively influenced in their own motivation and attitudes toward the test as well as in their actual test performance.

14. Findings concerning the lack of comparability of verbal intelligence tests and "cross-cultural" tests using nonverbal content have been reinforced by research in cognitive psychology which has repeatedly shown the _ _ _ _ _ _ _ _ _ _ _ _ _ _ _ _ of thinking processes.

15. The traditional approach to transcultural testing was focused on removing from the test those parts that would be affected by an individual's cultural background. It has been replaced by an approach focusing on the _ _ _ _ _ _ _ _ ' _ behavior in the test situation.

ANSWERS TO FILL-IN-THE-BLANKS: Key Terms and Concepts

1. longitudinal (studies)
2. prerequisite learning (skills)
3. acceleration (attempt)
4. developmental transformations
5. cohort
6. cross-sectional (comparisons)
7. cross-sequential (design)
8. Seattle Longitudinal Study (SLS)
9. cultural psychology
10. "culture-fair" (tests)
11. (cultural) differences / (cultural) handicaps
12. mediated learning (experiences)
13. stereotype vulnerability
14. content specificity (of thinking processes)
15. examiner's (behavior in the test situation)

TRUE/FALSE and WHY?

1. When the interval between tests is held constant, retest correlations tend to be higher in older than in younger children. (T/F) Why? _____

_____ _____

2. There is a growing amount of data which indicate that the psychological environments of siblings reared in the same family are far from identical. (T/F) Why? _____
_____

3. Correlational studies of IQ at various stages of childhood provide actuarial data applicable to group predictions but not necessarily to the prediction of an individual's future IQ. (T/F) Why? _____
_____

4. The object of compensatory educational programs for young children from disadvantaged backgrounds should be to raise their IQs. (T/F) Why? _____
_____

5. Emotional dependency on parents appears to be a condition that is associated with large IQ gains during the preschool years. (T/F) Why? _____
_____

6. The conclusion that emerges from longitudinal studies of infant intelligence test performance is that tests administered during the first year of life have little or no long-term predictive value. (T/F) Why? _____
_____

7. Infant tests are more helpful in predicting subsequent development within clinical, nonnormal populations than within normal populations. (T/F) Why? _____
_____

8. In general, the findings of research on the nature of early childhood intelligence support the conception of a developmentally constant and unitary intellectual ability in infancy. (T/F) Why? _____
_____

9. Longitudinal studies of tested intelligence in average or below average adults have shown the same age-related decrements found in cross-sectional comparisons. (T/F) Why? _____
_____

10. Intensive studies of persons in their 70s, 80s, and 90s suggest that their intellectual functioning is more closely related to health status than to chronological age. (T/F) Why? _____
_____

11. Whether the test scores of a given population rise, fall, or remain stable over time depends exclusively on the time period covered. (T/F) Why? _____

12. Empirical evidence, as well as logic, indicates that every test tends to favor persons from the culture in which it was developed. (T/F) Why? _____

13. The assumption that tests which employ nonverbal content provide a more culture-fair measure of intellectual functions than verbal tests has been thoroughly justified. (T/F) Why? _____

14. Cultural factors that affect test performance are such that they rarely influence the broader behavior domains that tests are designed to assess. (T/F) Why? _____

15. Even when intelligence tests have been accurately translated, they cannot be assumed to be comparable to the original version as far as reliability and validity are concerned. (T/F) Why? _____

ANSWERS TO TRUE/FALSE:

1. True	4. False	7. True	10. True	13. False
2. True	5. False	8. False	11. False	14. False
3. True	6. True	9. False	12. True	15. True

Multiple Choice: Test Yourself

1. In general, studies of the stability of intelligence test performance in elementary, high school, and college students over periods of from 1 to 10 years show test-retest correlations of approximately _____.
   a. .80 or higher
   b. .50 to .80
   c. .20 to .50
   d. these correlations vary more widely than any of the above

2. Research has shown that IQs are most reliable when they are obtained at ages _____.
   a. 0 to 18 months
   b. 18 months to 2 years
   c. 3 to 10 years
   d. 10 to 25 years

3. Which of the following is *not* a major factor in increasing the stability of the IQ in older children? _____.
   a. Regularities in their environments
   b. The cumulative nature of intellectual development
   c. The role of prerequisite learning skills
   d. An acceleration attempt by parents

4. The effectiveness of compensatory educational programs, such as Head Start, has been _____.
   a. substantial and enduring in most cases
   b. substantial but short-lived in most cases
   c. limited but enduring in most cases
   d. largely dependent on the quality of the programs

5. Longitudinal studies of test performance _____.
   a. compare different groups of people at different age levels
   b. are not as effective as cross-sectional studies
   c. follow the performance of the same group of persons over time
   d. emphasize wide-ranging skill areas

6. In the time-lag comparisons that are a part of cross-sequential designs for studying age changes in intelligence test performance _____.
   a. persons of different ages are examined at the same time
   b. the same persons are followed periodically over time
   c. same-age cohorts from different time periods are compared
   d. several same-age cohorts are tested at one point in time

7. Which of the following is the *least likely* reason for the decline cross-sectional studies show in the intelligence test performance of adults over 40? _____.
   a. Age, per se
   b. The fact that younger adults have had more education
   c. Cultural changes
   d. Experiential factors in the lives of adults

8. Which of the following is true about the IQ of people over 60? _____.
   a. There is a general decrease in IQ level on standard tests
   b. Some 60-year-olds still do better than the average 25-year-olds
   c. Intelligence test performance improves
   d. None of the above are true

9. All other things being equal, if a person were tested with the WAIS at ages 20, 30, and 40, how would you expect her/his IQ to vary? _____.
   a. The IQ would rise until age 40 and then drop

b. The IQ would drop on each successive examination
c. The person's IQ would remain about the same
d. There would be a slow increase in the IQ

10. What is the effect of continuing lifelong education on IQ? _____.
    a. IQ may actually increase
    b. There will be no effect on IQ
    c. The effect will be impossible to predict
    d. IQ will still decrease after age 40

11. Which of the following is the *least likely* reason for the decline in SAT scores during the 1960s and 1970s? _____.
    a. The test was getting harder each year because students were better prepared
    b. A broader range of people considered college and, therefore, took the test
    c. Schools reduced their academic requirements
    d. Social activities became more important to students

12. Of the following, the most important single influence on a person's performance in an intelligence test is _____.
    a. attitude
    b. environment
    c. ethnic background
    d. socioeconomic status

13. There is a growing body of empirical evidence which suggests that nonlanguage tests may be _____.
    a. more culturally loaded than language tests
    b. less culturally loaded than language tests
    c. virtually culture-free
    d. practically immune to training effects

14. If a test were designed to be totally culture-free, it _____.
    a. could be used with anyone of any background
    b. would be unbiased
    c. would measure only nonverbal content
    d. would probably not measure anything of value

15. Stereotype vulnerability has been found to affect the test performance of members of certain ethnic and gender groups through factors such as _____.
    a. increased effort
    b. self-concept
    c. high expectations
    d. none of the above

Miniprojects/Suggested Homework Activities:

1. Chapters 11 and 12 contain a distillation of a wide spectrum of psychological research and knowledge. Short summaries cannot really do justice to the depth and breadth of coverage of these chapters. Moreover, the ideas discussed in them are central not only to psychological testing but also to differential and developmental psychology as well as to the area of research methods. For these reasons, you would be well advised to study these chapters carefully and incorporate as much of them as possible into your working knowledge of the field. Supplement your insight into the issues discussed in Chapters 11 and 12, by reading some of Anastasi's major writings on these topics, such as the 1958 classic "Heredity, Environment, and the Question 'How?'" (*Psychological Review, 65,* 197-208) or her 1986 article on "Experiential Structuring of Psychological Traits" (*Developmental Review, 6,* 181-202). You might also note that if you ever need to prepare for a comprehensive examination in psychology, like the GRE Subject Test or a licensure exam, a review of these chapters should prove exceedingly worthwhile.

2. Another good source of information on many of the issues discussed in Chapters 11 and 12 of the text is the report of a task force of eleven psychologists, with expertise in various fields, established by the American Psychological Association in response to the debate sparked by R. J. Herrnstein & C. Murray's book *The Bell Curve: Intelligence and Class Structure in American Life* (New York: Free Press, 1994). The report—by Neisser et al.—is entitled "Intelligence: Knowns and Unknowns" and was published in the February 1996 issue of the *American Psychologist* (*AP, 51,* 77-101). In addition, several comments on it appeared in the January 1997 issue of the same journal (*AP, 52,* 69-81), along with a reply by Neisser.

3. Locate the *WAIS-R Manual,* by David Wechsler (San Antonio, TX: Psychological Corporation, 1981), and examine Table 20 (IQ Equivalents of Sums of Scaled Scores). Notice the differences in test scores needed to obtain a certain IQ, e.g., 100 or 120, at various age levels. For an even more detailed view of the "age decrements" mentioned in the textbook, look at Table 21 (Scaled Score Equivalents of Raw Scores). Contrast the raw scores needed to obtain a given scaled score, such as 10 or 8, on some of the WAIS-R subtests (e.g., Vocabulary and Block Design) at various age levels. Similar tables can be found in the manuals of other tests, such as the KAIT, which span a range of several decades of adulthood.

4. Review Chapter 12 of the textbook again. Then, based on the research findings that are described in it, prepare a "prescription" to be followed if one wanted to maximize a person's intelligence test performance from infancy to old age.

5. If the idea of improving your intellectual skills appeals to you, read *Intelligence Applied: Understanding and Increasing Your Intellectual Skills* by Robert J. Sternberg (San Diego: Harcourt Brace Jovanovich, 1986). This book—also mentioned in connection with Miniproject # 1 for Chapter 11—contains many suggestions, as well as practice problems, that should prove useful.

6. One of the most intriguing findings described in Chapter 12 concerns the large gains in the intelligence test scores of people of the United States and several other countries over the course of the past seven decades. This phenomenon, which has come to be known as the "Flynn effect," was identified and discussed at length by James R. Flynn. Two of the most pertinent articles on the subject, both by Flynn, appeared in the *Psychological Bulletin (PB)* in 1984 and 1987, respectively. They are: "The Mean IQ of Americans: Massive Gains 1932 to 1978" (*PB, 95*, 29-51) and "Massive IQ Gains in 14 Nations: What IQ Tests Really Measure" (*PB, 101*, 171-191). Since these studies were published, a good deal more has been written about the reasons for this trend and about its possible future course.

ANSWERS TO MULTIPLE CHOICE/TEST YOURSELF ITEMS:

1. b
2. d
3. d
4. d
5. c
6. c
7. a
8. b
9. c
10. a
11. a
12. b
13. a
14. d
15. b

PART IV   Personality Testing

∞ 13 ∞

SELF-REPORT PERSONALITY INVENTORIES

Chapter Summary

In conventional psychometric terminology, instruments for the measurement of emotional, motivational, interpersonal, and attitudinal characteristics are designated as "personality tests." The present chapter deals with self-report personality inventories which, along with the projective techniques discussed in Chapter 15, are the most numerous of personality assessment instruments.

Personality inventories can be developed through a variety of approaches. These approaches are not mutually exclusive; they can be, and recently have increasingly been, combined. The major procedures currently used in formulating, assembling, selecting, and grouping personality inventory items are based on content, empirical criterion keying, factor analysis, and the application of personality theory.

Content-related procedures were used in the development of the Woodworth Personal Data Sheet, the prototype of self-report inventories designed to screen military personnel during World War I for serious emotional disturbances. This inventory was an attempt to standardize a psychiatric interview and adapt it for mass testing. It consists of questions that deal directly with deviant or maladaptive behaviors. Among current inventories, the Symptom Checklist-90-Revised (SCL-90-R), designed simply to screen for psychological problems and symptoms of psychopathology, is one of the clearest examples of the use of content as a basis for selecting inventory items.

Empirical criterion keying is a procedure involving the selection of items, and the assignment of scoring weights to each response in an inventory, based on some external criterion. Typically, such criteria consist of differential rates of endorsement by people who belong to contrasted groups. Unlike content-related procedures, which rely on a literal interpretation of questionnaire items, the empirical criterion keying approach treats responses, regardless of their content or veracity, as symptomatic of the criterion behavior.

The Minnesota Multiphasic Personality Inventory (MMPI) is an outstanding example of criterion keying in personality test construction. The MMPI has been the most widely used personality inventory, and also one of the most assiduously investigated, of the past half century. It has recently been revised and reconstituted into two separate versions, the MMPI-2 and the MMPI-Adolescent (MMPI-A). The MMPI-2 consists of 567 statements to which the test taker gives the responses "True" or "False." It provides scores on the original 10 clinical and three "validity" scales of the MMPI and on many additional scales of various types. Eight of the original MMPI's clinical scales were empirically keyed on the basis of the responses of normal adults compared with those of clinical groups representing traditional psychiatric diagnoses. The other two were keyed on other contrasted samples. The "validity" scales are essentially checks on carelessness, misunderstanding, malingering, and the operation of special response sets. In addition to these basic scales, the MMPI-2 provides over 100 additional scales—both new and revised—including "validity" indicators, a large number of content-based scales made up of homogeneous item groupings, and several other supplementary scales. These additional scales, which can be scored only when examinees respond to the full complement of items, vary widely in their content, derivation, and psychometric characteristics. All of the MMPI-2 scales are scored by reference to the new normative sample of 2,600 adults.

The MMPI-A—which was developed on normative and clinical samples of contemporary adolescents—incorporates most of the features of the MMPI-2, including the 13 basic scales. However, it accommodates younger test takers through its reduced length and through the inclusion of several scales especially designed for the adolescent form. The primary method for interpreting the MMPI is based on profile codes or patterns and has evolved over many years. Because of this, the revision of the inventory has brought about a major debate concerning the equivalence of the original and new forms for interpretive purposes. One possible solution is to compare the scores generated by both versions. In addition, new approaches to MMPI interpretation continue to evolve. Only time will tell whether the Minnesota inventories will continue to dominate the field or whether they will be overtaken by a new generation of instruments for the assessment of psychopathology.

The California Psychological Inventory (CPI) and the Personality Inventory for Children-Revised (PIC-R) are two additional examples of major personality inventories, discussed in the textbook, that were developed at least partly through empirical criterion keying. The CPI draws almost half of its items from the MMPI but was designed specifically for use with normal adults. The PIC-R, like the MMPI, was developed at the University of Minnesota. It is really an inventory of observed behavior designed to assess personality functioning in children and adolescents—aged 3 to 16—through items answered by a knowledgeable adult, usually the mother. A parallel instrument, the Personality Inventory for Youth (PIY), has been developed to provide a self-report option for youngsters between the ages of 9 and 18. It can be used in conjunction with the PIC-R.

Factor analysis has been used extensively to classify personality traits and to develop personality tests. The Guilford-Zimmerman Temperament Survey and the Sixteen Personality Factor Questionnaire (16 PF) are well-known examples of personality inventories developed through factor analysis. They represent the two different traditions within this field: the use of personality questionnaire data and the use of ratings on scales made up of personality trait names. More recently, the Five-Factor Model (FFM) has managed to gather a considerable amount of consensus among workers from the different factor analytic traditions. The FFM uses a hierarchical structure to organize and simplify the collection of personality data. The two investigators most closely associated with the FFM have developed and revised the NEO Personality Inventory (NEO PI-R) to assess the major domains of personality they propose—which are Neuroticism, Extraversion, Openness to Experience, Agreeableness, and Conscientiousness—as well as their various facets. Furthermore, the model has spurred a great deal of research activity on cross-identification of factors, consolidation of various perspectives, and related work in test development. Still, disagreement remains concerning

158

the number and nature of the basic factors needed to account for the variance in personality description data. Although factor analysis is an effective technique for grouping personality inventory items into clusters that are relatively homogeneous and independent, it cannot substitute for empirical validation. Therefore, to the extent that inventories rely exclusively on factor analytic studies in their development, they are in need of further validation.

A number of personality tests have been constructed within the framework of one personality theory or another. The MCMI-III, for example, is based on Millon's biopsychosocial theories of personality and psychopathology. It is an instrument whose development used various methodologies and was aimed at meeting the criticisms leveled against the MMPI. The MCMI was designed specifically for diagnostic screening and its scales are largely consistent with the classification system used in the fourth edition of the Diagnostic and Statistical Manual of Mental Disorders (DSM-IV). Millon has also developed two other inventories that extend his theoretical perspectives to the assessment of adolescent personality and psychopathology. The manifest need system proposed by Murray and his associates at the Harvard Psychological Clinic in 1938 is another theoretical framework that has been used repeatedly in personality test construction. The Edwards Personal Preference Schedule (EPPS) and the Personality Research Form (PRF) are two examples of inventories that used Murray's system as their starting point. They are discussed in the textbook at some length, as are other Inventories developed by Douglas Jackson, author of the PRF.

Self-report inventories are particularly susceptible to malingering or faking. Numerous empirical investigations have demonstrated that respondents are able to create the impression they desire, whether favorable or unfavorable. In addition to such impression management, self-report data are also susceptible to unwitting distortions resulting from self-deception on the part of the test taker. Although self-deception may be too complex to assess through questionnaire methods directly, most of the major personality inventories do include one or more scales—such as the MMPI's validity indicators—that have been developed in an effort to evaluate the extent of *deliberate* dissembling by respondents. In addition, the forced-choice technique, used by the EPPS among others, was devised specifically to counteract the effect of social desirability in questionnaire responses. It requires the respondent to choose between descriptive terms or phrases that appear equally acceptable but differ in validity. However, there is evidence that the forced-choice format does not eliminate the influence of social desirability in inventory responses. Moreover, the procedure is most often applied in such a way, e.g., in the EPPS, that it produces ipsative scores wherein the frame of reference is the individual rather than the normative sample. This, in turn, introduces technical difficulties and eliminates information that may be significant in many testing situations.

Response sets include not only the tendency to choose socially desirable response alternatives, but also propensities toward acquiescence, deviant responding, or choosing the extreme ends of a rating scale. The voluminous research on these response sets first centered on efforts to rule out their influence because they were regarded as a source of irrelevant variance. Later, response sets came to be viewed by many as important indicators of personality traits and were investigated in their own right and described as "response styles." The controversy over the significance of response styles in personality measurement has stimulated extensive research and methodological advances in personality inventory construction, but has never been fully settled.

Another long-standing controversy in personality assessment concerns the issue of the generalizability of personality traits versus the situational specificity of behavior. The impetus toward behavioral specificity arose in the 1960s, largely from social learning theorists who were dissatisfied with the early view of traits as fixed, underlying causal entities. The results of subsequent research aimed at assessing the impact of situations on behavior highlighted the extent to which behavior variance depends upon both persons *and* situations, as well as their interaction, and has led to a growing consensus in this area. In spite of this consensus, many interesting questions remain concerning both sides of the person-situation debate. With regard to the person, for example, interindividual differences in consistency are of great interest. Similarly, cross-cultural comparisons of personality test results provide the opportunity to investigate the transportability of the tests—and of the conceptual systems on which they are based—across situations that differ in pervasive ways. The differentiation between traits and states, which is exemplified in Spielberger's State-Trait Anxiety Inventory (STAI), is another way of conceptualizing the behavior domain assessed by personality tests. It has had a salutary effect on the field, as have other methodological and theoretical innovations arising from earlier critiques of personality assessment.

Comprehensive Review

STUDY QUESTIONS:

1.   Define personality tests and describe the major areas in which they are used.

2.   List and explain each of the four main approaches to the development of self-report personality inventories.

3.   Describe the Symptom Checklist-90-Revised as a modern example of an inventory developed on the basis of content.

4.   Describe the background and major features of the Minnesota Multiphasic Personality Inventory-2 (MMPI-2), including its format and basic scales.

5.   Discuss the changes made in the revision of the MMPI and the consequences of those changes with regard to the interpretation of its scale scores and profile patterns.

6.   Discuss the advantages and limitations of the MMPI-2 and MMPI-A as instruments for the evaluation of personality.

7. Describe the California Psychological Inventory (CPI) and the Personality Inventory for Children (PIC), with special reference to how these instruments relate to the MMPI.

8. Discuss the role of factor analysis in the development of personality inventories as exemplified by Cattell's work.

9. Explain what the "Five-Factor Model" is and discuss the reasons for its current preeminence.

10. Describe the major characteristics that make the Millon Clinical Multiaxial Inventory different from other tests of its kind.

11. Identify the personality theory that was used as a basis for designing the Edwards Personal Preference Schedule (EPPS) and the Personality Research Form (PRF); describe the major features of those instruments.

12. Explain what "ipsative scores" are and how they affect the interpretation of test results.

13. Discuss the impact of impression management on personality testing and describe some of the procedures that have been devised to counteract this phenomenon.

14. Discuss the issue of response sets and response styles as it has been conceptualized in personality assessment over time.

15. Describe the relationships that exist between traits, states, persons, and situations and how they are understood to affect the consistency or inconsistency of behavior.

16. Discuss the present status of self-report inventories in personality assessment.

FILL IN THE BLANKS: Key Terms and Concepts

1. In conventional psychometric terminology, _ _ _ _ _ _ _ _ _ _ _ tests are instruments used for the measurement of emotional, motivational, interpersonal, and attitudinal characteristics, as distinguished from abilities.

2. The major approaches currently used in the development of personality inventories are based on _ _ _ _ _ _ _, _ _ _ _ _ _ _ _ _ _ _ _ _ _ _ _ _ _ keying, _ _ _ _ _ _ analysis, and _ _ _ _ _ _ _ _ _ _ theory.

3. Whereas _ _ _ _ _ _ _ – _ _ _ _ _ _ _ approaches rest essentially on a literal or veridical interpretation of questionnaire items, in _ _ _ _ _ _ _ _ _ _ _ _ _ _ _

_ _ _ _ _ _ responses are treated as diagnostic or symptomatic of the criterion behavior with which they are associated.

4. A(n) _ _ _ _ – _ _ _ _ _ inventory consists of a series of standardized verbal stimuli which are usually presented in a paper-and-pencil format suitable for group administration and are especially prone to malingering or faking.

5. In its original basic form, the MMPI provided scores on ten "_ _ _ _ _ _ _ _" scales, such as Hysteria and Paranoia, and on three "_ _ _ _ _ _ _ _" scales, which represent checks on carelessness, misunderstanding, and the operation of special response sets.

6. The norms on the MMPI-2 restandardization sample of approximately 2,600 adults, aged 16 to 84, are reported as uniform _ _ _ _ _ _ _, which are standard scores with a mean of 50 and SD of 10.

7. In retaining the basic scales of the MMPI fairly intact, the MMPI-2 developers sought to preserve information useful in profile interpretation. By the same token, they also retained problems associated with the original inventory, such as the _ _ _ _ _ _ _ and _ _ _ _ _ _ _ _ _ _ _ _ _ _ _ _ _ _ _ of the MMPI scales, which stemmed from its naive application of the empirical methods of contrasted criterion groups.

8. Among the new approaches to the interpretation of the MMPI, one of the most recent is the use of _ _ _ _ _ _ _ _ _ _ _ _ _ _ _ _ _ _ _ which attempt to bring coherence to the interpretive process by cutting across arbitrary sets of scale classifications and organizing categories into a format similar to the one Exner developed for the Rorschach.

9. The two major traditions of factor analytic research on the organization of personality traits are the one pioneered by Guilford, which centers on the use of data from personality _ _ _ _ _ _ _ _ _ _ _ _ _ _ _ _, and the _ _ _ _ _ _ _ tradition, which Cattell began by assembling personality trait names from the dictionary and elsewhere.

10. The various factor analytic traditions in personality research have reached an unusual, though far from universal, level of consensus around the "_ _ _ _ – _ _ _ _ _ _ _ _ _ _ _" which represents an attempt to use a hierarchical pattern of analysis to simplify the collection of behavioral data pertinent to personality.

11. The scales of the Millon Clinical Multiaxial Inventory (MCMI) are consistent with the classificatory system followed in the fourth edition of the _ _ _ _ _ _ _ _ _ _ and _ _ _ _ _ _ _ _ _ _ _ _ _ _ _ _ _ of _ _ _ _ _ _ _ _ _ _ _ _ _ _ (DSM-IV).

12. One of the significant innovations introduced by the MCMI is the use of standard scores called _ _ _ _ _ _ _ _ (BR) scores which are anchored to the prevalence rates

of the psychiatric conditions that the inventory assesses.

13. When an individual responds by expressing a preference for one item against one or more others, as in the _ _ _ _ _ _ – _ _ _ _ _ _ technique, the resulting score is usually _ _ _ _ _ _ _ _, which means that the frame of reference for its interpretation has to be the individual rather than the normative sample.

14. A. L. Edwards was the first to investigate the _ _ _ _ _ _ _ _ _ _ _ _ _ _ _ _ (SD) variable, which he conceptualized primarily as a tendency, of which the respondent is largely unaware, to "put up a good front."

15. _ is a contaminant of self-report data that consists of conscious dissembling in order to create a specific effect desired by the respondent when taking a test.

16. The influence of _ _ _ _ _ _ _ _ _ _ _ _, such as acquiescence and deviation, in both ability and personality tests was observed by investigators well before massive research into their operation in personality inventories began in the 1950s.

17. The use of forced-choice to control for SD requires two types of information about each response alternative, namely, its desirability or "_ _ _ _ _ _ _ _ _ _ index" and its validity or "_ _ _ _ _ _ _ _ _ _ _ _ _ _ index."

18. When response sets came to be regarded as indicators of broad and durable personality characteristics that were worth studying in their own right, they began to be commonly described as _ _ _ _ _ _ _ _ _ _ _ _ _ _.

19. The early view of _ _ _ _ _ _ as fixed, unchanging, underlying entities came under strong criticism in the 1960s and 1970s, especially from social learning theorists who emphasized the _ of behavior.

20. One way to investigate individual differences in intersituational consistency is by analyzing the interitem scale variances of self-rating data. Low interitem scale variances represent the quality of _ _ _ _ _ _ _ _ _ _ _ _ which has, in turn, been linked to higher validity levels in self-report data.

ANSWERS TO FILL-IN-THE-BLANKS: Key Terms and Concepts

1. personality (tests)
2. content / empirical criterion (keying) / factor (analysis) / personality (theory)
3. content-related (approaches) / empirical criterion keying
4. self-report (inventory)
5. "clinical" (scales) / "validity" (scales)

6. T scores
7. overlap (and) multidimensionality (of the MMPI scales)
8. structural summaries
9. (data from personality) questionnaires / lexical (tradition)
10. "Five-Factor Model"
11. Diagnostic (and) Statistical Manual of Mental Disorders (DSM-IV)
12. Base Rate (BR) (scores)
13. forced-choice (technique) / ipsative
14. social desirability (SD) (variable)
15. Impression management
16. response sets
17. "preference (index)" / "discriminative (index)"
18. response styles
19. traits / situational specificity
20. traitedness

MATCHING: Self-Report Personality Inventories (One letter per number)

_____ 1. Prototypical self-report personality inventory developed for use during World War I in an attempt to standardize a psychiatric interview.

_____ 2. Modern inventory that relies on content relevance to screen for psychological problems and symptoms of psychopathology and can be used as part of a battery to evaluate treatment outcomes.

_____ 3. Outstanding example of criterion keying in personality test construction—now in its second version—that has been the most widely used and extensively researched personality inventory to date.

_____ 4. Inventory which draws nearly half of its items from the MMPI but was developed specifically for use with normal adult populations.

_____ 5. Instrument for diagnostic screening whose development was undertaken specifically to meet the criticisms of the MMPI and to apply intervening advances in psychopathology and test construction.

_____ 6. Instrument devised by the two investigators most closely associated with the "Five-Factor Model" as a measure of the major dimensions and facets of personality.

_____ 7. The best known of the inventories developed by Cattell to assess the "primary source traits of personality" he identified through his factor analytic research.

_____ 8. Instrument designed to assess the strength of 15 of the needs proposed by Murray through a series of 210 pairs of statements; within each pair test takers must choose one statement as more characteristic of themselves than the other.

_____ 9. Instrument developed by Jackson which, while taking Murray's personality theory as its starting point, incorporates multiple strategies for personality test development and reflects many technical advances in test construction.

164

_____ 10. Instrument developed by Spielberger to differentiate between a transitory emotional condition characterized by feelings of tension and apprehension and a relatively stable tendency to respond to situations as threatening.

A. Millon Clinical Multiaxial Inventory (MCMI)
B. Personality Research Form (PRF)
C. Sixteen Personality Factor Questionnaire (16 PF)
D. California Psychological Inventory (CPI)
E. State-Trait Anxiety Inventory (STAI)
F. Edwards Personal Preference Schedule (EPPS)
G. Symptom Checklist-90-Revised (SCL-90-R)
H. Woodworth Personal Data Sheet
I. Minnesota Multiphasic Personality Inventory (MMPI)
J. Revised NEO Personality Inventory (NEO PI-R)

ANSWERS TO MATCHING ITEMS:

1-H   2-G   3-I   4-D   5-A   6-J   7-C   8-F   9-B   10-E

TRUE/FALSE and WHY?

1. The major approaches to the development of personality inventories, such as content validation and factor analysis, are mutually exclusive. (T/F) Why? _____
   _____

2. The so-called validity scales of the MMPI are not concerned with validity in the technical sense. (T/F) Why? _____
   _____

3. At the present time, the interpretation of the MMPI-2 is still based on a strictly construed empirical criterion keying approach, wherein T scores of 65 or higher on a given scale can be taken as an almost certain indication of the presence of the syndrome the scale represents. (T/F) Why? _____
   _____

4. The Personality Inventory for Children (PIC) is *not* a self-report inventory but an inventory of observed behavior. (T/F) Why? _____
   _____

5. The traits encompassed within the "Five-Factor Model" are seen by most theorists as *the* five basic factors that make-up personality. (T/F) Why?_____
   _____

6. According to its author, the MCMI is *not* a general personality instrument to be used for "normal" populations. (T/F) Why? _____

_____

7. Homogeneity and factorial purity of personality inventory scales are desirable goals in test construction but cannot substitute for empirical validation. (T/F) Why?_____

_____

_____

8. Campbell and Fiske's multitrait-multimethod matrix provides an optimal organizational structure for examining the construct validity of personality inventories. (T/F) Why?

_____

_____

9. There is a good deal of evidence that suggests that respondents *cannot* dissemble successfully on personality inventories when asked to simulate responses characteristic of specific role, such as that of a person with a given vocational objective. (T/F) Why?

_____

_____

10. Independent research with the EPPS indicates that the forced-choice technique successfully eliminates the influence of the SD variable and also prevents test takers from faking to create a desired impression for specific purposes. (T/F) Why?_____

_____

_____

11. There is a growing consensus that people differ in the degree of behavioral specificity they display across situations and that situations also differ in the behavioral constraints they impose. (T/F) Why? _____

_____

12. Ample evidence has already been gathered to support the notion that personality inventories and their items are easily transportable across most cultures both for the assessment of "normal" personality and for the assessment of psychopathology. (T/F) Why? _____

_____

ANSWERS TO TRUE/FALSE:

1.	False	4.	True	7.	True	10.	False
2.	True	5.	False	8.	True	11.	True
3.	False	6.	True	9.	False	12.	False

Multiple Choice: Test Yourself

1. The primary use for self-report inventories is as a tool in_____
   _____.
   a. career decision making
   b. counseling and diagnosis
   c. self-evaluation of personality
   d. selection of employees

2. Which of the following is *not* one of the basic methods for formulating a self-report inventory? _____.
   a. Content-related procedures
   b. Self-constructed response analysis
   c. Factor analysis
   d. Empirical criterion keying

3. Which of the following instruments is based on content?_____
   _____.
   a. Symptom Checklist-90-Revised
   b. Minnesota Multiphasic Personality Inventory (MMPI)
   c. Sixteen Personality Factor Questionnaire (16 PF)
   d. Millon Clinical Multiaxial Inventory

4. The use of contrasted groups to develop a self-report inventory is a procedure followed in _____.
   a. content validation
   b. factor analysis
   c. the forced-choice technique
   d. empirical criterion keying

5. The lie (L) score on the MMPI and MMPI-2 is based upon_____
   _____.
   a. the consistency of a person's responses across similar items in the inventory
   b. the test taker's tendency to answer key questions in a favorable direction
   c. interscale consistency
   d. none of the above

6. Which of the following is *not* one of the major changes that took place in the process of revising the MMPI?_____
   _____.
   a. A complete renorming of the inventory
   b. The development of uniform T scores for several clinical and content scales

c.   The separation of the inventory into versions suitable for different age groups

d.   All of the above changes took place in the process of revision

7.   As contrasted with the MMPI, the California Psychological Inventory (CPI)_____
_____.

a.   has more items and fewer scales

b.   is more suited for use with normal populations

c.   does not have a validity scale

d.   is specifically designed for children

8.   A distinguishing feature of the Personality Inventory for Children (PIC) is that it___
_____.

a.   is an inventory of observed behavior

b.   requires all responses to be given orally

c.   has a built-in diagnostic scale

d.   has no validity scales

9.   Cattell's 16 PF is based upon_____.

a.   factorial research

b.   content validation

c.   multiple regression formulas

d.   empirical criterion keying

10.   When using the EPPS, one must be cautious about comparing the scores of two individuals because_____
_____.

a.   the EPPS has very low reliability

b.   its scores are based on percentile ranks

c.   its scores are ipsative

d.   the meaning of the EPPS scales is not very clear

11.   The forced-choice technique is used to_____
_____.

a.   increase reliability

b.   reduce faking

c.   counteract the ipsative nature of the items

d.   increase test validity

12.   Self-report inventories are especially susceptible to_____.

a.   faking

b.   low scorer reliability

c.   ipsative scoring

d.   criterion contamination

13. Persons who are more likely to answer "True" or "Yes" than "False" or "No" demonstrate a response bias known as _____.
    a.   deviation
    b.   acquiescence
    c.   social desirability
    d.   none of the above

14. People often behave quite differently in different settings or situations. Psychologists term this _____
_____.
    a.   unreliability
    b.   state specificity
    c.   situational specificity
    d.   trait analysis

15. The current state of self-report inventories can best be described as _____
_____.
    a.   neutral, with neither growth nor decline
    b.   moving into a period of slower growth
    c.   grim, since empirical analysis shows the poor validity of these tests
    d.   good, with a strong possibility of additional growth and technical improvement

Miniprojects/Suggested Homework Activities:

1.   The area of personality testing is inextricably tied to the field of personality theory, a large subspecialty within psychology. If you have already had a course in "Theories of Personality," you will find the material in this and subsequent chapters easier to grasp because you will be able to place it within that context. If you have not had such a course, you may wish to review a textbook in the area, with special reference to theories, like Murray's need system, which have served as a framework for the development of personality assessment instruments. Two representative textbooks in this field are: *Theories of Personality* (3rd ed.) by C. S. Hall and G. Lindzey (New York: Wiley, 1978), and *Personality Theories: A Comparative Analysis* (5th ed.) by Salvatore Maddi (Chicago: Dorsey Press, 1989).

2.   If you are intrigued by the MMPI-2, and would like a relatively brief but comprehensive introduction to that inventory, John Graham's book *MMPI-2: Assessing Personality and Psychopathology* (New York: Oxford University Press, 1993), now in its second edition, is probably the best place to start. For a thorough understanding of the MMPI and its history, the two-volume work entitled *An MMPI Handbook—Volume I: Clinical Interpretation* and *An MMPI Handbook—Volume II: Research Applications* by W. G.

Dahlstrom, G. S. Welsh, and L. E. Dahlstrom (University of Minnesota Press, 1972, 1975) is unsurpassed in its depth of coverage of the original inventory.

3. For those who are more attuned to the Internet as a source of information, the University of Minnesota's division of MMPI-2 Workshops & Symposia has a home page that provides information about forthcoming educational activities centered on the MMPI-2 and MMPI-A, as well as new developments concerning both instruments. The *MMPI-2/MMPI-A News & Profiles* newsletter is also available at the site, which can be accessed through the following address:

http://www.umn.edu/mmpi

4. Over the many years that the MMPI has been in heavy use by both clinicians and academicians, several humorous versions of that instrument have been circulated. The amusement these MMPI parodies provide stems mainly from the fact that many of the real MMPI items (especially in the original version) are rather awkward in either their wording or content and, therefore, easy to caricature. However, in order to be able to appreciate the humor in the parodies, you first need to familiarize yourself with the actual inventory. After you have had a chance to read the real items of the MMPI, the MMPI-2, or the MMPI-A, you would probably enjoy two very short satirical "revisions" that appear in the book *Oral Sadism and the Vegetarian Personality*, edited by G. C. Ellenbogen (New York: Brunner/Mazel, 1986). In spite of its title, this book contains some genuinely funny pieces that take a lighthearted view of various psychological topics, including several related to testing and assessment.

5. One of the problems attendant to the research on the "Big Five," or Five-Factor, model of personality is the proliferation of different terms that have been used to refer to its five ($\pm$ 2) broad dimensions of personality. A very brief but helpful compendium of many of these terms—along with citations of sources—can be found in the Appendix of an article by Robert Hogan, Gordon J. Curphy, and Joyce Hogan, entitled "What We Know about Leadership: Effectiveness and Personality," in the June 1994 issue of the *American Psychologist* (*49*, 493-504).

6. Some of the most up-to-date information on the inventories and issues covered in Chapter 13 appears in the *Journal of Personality Assessment*. See, for example, the special section on the current status and future direction of research on the MMPI-2, MMPI-A, MCMI-III, and NEO PI-R (Vol. 68, #1, February 1997) and the articles about assessment of the Five-Factor Model, dimensions of deception in personality assessment, and other important topics in the April 1997 issue (Vol. 68, #2).

7. One of the best ways to explore the notion of ipsative scores is to become familiar with the EPPS. This inventory, described in the textbook, produces raw scores on each

of 15 needs, along with their corresponding percentile scores. Each raw score represents the number of times that the respondent chose a statement of a given need over a statement of another one of the 14 needs with which it was paired. Each of the 15 needs is paired twice with the other 14 needs. Thus, depending on how many times a need is chosen, its raw score can range from zero to 28. However, since there are only 210 (14 x 15) choices to be made altogether, each choice necessarily entails an increase in the total score for one need and a reduction in the possible total score of another need. The result is that the scores of each respondent for each need do not represent the absolute strength of each need for that respondent but, rather, the rank order or relative positions of each need—vis-a-vis the other needs—for the respondent. To understand the difference between ipsative and normative scores more clearly, take the EPPS yourself, read the manual, and score the test carefully. Then, proceed to : (a) rank each of the 15 needs according to its percentile score—based on one of two sets of norms for groups of males and females; (b) rank each need according to its raw score; (c) compare the positions of each need on each set of ranks and note the changes that occur; and (d) compare the percentile scores for needs with identical raw scores and note discrepancies.

ANSWERS TO MULTIPLE CHOICE/TEST YOURSELF ITEMS:

1.   b
2.   b
3.   a
4.   d
5.   b
6.   d
7.   b
8.   a
9.   a
10. c
11. b
12. a
13. b
14. c
15. d

MEASURING INTERESTS AND ATTITUDES

Chapter Outline

Interest Inventories: Current Setting

The Strong Interest Inventory™ (SII)
      Origins and Development of the SII
      The SII-Form T317: General Description
      Scoring and Interpretation
      Psychometric Evaluation

Interest Inventories: Overview and Some Highlights
      Jackson Vocational Interest Survey (JVIS)
      The Kuder Occupational Interest Survey and Its Predecessors
      Career Assessment Inventory-The Vocational Version (CAI-VV)
      Self-Directed Search (SDS)

Some Significant Trends
      Inventory Development and Use
      Models of Occupations

Opinion Surveys and Attitude Scales
      Nature of Instruments
      Major Types of Attitude Scales
      A Note on Gender-Related Variables and Measures

Locus of Control

Chapter Summary

      The present chapter surveys a variety of self-report inventories that evaluate important aspects of personality, such as interests and attitudes, which determine life choices. These instruments cannot be rigidly categorized because they overlap with each other and with measures of values. The assessment of interests received its strongest impetus from educational and career counseling and is carried out primarily in that context. The assessment of opinions and attitudes, on the other hand, originated in social psychology and is used in that field as well as in applied areas that require the gauging and prediction of public opinion. As far as values are concerned, although a great deal of research has been done on the topic, new developments in the area of their measurement are relatively scarce.

In career counseling, the use of interest inventories—which are tests designed to assess the individual's interest in different fields of work and study—has increased relative to that of ability tests since the 1950s. During that time, career counseling itself has undergone major changes. Many of these have resulted from an increased emphasis on self-exploration and on expanding the career options open to all individuals, especially to women and—more recently—to individuals with disabilities.

The Strong Interest Inventory (SII-Form T317) is the current version of one of the most widely used interest inventories, first published in 1927. The Strong introduced empirical criterion keying of items, to which test takers respond primarily by expressing their like or dislike; the items are scored according to the responses of people in different occupations. The SII has undergone extensive revisions over the years, including: (a) the introduction of a theoretical framework to guide score organization and interpretation, (b) the merging of men's and women's forms and renorming of all occupational scales on both sexes, and (c) a substantial increase in the number of scales for occupations that require less than a college degree for entry. In addition, extensive data have been accumulated about the Strong's reliability and validity through a continuing research program. These data suggest a good deal of stability for occupational scales and occupational group profiles over periods of two to three decades. Concurrent and predictive validity as well as construct validation data have also been found to be satisfactory for previous forms of the SII, but new studies of the predictive validity of the latest revision need to be undertaken.

Four additional interest inventories, each one illustrating some noteworthy feature, are discussed in the textbook. The Jackson Vocational Interest Survey (JVIS), which contrasts sharply with the SII in its approach, exemplifies sophisticated test construction procedures. Its development started with a definition of the constructs to be measured—i.e., work roles and work styles—and included exhaustive statistical analyses, such as the establishment of an empirical linkage with the occupational database of the Strong. The Kuder Occupational Interest Survey (KOIS), the Career Assessment Inventory (CAI), and the Self-Directed Search (SDS) are the three additional interest inventories chosen for discussion in the textbook.

The major trends in the measurement of interests include the increasing use of Holland's model of general occupational themes as a theoretical basis, the provision of scores on both broad interest scales and specific occupational scales, as well as the cross-utilization of empirical data banks for interpretive purposes. In addition to these trends, which have been apparent for some time, the occupations that inventories cover have been expanded into the vocational/technical arena. There has also been a recognition that inventories can be seen as intervention techniques, which will probably lead to greater use of individualized methods in their development, administration, and interpretation. Recently, the field of vocational choice has also been enriched by the use of paradigms from cognitive psychology which view such decision making as a problem-solving activity that may recur through the lifespan. Furthermore, efforts to modify and expand Holland's model—currently under way—are likely to result in increased integration and advances in vocational theory and measurement.

Attitudes, which are commonly defined as tendencies to react favorably or unfavorably to certain classes of stimuli, cannot be differentiated from opinions in a consistent or defensible fashion. However, in terms of assessment methodology, opinion surveys have traditionally been distinguished from attitude scales. The former are usually concerned with isolated answers to specific questions—tabulated and analyzed separately—whereas the latter typically yield a total score based on the individual's agreement or disagreement with a series of statements about a given stimulus category. The three major approaches to attitude scale construction commonly encountered in the psychological testing literature are the Thurstone-, Guttman-, and Likert-type scales. Of these, the Likert-type are used most frequently because they are easier to construct than the other two types and still yield comparable reliabilities.

One illustration of a set of psychological variables that has been widely used in research and has served as the basis for the development of many self-report inventories is the concept of sex roles, and related constructs, such as masculinity-femininity and androgyny. These, however, have not proven to be effective constructs for categorizing human personality or for explaining empirical findings. It appears that, for further progress to occur in this area, the conceptualization of gender-related variables needs to be refined and placed within a more coherent theoretical framework.

The construct of "locus of control," as described by Rotter, has also served as the basis for a great deal of research and has led to the development of several scales, of which the best known is Rotter's own I-E scale. This instrument, which examines the individual's generalized expectancies for internal versus external control of reinforcement, and other locus of control scales, illustrate a remarkably productive use of psychometric tools in the conduct of investigations on central aspects of personality.

Comprehensive Review

STUDY QUESTIONS:

1. Discuss the major changes that have occurred in the area of career counseling and explain how those changes have affected interest inventories.

2. Describe the history and evolution of the Strong Interest Inventory, including the characteristics that distinguish it from other inventories.

3. Describe the information that can be obtained from the current Strong Interest Inventory (SII) and discuss the psychometric features of that instrument.

4. Contrast and compare the SII with the Jackson Vocational Interest Survey (JVIS).

5. Discuss the history of the Kuder interest inventories and compare the current Kuder Occupational Interest Survey (KOIS) with the SII.

6. Describe the Career Assessment Inventory (CAI) in terms of its similarities to, and differences from, other interest inventories.

7. Discuss Holland's general approach to the assessment of vocational interests and how the Self-Directed Search (SDS) fits into that approach.

8. List and describe the significant trends that become apparent from an overview of the current major interest inventories.

9. Describe the current status of Holland's model and the efforts that are being made to modify and expand it.

10. Compare and contrast opinion surveys with attitude scales.

11. Describe the three major approaches to attitude scale construction discussed in the textbook.

12. Discuss the history and current issues in the measurement of gender-related variables, such as masculinity and femininity.

13. Discuss the construct of locus of control and describe how it is assessed.

FILL IN THE BLANKS: Key Terms, Concepts, and Names

1. The development of _____ _____, which often compare an individual's expressed preferences with those typical of people in various occupations, received its strongest impetus from educational and career counseling.

2. The term _____ _____ designates the effect that interest inventories can have in increasing behaviors instrumental in expanding the career options of individuals.

3. The theoretical model used in most of the current interest inventories discussed in the text is _____ ' _____ (R-I-A-S-E-C) model of general occupational themes.

4. The results of many current interest inventories, e.g., the SII and the SDS, are linked with the occupations listed in the _____ of _____ _____ (DOT) and other materials developed by the U.S. Employment Service.

5. The major dimensions or constructs that the JVIS set out to assess were defined in terms of _ _ _ _ _ _ _ _ _ _, which refer to the specific kinds of behavior expected in different working environments, and _ _ _ _ _ _ _ _ _, which pertain to what a person does on the job.

6. When interest inventories serve to support and strengthen existing vocational aspirations or to provide increased self-understanding, they move beyond the realm of assessment and can be viewed as _ _ _ _ _ _ _ _ _ _ _ _ techniques.

7. Tracey and Rounds have expanded Holland's hexagonal R-I-A-S-E-C typology of occupations and developed an expanded _ _ _ _ _ _ _ _ _ model that can accommodate the dimension of _ _ _ _ _ _ _ _.

8. A(n) _ _ _ _ _ _ _ _ is defined as a tendency to react favorably or unfavorably toward a designated class of stimuli, such as an ethnic group, a custom, or an institution; the key connotation of that concept is one of response _ _ _ _ _ _ _ _ _ _ _ toward certain categories of stimuli.

9. Whereas _ _ _ _ _ _ _ surveys are typically concerned with answers to specific questions that need not be related, _ _ _ _ _ _ _ _ scales usually yield a total score that indicates the direction and intensity of the individual's response to a stimulus category.

10. The development of a(n) _ _ _ _ _ _ _ _ _ _ –type scale involves the gathering of statements that express a wide range of attitudes toward an object and the assignment of values to those statements according to how judges classify them.

11. The development of _ _ _ _ _ _ _ –type scales, which were originally meant to assess whether a set of attitude statements is unidimensional, involves the identification of a set of items that fall into an ordered sequence in terms of their endorsement by respondents.

12. _ _ _ _ _ _ –type scales call for graded responses—usually expressed in terms of five categories ranging from "strongly agree" to "strongly disagree"—to each statement in the scale.

13. Over the past decade it has become evident that global explanatory concepts for gender-related differences, such as _ _ _ _ _ _ _ _ _ _ _ _ – _ _ _ _ _ _ _ _ _ _ or sex roles, have not been supported by empirical findings.

14. Rotter's construct of _ _ _ _ _ of _ _ _ _ _ _ _ _ refers to whether individuals perceive a causal relationship between their own behavior and a consequent event or whether reinforcement following some action is perceived as being the result of chance, fate, or other external forces.

15. By the mid- to late 1970s, it had been empirically well established that _ _ _ _ _ _ _
_ _ _ _ _ _ _ _ _ _ _ of the sort tapped by the I-E Scale can play a meaningful role
in the prediction of some behaviors.

ANSWERS TO FILL-IN-THE-BLANKS: Key Terms, Concepts, and Names

1. interest inventories
2. exploration validity
3. Holland's hexagonal (R-I-A-S-E-C) (model of general occupational themes)
4. Dictionary (of) Occupational Titles (DOT)
5. work styles / work roles
6. intervention (techniques)
7. spherical / prestige
8. attitude / (response) consistency
9. opinion (surveys) / attitude (scales)
10. Thurstone (-type scale)
11. Guttman (-type scales)
12. Likert (-type scales)
13. masculinity-femininity
14. locus (of) control
15. control expectancies

MATCHING: Measures of Interests and Attitudes (One letter per number)

_____ 1. Name of the original version of the instrument, first published in 1927, whose empirical criterion keying of items in terms of the likes and dislikes of individuals in various occupations has had a pervasive influence in the measurement of interests.

_____ 2. Current version of the pioneering instrument for the assessment of occupational interests, which provides scores on six General Occupational Themes, 25 Basic Interest Scales, 211 Occupational Scales, as well as a set of Administrative Indexes and four Personal Style Scales.

_____ 3. Instrument which exemplifies construct validation and a generally sophisticated approach to test construction, at every stage of its development; it is one of the newest interest inventories.

_____ 4. The earliest one of a series of interest measures that have been in use almost as long as the Strong series and use forced-choice triad items—wherein respondents indicate which activity they would like most and which they would like least.

_____ 5. Current version of one of the oldest interest inventory series, which now provides occupational scale scores expressed in terms of correlations between the test taker's interest pattern and the interest patterns of over 100 occupational groups.

177

_____ 6. Vocational inventory patterned on the Strong but designed specifically for persons seeking a career that does *not* require a four-year college degree or advanced professional training.

_____ 7. Instrument developed by Holland, which is self-administered, self-scored, and self-interpreted; though organized around interests, it also calls for self-ratings of abilities and reported competencies.

_____ 8. Interest inventory that can be used in conjunction with the Differential Aptitude Tests with which it was standardized.

_____ 9. Instrument that measures self-reported interests and skills and is organized in a way similar to the Strong inventory, with which the author of this instrument was involved for some time.

_____ 10. Instrument developed by Rotter to assess the individual's generalized expectancies regarding the locus of control of reinforcements.

- A. Career Assessment Inventory (CAI)
- B. Self-Directed Search (SDS)
- C. Campbell Interest and Skill Survey (CISS)
- D. Strong Interest Inventory (SII-Form T 317)
- E. I-E Scale
- F. Kuder Preference Record-Vocational
- G. Jackson Vocational Interest Survey (JVIS)
- H. Strong Vocational Interest Blank® (SVIB)
- I. Kuder Occupational Interest Survey (KOIS)
- J. Career Interest Inventory

ANSWERS TO MATCHING ITEMS:

I-H   2-D   3-G   4-F   5-I   6-A   7-B   8-J   9-C   10-E

TRUE/FALSE and WHY?

1. In counseling, the use of interest tests, relative to that of ability tests, has decreased since the 1950s. (T/F) Why? _____

    _____

2. The fact that interest inventories often compare an individual's expressed interests with those typical of persons in different occupations tends to perpetuate existing group differences. (T/F) Why? _____

    _____

3. In Holland's R-I-A-S-E-C model of occupations, each theme characterizes not only a type of person, but also the type of working environment that a person finds most

congenial. (T/F) Why? _____

_____

4. The occupational criterion groups used in developing the latest Occupational Scales of the Strong were made up of persons selected solely on the basis of age and current occupation. (T/F) Why? _____

_____

5. The interrelations among the General Occupational Themes found in the general reference samples of the SII are of special relevance to construct validation. (T/F) Why? _____

_____

6. One of the most recent developments in interest inventory construction is the attempt to design them so as to bypass the reading requirements of traditional paper-and-pencil measures. (T/F) Why? _____

_____

7. Cross-cultural research on Holland's model of occupational themes has uniformly suggested that the model is equally applicable across cultures in most of its aspects. (T/F) Why? _____

_____

8. One of the most extensive applications of attitude measurement is found in research in social psychology. (T/F) Why? _____

_____

9. The constructs of masculinity and femininity have proven to be quite effective for categorizing human personality and also as a basis for test development. (T/F) Why?

_____

_____

10. Various factor analytic studies of Rotter's I-E Scale have found that the construct assessed by that scale may be subdivided into several distinct factors. (T/F) Why?

_____

_____

ANSWERS TO TRUE/FALSE:

| 1. False | 3. True | 5. True | 7. False | 9. False |
| 2. True | 4. False | 6. True | 8. True | 10. True |

Multiple Choice: Test Yourself

1. The use of interest inventories is of greatest value in_____
_____.
   a. industrial employment offices
   b. psychological research
   c. individual guidance and counseling
   d. the selection of applicants for a specific job

2. A high score on an Occupational Scale of the SII means that_____
_____.
   a. the individual would be successful in that occupation
   b. the individual is talented in that field of endeavor
   c. the individual shares common interests with people already in that occupation
   d. none of the above

3. The scoring for the SII Occupational Scales was developed by means of_____
_____.
   a. criterion keying
   b. content validation
   c. factor analysis
   d. regression equations

4. Studies of the long-term stability of the Strong Occupational Scales, over periods of as long as 20 years, yield correlations that fall mostly in the range of _____.
   a. .90 to .95
   b. .60 to .80
   c. .40 to .45
   d. .20 to .30

5. In contrast with the SII, the JVIS_____
_____.
   a. focuses on broader interest areas
   b. is more anchored in construct validation
   c. utilizes the forced-choice format
   d. all of the above

6. Throughout their history, the Kuder interest inventories have provided a set of scores which_____.
   a. cover 10 broad interest areas
   b. rely on empirical criterion keying
   c. cover 207 occupational areas
   d. are based on true/false items

7. The Career Assessment Inventory_____
   _____.
   a.   has been in use almost as long as the Strong inventories
   b.   concentrates on technical and semiprofessional occupations
   c.   requires a higher level of reading skills than most other inventories
   d.   is one of the few interest inventories which does not use Holland's general themes

8. A unique characteristic of the SDS is that it is_____.
   a.   self-administered
   b.   self-scored
   c.   self-interpreted
   d.   all of the above

9. Which of the following is *not* a significant trend among current interest inventories?
   _____.
   a.   The merging of major theoretical approaches
   b.   The cross-utilization of empirical data banks
   c.   A reduction in the number and range of occupations covered
   d.   A recognition of such inventories as intervention techniques

10. The search for the nature, number, and organization of basic interests resembles the search(es) conducted to identify the primary factors in the realm(s) of _____
    _____.
    a.   ability
    b.   personality
    c.   neither a nor b
    d.   both a and b

11. Which of the following is *not* one of the names associated with the three major approaches to attitude scale construction? _____.
    a.   Thurstone
    b.   Guttman
    c.   Likert
    d.   Lindzey

12. The numerical values for a Thurstone-type scale are determined by_____
    _____.
    a.   experts in attitude measurement
    b.   a panel of judges
    c.   statistical analysis from a sample administration
    d.   none of the above

13. The simplest scale to construct, and the most often used, is the_____
_____.

    a.   Thurstone-type scale
    b.   Guttman-type scale
    c.   Likert-type scale
    d.   all of the above are equally difficult to construct

14. Which of the following circumstances is *not* related to the current disarray that many perceive with regard to the measurement of sex roles and related constructs?_____
_____.

    a.   Investigators' lack of interest in gender-related phenomena
    b.   Lack of a theoretical framework and good conceptual definitions
    c.   The unprecedented cultural changes of the past few decades
    d.   Lack of empirical support for the role of these constructs in explaining gender differences

15. The Rotter I-E Scale assesses one's expectancies about_____
_____.

    a.   the attitudes of others towards one's own behavior
    b.   the locus of control of reinforcement
    c.   success in one's chosen occupation
    d.   the typical response style of other people

Miniprojects/Suggested Homework Activities:

1. A review of the *Applications and Technical Guide* for the SII was already suggested in Miniproject #3 for Chapter 5. If you have not had a chance to take the SII or to review that instrument, this would be a good time to do so. The Strong is an interesting inventory to take, as it requires one to consider and express one's preferences about a wide range of occupations, activities, and pursuits. It is also an excellent instrument to review from a psychometric standpoint; it incorporates many of the concepts that are central to testing and its properties have been investigated continuously and exhaustively. In addition, if you are able to take the inventory yourself, the report you receive with the results would provide you with an opportunity to interpret a great number of scores and, in conjunction with the *Guide*, would probably be helpful in crystallizing or reaffirming your vocational goals.

2. Whether or not you are able to take the Strong inventory, it would also be desirable to take and review either the Self-Directed Search or an inventory of values, such as The Values Scale or the Life Values Inventory (see p. 387 of the textbook for references). Taking the SII, along with the SDS and a values inventory, would provide

you with an opportunity to compare instruments that purportedly assess similar constructs.

3. You can investigate the principal conceptual basis underlying the SII by conducting structured interviews with samples of students in each of four very different fields of study. The purpose of the interviews would be to ascertain students' preferences in terms of leisure activities, academic interests, and any other pursuits that might differentiate among the groups (e.g., musical tastes, political philosophies, etc.). If you conduct your interviews in a standardized fashion—and use a format that calls for selection of options from a given list—you would be able to quantify the results, assess the group differences and similarities that you find, and provide feedback to the participants. You might even have a pilot version of a new interest inventory!

4. As you probably have surmised already, the field of attitude measurement is a vast and diverse one. To ascertain that diversity directly, locate and review the compendium of *Measures of Personality and Social Psychological Attitudes* edited by J.P. Robinson, P.R. Shaver, and L.S. Wrightsman (San Diego, CA: Academic Press, 1991). A first-hand look at the instruments contained in that book, which include measures of constructs such as Machiavellianism, helplessness, and self-esteem, is almost guaranteed to stimulate your investigative propensities.

5. The historical evolution of masculinity and femininity as psychological constructs, and of the measures designed to assess them, is one of the liveliest topics discussed in Chapter 14. If you are interested in pursuing it, Anne Constantinople's classic review entitled "Masculinity-Femininity: An Exception to a Famous Dictum?" (*Psychological Review*, 1973, *80*, 389–407) would provide some good background. For information about subsequent work in that area, including the current disarray in the field, see one of the reviews cited in pages 407–408 of the textbook (e.g., Betz, 1995, or Lenney, 1991).

ANSWERS TO MULTIPLE CHOICE/TEST YOURSELF ITEMS:

1.	c	6.	a	11.	d
2.	c	7.	b	12.	b
3.	a	8.	d	13.	c
4.	b	9.	c	14.	a
5.	d	10.	d	15.	b

PROJECTIVE TECHNIQUES

Chapter Outline

Nature of Projective Techniques

Inkblot Techniques
    The Rorschach
    Exner's Comprehensive System
    Alternative Approaches
    The Holtzman Inkblot Technique

Pictorial Techniques
    Thematic Apperception Test
    Adaptations of the TAT and Related Tests
    The Rosenzweig Picture-Frustration Study

Verbal Techniques

Autobiographical Memories

Performance Techniques
    Drawing Techniques
    Play Techniques and Toy Tests

Evaluation of Projective Techniques
    Rapport and Applicability
    Faking
    Examiner and Situational Variables
    Norms
    Reliability
    Validity
    The Projective Hypothesis
    Projective Techniques as Psychometric Instruments
    Projective Techniques as Clinical Tools

Chapter Summary

Projective techniques are instruments characterized by the assignment of a relatively unstructured task to test takers, who are often unaware of the type of interpretations that will be made of their responses. These instruments typically represent a global approach to the assessment of personality and are regarded as especially effective in revealing its unconscious or covert aspects. Projective methods originated in the clinical setting, and have remained a predominantly clinical tool, often reflecting the influence of psychoanalytic concepts.

The Rorschach inkblot series, one of the most popular projective techniques, was developed by a Swiss psychiatrist in the early part of this century, on the basis of clinical observations of the differential responses of patients with various psychiatric syndromes. The technique that Rorschach developed involves the sequential presentation of 10 stimulus cards on each of which is printed a bilaterally symmetrical inkblot. The respondent is first asked to tell what each blot could represent and later, during the inquiry phase of the administration, is questioned about the location and other aspects of the associations given for each blot. After Rorschach's death, several systems for using his inkblots evolved over the years. Although these systems shared some common features—such as the fact that they included the location, determinants, and content of responses among their main scoring and interpretive categories—the lack of standardization in the Rorschach method caused it to fall into disrepute as an assessment tool.

Over the past two decades, John Exner has led an ambitious, and largely successful, effort to improve the psychometric soundness of the Rorschach. Exner's Comprehensive System integrates five of the major approaches to the Rorschach and provides standardized administration, scoring, and interpretive procedures. Nevertheless, questions about the validity of the Roschach still remain. In addition, there are other issues that greatly complicate the study and interpretation of Rorschach scores, such as individual variability in response productivity (R) and the possible link between variability in R and extraneous factors. In spite of these methodological problems, the popularity of the Rorschach—which remained high in clinical circles all along—has been rekindled in recent years. Furthermore, the Holtzman Inkblot Technique (HIT), an entirely new instrument modeled after the Rorschach but designed to eliminate its principal technical deficiencies, has been devised as an alternative. Although it is apparent that the HIT has some psychometric advantages, there is much less information on it than on the Rorschach and more data are needed to establish its diagnostic significance and validity.

The Thematic Apperception Test (TAT) developed by Murray and his associates at the Harvard Psychological Clinic is another well-known projective instrument. In contrast to the inkblot techniques, the TAT uses more highly structured stimuli and requires more complex and meaningfully organized verbal responses. It consists of stories made up by the respondent upon presentation of cards that contain vague pictures, and it is usually interpreted qualitatively. Analysis of the content of TAT stories is usually done in reference to Murray's list of "needs," such as achievement and affiliation, and "press," which refers to environmental forces that facilitate or interfere with the satisfaction of needs. Although a number of quantitative scoring schemes, and a fair amount of normative information, have been published for use with the TAT, in clinical practice such procedures are seldom used.

Many adaptations of the TAT, of varying quality and degrees of resemblance to the original, have been developed for special purposes. The Children's Apperception Test (CAT), for example, uses cards that substitute animals for people in an effort to stimulate projection in young test takers, but has apparently not been very successful. Two other instruments developed especially for youngsters are the Roberts Apperception Test for Children (RATC) and "Tell-Me-A-Story" (TEMAS), a test which provides parallel sets of stimulus cards for ethnic minority and for White children. There are also some tools, such as the Senior Apperception Technique, that have been developed especially for the aged and feature elderly persons in the stimulus cards. Still others employ pictorial material in ways that differ from those of the inkblot and TAT techniques. The Rosenzweig Picture-Frustration Study (P-F Study), for example, presents a series of cartoons in which frustrating circumstances are portrayed; it requires the respondent to write what the frustrated person would reply under such circumstances.

Some projective techniques, such as word association and sentence completion tests, are wholly verbal, in that they use only words in both stimulus materials and responses. The diagnostic use of word association techniques predated all other projective techniques by almost half a century but has almost disappeared due to the realization that response frequency is significantly affected by the demographic characteristics of respondents. Sentence completion tests, on the other hand, continue to be widely used both in research and clinical practice. The use of autobiographical memories—which is one of the newest projective tools—can also be classified as a verbal technique. Although the analysis of early memories has been a part of psychodynamic therapies since Freud's time, recently Arnold Bruhn has proposed a new conceptual framework for these memories, as well as a method of employing them that is more systematic than those that existed before. Bruhn's Early Memories Procedure (EMP) is still under development, but it seems to have the potential to become a useful tool for assessing personality in the context of psychotherapy.

Still another category of projective devices, one that is rather large and amorphous, is comprised of performance techniques that call for relatively free self-expression. All of these techniques, which include activities such as drawing and the dramatic use of toys, have been employed for therapeutic as well as diagnostic purposes. A well-known example of these expressive projective techniques is the Machover Draw-a-Person Test (D-A-P). Because of its highly questionable validity, the D-A-P can probably serve best as part of a clinical interview rather than as a psychometric instrument. In spite of the generally poor psychometric characteristics of drawings as tools for assessment, their popularity continues unabated and new variations, such as the Kinetic Family Drawing (KFD), are still appearing. Moreover, a diverse collection of play techniques, ranging from formalized observation of play activities to highly unstructured free play, is also growing.

Projective techniques differ widely in their theoretical soundness as well as in the amount and quality of data available with which to evaluate and interpret them. Nevertheless, certain general observations can be made about most instruments in this category. On the positive side, projective techniques, which are usually intrinsically interesting and nonthreatening, may be quite effective in building rapport and in testing persons who are verbally limited. Similarly, although it cannot be assumed that projective tools are completely immune to faking, they are less susceptible to it than self-report inventories. On the other hand, most projective techniques are inadequately standardized with respect to both administration and scoring and many of them lack adequate normative data. These and other features typical of projective devices, such as the small number and wide diversity of responses, also make it extremely difficult to gather appropriate data on their reliability. In addition, the large majority of published validation studies on projective techniques are inconclusive due to procedural deficiencies in either experimental controls or statistical analyses, or both. With regard to the validity of projective instruments, it should be noted that the methodological problems inherent in their study can sometimes produce spurious evidence of validity, where none exists, and—at other times—can result in underestimating their validity. Additional, and better-designed, studies of most of the projective techniques available are needed to answer the questions concerning whether, when, with whom, and how they work.

The fundamental assumption of the projective hypothesis is that the individual's responses to the ambiguous stimuli presented to her or him reflect significant, often covert, and relatively enduring personality attributes. This has not been supported by research. Indeed, there is ample evidence that other explanations may account as well or better for the individual's responses to unstructured test stimuli. Furthermore, there is an impressive accumulation of studies that have failed to demonstrate any validity for some projective techniques, such as the traditional Rorschach and the D-A-P. In spite of these circumstances, the status of projective techniques remains substantially unchanged, with enthusiastic support for them from clinicians and doubts about them from statisticians.

The seeming contradiction between the largely negative results accumulated over six decades of research with projective techniques and their continued use can be understood if it is recognized that, with a few exceptions, these techniques are not truly tests. Rather, projective devices are coming to be regarded as supplementary qualitative interviewing aids whose value is proportional to the skill of the clinician and whose proper input consists of the suggestion of leads for further exploration.

Comprehensive Review

STUDY QUESTIONS:

1.   List and discuss the major features that distinguish projective techniques from other personality assessment tools.

2.   Describe the procedures used to administer and score the Rorschach inkblots.

3. Discuss the methodological problems involved in the use and interpretation of the Rorschach.

4. Describe the efforts that Exner and his associates have made to put the Rorschach on a psychometrically sound basis.

5. Compare and contrast the Holtzman Inkblot Technique (HIT) with the Rorschach.

6. Describe the main features of the Thematic Apperception Test (TAT), including its administration, scoring, and interpretation.

7. Describe the major adaptations of the TAT developed for special populations.

8. Describe the purpose and procedures of the Rosenzweig Picture-Frustration Study (P-F Study).

9. Describe the history and present status of word association tests.

10. Discuss sentence completion techniques and describe an example of this type of projective device.

11. Explain how autobiographical memories are being used as tools in personality assessment.

12. Enumerate the major types of performance techniques used in projective assessment and explain why they might best serve as part of a clinical interview.

13. Identify and discuss the major advantages of projective techniques as assessment devices.

14. List and discuss the major disadvantages of projective techniques as assessment devices.

15. Explain how the unique characteristics of projective techniques may lead to overestimating or underestimating their validity.

16. Describe the current status of the projective hypothesis and of projective techniques.

FILL IN THE BLANKS: Key Terms, Concepts, and Names

1. _____ _____ are relatively unstructured tasks whose often disguised purpose is to assess personality, especially its unconscious aspects, in a global fashion.

2. The major varieties of projective instruments discussed in the text are _ _ _ _ _ _ _ _ techniques, such as the Rorschach; _ _ _ _ _ _ _ _ _ techniques, such as the TAT; _ _ _ _ _ _ techniques, such as sentence completion tests; and _ _ _ _ _ _ _ _ _ _ techniques, such as drawings and toy tests.

3. _ _ _ _ _ _ _ _ developed the scoring system he applied to the innovative diagnostic tool that he first described in 1921 on the basis of his clinical observations of the responses typical of various psychiatric groups.

4. The most common scoring categories for the Rorschach are _ _ _ _ _ _ _ _ , which refers to the part of the blot associated with each response; _ _ _ _ _ _ _ _ _ _ _ _ , such as color and form; and _ _ _ _ _ _ _ , which typically includes categories such as human and animal figures. In addition, a _ _ _ _ _ _ _ _ _ _ score is often found on the basis of the relative frequency of different responses. The _ _ _ _ _ _ _ _ _ _ _ or precision with which responses match the blots may also be scored.

5. A variable that greatly complicates the interpretation of Rorschach scores is the total number of responses, known as _ _ _ _ _ _ _ _ _ _ _ _ _ _ _ _ _ _ _ _ , or R.

6. The most ambitious effort to put the Rorschach on a psychometrically sound basis was undertaken by _ _ _ _ _ , who has developed a _ _ _ _ _ _ _ _ _ _ _ _ _ system for administering, scoring, and interpreting the test and has collected a considerable body of psychometric data on many of its variables.

7. The _ _ _ _ _ _ _ _ Rorschach is a special clinical adaptation wherein the inkblots are presented for joint interpretation by married couples and other natural groups.

8. The _ _ _ _ _ _ _ _ _ _ _ _ _ _ _ _ _ _ _ _ _ _ _ _ (HIT), which is modeled after the Rorschach, represents a genuine attempt to achieve acceptable psychometric standards and eliminate the main deficiencies of the earlier instrument.

9. Thematic Apperception Test stories are typically interpreted by first determining who is the " _ _ _ _ ," or character with whom the respondent has identified. Then, the content of the stories is analyzed in terms of Henry Murray's list of " _ _ _ _ _ " and " _ _ _ _ _ "; the latter refers to the environmental forces that facilitate or interfere with the satisfaction of needs.

10. One of the most extensive research programs utilizing a TAT adaptation is the one conducted by McClelland and his coworkers on the _ _ _ _ _ _ _ _ _ _ _ _ _ _ _ (n-Ach).

11. The _ _ _ _ _ _ _ _ _ _ _ _ _ _ _ _ _ _ _ _ _ _ _ for Children (RATC) is an adaptation of the TAT that uses stimulus cards depicting familiar interpersonal

situations involving children and represents a serious effort to combine the projective method with good psychometric practices.

12. The _____ _____ – _____ Study (P-F Study) is an ingenious application of pictorial material to projective assessment that consists of a series of cartoons wherein the respondent must project what the frustrated person who is depicted would reply in a given situation.

13. A verbal technique that preceded the flood of projective tests by more than 50 years is the ____ _____ test, which was used by early experimental psychologists, such as Wundt and Cattell, and was systematized as a clinical tool by Jung. In recent decades the diagnostic use of this technique has declined.

14. The ____ – _____ Free Association Test, which was designed as a psychiatric screening instrument, used a list of 100 stimulus words and was scored on the basis of the "commonality" of responses given by the examinee.

15. Fill-in-the-blanks items, such as the ones in this segment of your review, are similar in format to a verbal projective technique known as _____ _____ tests, although the latter are designed for a different purpose and permit an almost unlimited variety of possible responses.

16. The most prominent proponent of the construct of locus of control, discussed in Chapter 14, is also the author of one of the most widely used sentence completion tests, namely, the _____ Incomplete Sentences Blank.

17. Recent interest in the role of autobiographical memories in personality organization is reflected in the development of the ____ _____ _____ (EMP), a self-administered instrument, devised by Arnold Bruhn, which samples memories from throughout one's life span.

18. _____ techniques are a large and varied category of projective devices that use almost every art medium and type of subject matter and can be applied in therapy as well as diagnosis. _____ and ____ techniques are the most numerous within this category.

19. One of the newest drawing techniques, with seemingly great potential as a clinical instrument, is the _____ _____ _____ (KFD), which asks children to draw a picture of everyone in their family, including themselves, "doing something."

20. The most common reasons why studies of projective techniques may produce spurious evidence of validity are (a) the _____ of criterion or test data with

knowledge acquired by criterion judges or examiners; (b) the failure to _ _ _ _ _ –
_ _ _ _ _ _ _ _ the signs that differentiate significantly between criterion groups; (c)
_ _ _ _ _ _ _ _ _ _ accuracy, which is an example of the "Barnum effect;" and (d)
_ _ _ _ _ _ _ _ validation, which is a special example of the mechanism that underlies
the survival of superstitions.

21.   Borrowing a concept from information theory, Cronbach and Gleser characterized
interviewing and projective techniques as procedures wherein_ _ _ _ _ _ _ _ _, or
breadth of coverage, is achieved at the expense of lowered _ _ _ _ _ _ _ _, or
dependability of information.

ANSWERS TO FILL-IN-THE-BLANKS: Key Terms, Concepts, and Names

1.   projective techniques
2.   inkblot (techniques) / pictorial (techniques) / verbal (techniques) / performance
(techniques)
3.   Rorschach
4.   location / determinants / content / popularity / form quality
5.   response productivity (or R)
6.   Exner / comprehensive (system)
7.   consensus (Rorschach)
8.   Holtzman Inkblot Technique (HIT)
9.   "hero" / "needs" / "press"
10.   achievement need (n-Ach)
11.   Roberts Apperception Test (for Children) (RATC)
12.   Rosenzweig Picture-Frustration (Study) (P-F Study)
13.   word association (test)
14.   Kent-Rosanoff (Free Association Test)
15.   sentence completion (tests)
16.   Rotter (Incomplete Sentences Blank)
17.   Early Memories Procedure (EMP)
18.   performance (techniques) / drawing / play (techniques)
19.   Kinetic Family Drawing (KFD)
20.   (a) contamination (of criterion or test data) / (b) (failure to) cross-validate / (c)
stereotype (accuracy) / (d) illusory (validation)
21.   bandwidth/fidelity

TRUE/FALSE and WHY?

1.   Test takers are usually aware of the type of psychological interpretation that will be
made of their responses to projective instruments. (T/F) Why? _____
_____

2. By the 1960s the use of the Rorschach had become indefensible from the point of view of its psychometric characteristics. (T/F) Why? _____

_____

3. Rorschach investigators agree that differences in response productivity or R can be ignored without detrimental consequences. (T/F) Why? _____

_____

4. Experimental data suggest that TAT responses are significantly affected by conditions such as hunger, sleep deprivation, and social frustration. (T/F) Why? _____

_____

5. The Gerontological Apperception Test and the Senior Apperception Test have both been shown to have definite advantages over the TAT when testing is conducted with elderly persons. (T/F) Why? _____

_____

6. Although the Kent-Rosanoff Free Association Test has retained its position as a standard laboratory technique, its diagnostic use has declined. (T/F) Why?_____

_____

7. The reliability and validity of the Comprehensive Early Memories Scoring System devised by Bruhn and his associates have been amply documented. (T/F) Why? ___

_____

8. The interpretive guidelines for the Machover D-A-P Test abound in sweeping generalizations for which no substantial evidence is provided. (T/F) Why? _____

_____

_____

9. Basically, projective techniques and self-report inventories differ from each other in degree, rather than in kind, with regard to their psychometric properties and nature of their task. (T/F) Why? _____

_____

10. For all practical purposes it can be assumed that projective tests are immune to faking. (T/F) Why? _____

_____

11. The final interpretation of projective test responses may reveal more about the examiner than it does about the examinee's personality dynamics. (T/F) Why?

_____

_____

12. Projective devices frequently require special statistical procedures for ascertaining such psychometric characteristics as reliability. (T/F) Why? _____

_____

_____

13. In the context of projective testing, fantasy productions with high aggressive content are consistently associated with high aggression in overt behavior. (T/F) Why?

_____

_____

14. The relation between ambiguity of stimuli and projective productivity appears to be linear, in that the less structured the stimuli, the more likely they are to elicit projection and tap deep layers of personality. (T/F) Why? _____

_____

_____

15. There is ample evidence that responses to unstructured test stimuli can be best explained by the projective hypothesis. (T/F) Why? _____

_____

_____

ANSWERS TO TRUE/FALSE:

1. False	4. True	7. False	10. False	13. False
2. True	5. False	8. True	11. True	14. False
3. False	6. True	9. True	12. True	15. False

Multiple Choice: Test Yourself

1. Compared to the more objective measures of personality, projective techniques are_____.
   a.   less structured
   b.   more difficult to evaluate
   c.   less reliable
   d.   all of the above

2. The original scoring procedures for the Rorschach can best be described as_____

   _____.
   a.   based primarily on the intuition of Rorschach
   b.   refined through statistical manipulation
   c.   based on an informal and subjective application of criterion keying
   d.   relatively simple, straightforward, and easy to master

3. The various Rorschach systems that flourished from the 1930s to the 1960s differed mainly in terms of _____.
   a. the number of cards that were used
   b. scoring and interpretation
   c. their emphasis on the significance of color as a determinant
   d. administration procedures

4. Exner's efforts to improve the Rorschach as a psychometric instrument have centered on _____.
   a. more standardized procedures for administration and scoring
   b. additional emphasis on structural variables
   c. more data-based interpretations
   d. all of the above

5. An alternative to Exner's approach to the Rorschach that has evolved since the 1970s and is grounded in modern psychoanalytic theory is the one developed by _____
   _____.
   a. Arnold Bruhn
   b. Wayne Holtzman
   c. Paul Lerner
   d. Bruno Klopfer

6. When compared to the Rorschach, the Holtzman Inkblot Technique (HIT) _____
   _____.
   a. allows for greater response productivity
   b. is more standardized
   c. uses fewer stimulus cards
   d. all of the above

7. The Thematic Apperception Test (TAT) involves_____
   _____.
   a. presenting the respondent with a series of incomplete statements
   b. creating stories after exposure to vague pictures
   c. responding to a set of multicolored inkblots
   d. a set of 250 forced-choice-type questions

8. Compared with the Rorschach, the TAT is _____
   _____.
   a. more structured
   b. less structured
   c. less influenced by examiner variables
   d. unaffected by the respondent's motivation

9. "My mother ...," "What worries me ...," and "I am ..." are all examples of items that might appear on _____.
   a. the TAT
   b. a word association test
   c. a sentence completion test
   d. the Kent-Rosanoff Free Association Test

10. Which of the following pictorial techniques comes closer to meeting psychometric standards of test construction than the rest?_____.
    a. Tell-Me-A-Story (TEMAS)
    b. The Children's Apperception Test (CAT)
    c. The Gerontological Apperception Test
    d. Roberts Apperception Test for Children

11. Playing with toys while being observed, drawing pictures of people, and drawing familiar things can be classified as _____.
    a. performance techniques
    b. pictorial techniques
    c. psychometric instruments
    d. dramatic techniques

12. Which of the following is *not* one of the human figure drawings' "emotional indicators" mentioned in the textbook?_____.
    a. transparencies and shading of the face
    b. drawings of stick figures
    c. tiny heads and other grotesque features
    d. omissions of expected parts, such as the eyes

13. The reliability of most projective techniques is _____.
    a. lower than desirable
    b. difficult to assess
    c. heavily dependent on the training of the clinician who administers and scores the procedure
    d. all of the above

14. The "projective hypothesis" _____.
    a. assumes that the individual's responses reflect significant and lasting personality attributes
    b. has been supported surprisingly well by empirical findings
    c. has become less and less favored by clinicians
    d. all of the above

15. Projective techniques are best used for_____

    _____.

    a.   detecting deep-seated emotional disorders
    b.   accurate assessment of global personality characteristics
    c.   developing leads for further exploration
    d.   evaluating verbally gifted individuals

Miniprojects/Suggested Homework Activities:

1.   A sizable portion of what has been written and said about projective techniques has dealt with the Rorschach. Exner's three-volume work, *The Rorschach: A Comprehensive System* (New York: Wiley), is among the most thorough current sources on the subject. Each volume has been revised at least once. *Volume 1: Basic Foundations*, is now in its third edition (1993), *Volume 2: Interpretation*, is in its second edition (1991), and *Volume 3: Assessment of Children and Adolescents*—coauthored by Exner and I.B. Weiner—is also its second edition (1995). This monumental work, however, is well beyond the scope of a "miniproject" and would only be appropriate for those wanting to become serious "Rorschachers." For a briefer overview of Exner's Comprehensive System (ECS), see Chapter 9 (pp. 393-457) of the *Handbook of Psychological Assessment*, 3rd ed., by Gary Groth-Marnat (New York: Wiley, 1997). Critical commentaries on the ECS by J.M. Wood, M.T. Nezworski, and W.J. Stejskal, and a rebuttal by Exner, can be found in the January 1996 issue of *Psychological Science* (*7*, 3-17).

2.   An entirely different view of the Rorschach, is presented in *The Rorschach Technique*: *Perceptual Basics, Content Interpretation, and Applications,* by Edward Aronow, Marvin Reznikoff, and Kevin Moreland (Boston: Allyn & Bacon, 1994). This work provides a history of the technique and discusses various approaches, with particular emphasis on sophisticated content-based interpretation. Another good source of current information about the Rorschach, other projective techniques, and personality tests in general, is the *Journal of Personality Assessment.* The evolution of this quarterly publication, which started out as a mimeographed newsletter called *The Rorschach Research Exchange* and later became the *Journal of Projective Techniques,* reflects the development of personality assessment.

3.   If you can obtain a set of TAT cards and a manual, select about 10 of the pictures and write stories based on them, following the directions in the manual. After you have written the stories, set them aside for a couple of days. Then, reread them and analyze them as objectively as you can, using the manual and any other TAT references you can locate (see, for example, Chapter 10, pp. 458–498, of Groth-Marnat's *Handbook*, cited in Miniproject # 1 for this chapter). Note particularly whether the "needs" and "presses" expressed in your stories bear any relationship to

your mental or physical state at the time you wrote them, or whether they reflect "themes" that concern you on an ongoing basis. If you cannot obtain TAT cards, the thematic analysis of records of daily events—described in an article by R. Karl Hanson in the *Journal of Personality Assessment, 58,* 606-620—provides an interesting alternative.

4. Another activity you might wish to undertake in order to deepen your understanding of the material in Chapter 15 is a replication of Chapman and Chapman's demonstration of the phenomenon of "illusory validation" (*Journal of Abnormal Psychology,* 1967, *72,* 193–204). After you read the article describing the experiments, duplicate the materials they used or fashion your own, along similar lines. Then, present them to a small sample of college students, preferably in majors other than psychology.

5. One great advantage of longevity, in a psychological test, is that it permits the accumulation of data that can be used for analyses which are of historical as well as psychological interest. An extraordinary example of this circumstance is the test data available on some members of the Nazi German elite who were defendants at the Nuremberg trials. For a description and discussion of these data, as well as some verbatim Rorschach records, read *The Quest for the Nazi Personality: A Psychological Investigation of Nazi War Criminals* by Eric A. Zillmer, Molly Harrower, Barry A. Ritzler, and Robert P. Archer (Hillsdale, NJ: Erlbaum, 1995).

6. Those who are interested in the projective use of autobiographical memories may wish to consult Arnold Bruhn's informative chapter on "Early Memories in Personality Asssessment." It appears in the book *Clinical Personality Assessment: Practical Approaches,* edited by James N. Butcher (New York: Oxford, 1995). The chapter (pp. 278–301) presents a historical overview of the use of autobiographical memories as well as a description of Bruhn's Early Memories Procedure (EMP).

7. The continued popularity of projective techniques, even in light of the unabated criticisms they have received for their psychometric weaknesses, is evident in a number of ways. One is in surveys of psychodiagnostic test usage (see, for example, the Piotrowski et al. survey in the *Journal of Personality Assessment,* 1985, *49,* 115–119). Another is in the frequency with which such techniques are taught (see, e.g., Piotrowski & Zalewski's article on training in psychodiagnostic testing in the *Journal of Personality Assessment,* 1993, *61,* 394–405). To ascertain this phenomenon more directly, survey clinicians in your area, with a questionnaire, asking them to report on their use of the major techniques cited in Chapter 15.

ANSWERS TO MULTIPLE CHOICE/TEST YOURSELF ITEMS:

1.	d	6.	b	11.	a
2.	c	7.	b	12.	b
3.	b	8.	a	13.	d
4.	d	9.	c	14.	a
5.	c	10.	d	15.	c

OTHER ASSESSMENT TECHNIQUES

Chapter Outline

Measures of Styles and Types
      Cognitive Styles
      Personality Types
      Myers-Briggs Type Indicator

Situational Tests
      Tests of the Character Education Inquiry
      Situational Tests in Assessment Centers and Roleplaying Techniques

Self-Concepts and Personal Constructs
      Washington University Sentence Completion Test
      Self-Esteem Inventories and Related Measures
      The Adjective Check List
      Q Sort
      The Semantic Differential
      Role Construct Repertory Test
      Perceived Environment and Social Climate

Observer Reports
      Naturalistic Observation
      The Interview
      Ratings
      Nominating Technique
      Checklists and Q Sorts

Biodata

Chapter Summary

Chapter 16 considers a diverse array of personality assessment tools that differ from the self-report inventories and projective techniques described earlier in the text. These instruments—which include measures of styles and types, situational tests, as well as techniques for the assessment of self-concepts and personal constructs—are used mainly in research, although some can also serve as clinical aids. In addition, the chapter describes nontest techniques used in personality appraisal, including naturalistic observation, interviewing, ratings, and the analysis of life-history data.

The notion of cognitive styles has been used primarily to explain differences in the way individuals perceive, remember, think, and solve problems. Among the most common features used to differentiate cognitive styles are perceptual characteristics—such as field independence (FI) and field dependence (FD). These terms refer to the ability and inability, respectively, to resist disruption in what one perceives when conflicting contextual cues are present. Field independence and dependence are relatively stable cognitive characteristics that have been widely studied with the use of the Embedded Figures Test. Personality types, on the other hand, are categories that have been employed since ancient times to explain a wide variety of behavioral tendencies within individuals and differences between individuals. One of the most enduring typologies was devised by Jung and has served as the basis for a widely used personality inventory known as the Myers-Briggs Type Indicator (MBTI). Cognitive styles and personality types exemplify attempts to capture qualitative differences in the patterns of human behavior. Both of these sets of constructs cut across the realms of ability and personality. They are both enjoying renewed popularity as the need to integrate the cognitive and affective domains in theory and practice is increasingly recognized. At the same time, the reluctance that many psychologists traditionally have felt about using typologies to explain differences in human behavior is, to some extent, being overcome.

Situational tests are techniques that place the test taker in a circumstance that simulates "real life." The most notable forerunners of such tests were the situations that Hartshorne and May devised in the course of the Character Education Inquiry (CEI) investigations they conducted in the late 1920s. The CEI tests were designed to measure behavior characteristics such as honesty and self-control in children; they produced results that underscored the situational specificity of those traits. The quintessential examples of situational tests are the techniques devised as part of the assessment-center program introduced by the U.S. Office of Strategic Services (OSS) during World War II. These techniques—which include situational stress tests and leaderless groups among others—were later adapted for other uses, such as the selection of high level executives in industry. The Leaderless Group Discussion (LGD), for example, has proved to be effective for predicting performance in jobs that require good communication skills and acceptance by peers. Another ubiquitous type of situational test is the roleplaying or improvisation technique wherein the individual is instructed to play a part either overtly or by reporting what he or she would do or say in a given situation. This tool has enjoyed great popularity in the selection and training of people whose jobs require interpersonal skills. Although no generalizations can be made about the validity of *the* assessment center technique, in general, the studies showing the highest validity coefficients are those which use multiple sources of data and focus on relevant and directly observable behaviors.

Several current approaches to personality assessment concentrate on the way people view themselves and others. The Washington University Sentence Completion Test, for example, measures the trait of self-conceptualization—designated as ego development or ego level—that is so prominent in Loevinger's theoretical approach to personality development. The Student Self-Concept Scale (SSCS) and the Personal and Academic Self-Concept

Inventory (PASCI) are examples of instruments for the measurement of evaluative self-concept, a multifaceted construct that is thought to influence the development of many affective as well as cognitive traits. Other broadly oriented techniques especially useful for the assessment of self-concepts include the Adjective Check List (ACL) and the Q sort procedure originated by Stephenson. Two representative examples of techniques used for investigating how individuals perceive others are the Semantic Differential, developed by Osgood for his research on the psychology of meaning, and the Role Construct Repertory Test (Rep Test) devised by G.A. Kelly and intimately related to his personal construct theory. A variety of assessment techniques are also being explored in order to evaluate physical and social aspects of various environments. Among these are the ten Social Climate Scales which were developed by Rudolph Moos and are described in the text.

Direct observations of behavior are an essential supplement to standardized tests in the assessment of personality. Naturalistic observations, interviewing, ratings, nominating techniques, checklists, and Q sorts are some of the most prominent approaches that have been devised or adapted for gathering and reporting observational data in personality appraisal. Although much can be done to improve the accuracy and communicability of these procedures, their input is extremely valuable because they allow for more extensive and flexible sampling of behavioral data than do standardized tests.

Life-history data are a critical component of the information base that must be gathered by clinicians and others who are involved in the assessment of individuals. Although interviewing can and does supply much of these data, structured biographical inventories or scales—now designated as biodata measures—are an important alternative or additional source of information on the individual's life history. Biographical inventories bring the advantages of uniformity and economy to the gathering of biodata. In addition, when their items are selected and weighted by criterion keying—and cross-validated—such inventories have proven to be good predictors of performance albeit, typically, only for the specific purposes or contexts for which they were designed. New methods of generating, analyzing, and keying biodata items are being tried in an effort to make instruments more flexible and transportable. The use of clustering techniques to identify subgroups of individuals who share common patterns of experience was pioneered by William Owens. It has been one of the most fruitful avenues of biodata research and has both theoretical and practical applications that appear very promising. In spite of their effectiveness, the implementation of biodata measures is also the subject of some concerns, such as invasion of privacy issues and the susceptibility of these data to faking or other sources of inaccuracy.

Comprehensive Review

STUDY QUESTIONS:

1. Define what is meant by cognitive styles and discuss the role these constructs can play in explaining behavior.

2. Discuss the notion of field dependence and describe some of the research findings related to the field dependence-independence dichotomy.

3. Describe the role that personality types have played in explaining human behavior and cite two examples of typologies.

4. Discuss the theoretical basis and psychometric characteristics of the Myers-Briggs Type Indicator.

5. Explain why scientific psychology has traditionally been reluctant to embrace the use of typologies and describe some of the reasons why this reluctance seems to be diminishing.

6. Describe the methodology and major findings of Hartshorne and May's Character Education Inquiry (CEI).

7. Describe two examples of situational tests that were developed through the assessment-center program of the Office of Strategic Services (OSS) and discuss their value in personality assessment.

8. Discuss the various current uses of roleplaying or improvisation techniques in individual assessment.

9. Describe the background and purpose of the Washington University Sentence Completion Test.

10. Discuss the construct of self-esteem, its relationship to self-concept, and the principal ways in which it can be assessed.

11. Describe how the Adjective Check List (ACL), the Q sort, and the Semantic Differential technique can be used in the assessment of self-concepts.

12. Explain the theoretical basis and procedures of the Role Construct Repertory Test (Rep Test).

13. Describe the Social Climate Scales and discuss the role that such measures can play in the assessment of environments.

14. Enumerate and discuss the functions of naturalistic observations and interviews in personality assessment.

15. Compare and contrast ratings and the nominating technique as they are used in the evaluation of individuals.

16. Explain how checklists, Q sorts, and other self-report instruments may be used by an observer to describe another person; indicate what the advantages of using such standardized tools for observer evaluations might be.

17. Describe how life-history data are typically gathered and how biodata measures are developed and used in the industrial and educational settings.

FILL IN THE BLANKS: Key Terms, Concepts, and Names

1. _ _ _ _ _ _ _ _ _ _   _ _ _ _ _ _ refer to people's preferred and typical modes of perceiving, remembering, thinking, and problem solving; regarded as broad stylistic behavioral characteristics, they cut across abilities and personality and are manifested in many activities.

2. Instruments such as the Gottschaldt Figures and the _ _ _ _ _ _ _ Figures Test have been used to assess personality characteristics through an analysis of differences in _ _ _ _ _ _ _ _ _ functions.

3. Witkin and his associates identified a relatively stable and consistent cognitive trait designated as _ _ _ _ _   _ _ _ _ _ _ _ _ _ _ _, which refers to the extent to which individuals' perceptions are influenced or disrupted by conflicting contextual cues and is apparently related to a number of personality variables.

4. _ _ _ _ _ _ _ _ _ _ _ _   _ _ _ _ _ are categories defined by patterns of two or more attributes; they have been used since ancient times to explain behavioral similarities and differences within and across individuals.

5. The _ _ _ _ _   -   _ _ _ _ _ _ _ _ _ _ _ _   _ _ _ _ _ _ _ _ _ _ (MBTI) is a personality inventory that uses Jung's dichotomy of introverted and extraverted attitudes as well as his classifications of the ways in which people perceive and judge.

6. _ _ _ _ _ _ _ _ _ _ _ tests of personality place the test taker in a circumstance that simulates "real life" in order to sample complex criterion behavior of an emotional, interpersonal, or attitudinal nature.

7. Some of the earliest situational tests were constructed by Hartshorne, May, and their associates in the course of the _ _ _ _ _ _ _ _ _   _ _ _ _ _ _ _ _ _ _   _ _ _ _ _ _ _ (CEI), which was an extensive project that investigated such traits as honesty and self-control in children.

8. The _ _ _ _ _ _ _ _ _ _   -   _ _ _ _ _ _ program introduced by the U.S. Office of Strategic Services during World War II resulted in the development of a number of

203

techniques later adapted for other settings. One of those, designed to sample behavior under frustrating or disruptive conditions, was the _ _ _ _ _ _ _ _ _ _ _ _ _ _ _ test; another was the use of a _ _ _ _ _ _ _ _ _ _ _ _ _ _ to carry out assigned tasks, such as transporting men and materials across a brook, without designating the specific responsibilities of group members.

9. The _ _ _ _ _ _ _ _ _ _ _ technique, which is used most extensively in the evaluation of interpersonal behavior, involves explicitly instructing the individual to play a part either overtly or by reporting what he or she would do or say in a given situation.

10. In the Washington University Sentence Completion Test, _ _ _ _ _ _ _ _ _ and her associates undertook to measure the trait of _ _ _ _ – _ _ _ _ _ _ _ _ _ _ _ _ _ _ _ _ _, designated as ego development or ego level, which is defined as the capacity to "assume distance" from oneself and one's impulses.

11. _ _ _ _ – _ _ _ _ _, which is often described as the evaluative component of the self-concept, is a multifaceted construct that has been extensively investigated in recent years, especially with regard to its impact on academic achievement.

12. In the investigation of self-concepts, two of the most widely used techniques are: (a) the _ _ _ _ _ _ _ _ _ _ _ _ _ _ _ _ _ _ _ (ACL), which consists of items ranging from "absentminded" to "zany," and (b) the _ _ _ _ _ _, wherein the respondent classifies a set of cards, with statements or trait names on them, into piles ranging from most to least characteristic of himself or herself.

13. The _, first developed by Osgood for research on the psychology of meaning, provides a standardized and quantified procedure for assessing the connotations that any given concept has for the individual through ratings of each concept along a series of bipolar adjectival scales.

14. The _ Test (Rep Test) was developed by Kelly to help the clinician identify some of the client's important constructs about people, but has been modified and used extensively in personality research. An important index derived from the Rep Test, and based on the number of constructs used by an individual, is designated as _ _ _ _ _ _ _ _ _ _ _ _ _ _ _ _ and is regarded as a measure of cognitive style.

15. An important application of assessment techniques to environmental psychology is represented by measures devised to describe and evaluate physical and social aspects of environment, such as the ten _ _ _ _ _ _ _ _ _ _ _ _ _ _ _ _ _ _ developed by Rudolph Moos.

16. Personality assessment cannot rely entirely on standardized tests and must be

supplemented by direct _ _ _ _ _ _ _ _ _ _ _ of behavior and by life-history data usually gathered through _ _ _ _ _ _ _ _ _ _.

17. In the assessment of individuals, evaluations from observers can be reported through simple _ _ _ _ _ _ _ _ , which are often used to obtain criterion information, or through a variation known as the _ _ _ _ _ _ _ _ _ _ technique, which is especially useful in gathering peer assessments, as well as from _ _ _ _ _ _ _ _ _ _ , such as the ACL, and decks of _ – _ _ _ _ items.

18. Ratings are subject to a number of constant errors, such as the _ _ _ _ _ _ _ _ _ _ , which has traditionally been defined as the tendency of raters to be influenced by a single favorable or unfavorable trait, the _ _ _ _ _ _ _ _ _ _ _ _ _ _ error, which results in a bunching of ratings in the middle of the scale, and the _ _ _ _ _ _ _ _ error, which refers to the reluctance of raters to assign unfavorable ratings. One way to correct the latter two types of errors is to use rankings or other _ _ _ _ _ – _ _ – _ _ _ _ _ procedures.

19. _ _ _ _ _ _ _ _ _ _ _ _ _ inventories are standardized self-report instruments that attempt to obtain life-history data in a structured fashion and/or when interviews are not feasible.

20. The collective term currently used to designate biographical inventories and scales that are devised for the prediction of performance in industrial and educational settings is _ _ _ _ _ _ _ measures.

ANSWERS TO FILL-IN-THE-BLANKS: Key Terms, Concepts, and Names

 1. cognitive styles
 2. Embedded (Figures Test) / perceptual (functions)
 3. field dependence
 4. personality types
 5. Myers–Briggs Type Indicator (MBTI)
 6. situational (tests)
 7. Character Education Inquiry (CEI)
 8. assessment-center (program) / situational stress (test) / leaderless group
 9. roleplaying (technique)
10. Loevinger/self-conceptualization
11. self-esteem
12. (a) Adjective Check List (ACL) / (b) Q sort
13. Semantic Differential
14. Role Construct Repertory (Test) (Rep Test) / cognitive complexity
15. Social Climate Scales
16. (direct) observation (of behavior) / interviews

17. ratings / nominating (technique) / checklists / Q-sort (items)
18. halo effect / central tendency (error) / leniency (error) / order-of-merit (procedures)
19. biographical (inventories)
20. biodata (measures)

TRUE/FALSE and WHY?

1. A number of projective techniques, most notably the Rorschach, are essentially tests of perceptual functions. (T/F) Why? _____

_____

2. Surveys of studies of the field dependent–field independent continuum suggest that field independent persons are generally more effective and well adapted than those who are field dependent. (T/F) Why? _____

_____

3. Traditionally, typological systems have had enormous popular appeal but relatively little acceptance in scientific psychology. (T/F) Why? _____

_____

4. The responses of children who were studied in the CEI tended to vary across situations and contexts, probably as a function of moral character and motivational factors. (T/F) Why? _____

_____

5. The convergent validity of assessment-center techniques, when used for the evaluation of specific dimensions of performance, has been well established across different methods. (T/F) Why? _____

_____

6. According to the theory formulated by Loevinger, it would be accurate to say that self-report inventories, such as the MMPI, are actually measures of self-concept. (T/F) Why? _____

_____

7. Many investigators have found that the relationship between self-concept and behavior can be demonstrated most clearly if the self-concept is assessed with a single, global measure. (T/F) Why? _____

_____

8. One of the advantages of gathering data through the Role Construct Repertory Test is the ease and simplicity of its scoring and interpretation procedures. (T/F) Why?

_____

9. Naturalistic observations differ from situational tests in that the former do not involve control of the stimulus situation and usually provide a more extensive behavior sample than the latter. (T/F) Why? _____

_____

10. Adept interviewers concern themselves only with what has happened to the individual in the past and what is presently happening to her or him. (T/F) Why? _____

_____

_____

11. The accuracy and validity of ratings can be vastly improved through the use of numbers or general descriptive adjectives and also by ascertaining that the rater has known the person to be rated for a long time. (T/F) Why? _____

_____

12. Peer assessments have generally proven to be one of the most dependable rating techniques in a diverse range of groups. (T/F) Why? _____

_____

13. One of the limitations of many biographical inventories developed for specific jobs by empirical methods is their narrow applicability. (T/F) Why? _____

_____

14. The history of biodata research exemplifies, in a very clear-cut fashion, the mutual interdependence of basic and applied psychological science. (T/F) Why?_____

_____

ANSWERS TO TRUE/FALSE:

1.	True	5.	False	9.	True	13.	True
2.	False	6.	True	10.	False	14.	True
3.	True	7.	False	11.	False		
4.	True	8.	False	12.	True		

Multiple Choice: Test Yourself

1. The Gottschaldt Figures and the Embedded Figures Test are basically tests of_____

_____.

    a.   perceptual functions
    b.   aesthetic preferences
    c.   motivational traits
    d.   none of the above

2. The Embedded Figures Test _____.
   a.   is difficult to administer
   b.   is a purely visual, paper-and-pencil measure of field dependence
   c.   is a personality measure useful in clinical assessment
   d.   lacks a form suitable for use with adults

3. Which of the following typological classifications has endured from the time of its inception up to the present? _____

   _____.
   a.   The Greek theory of body humors
   b.   Sheldon's classification of personalities and physiques
   c.   Jung's dichotomy of introversion and extraversion
   d.   The classification of mentally retarded persons

4. The Myers-Briggs Type Indicator produces scores on_____ independent dimensions which are then used to classify the respondent into any one of_____ possible types.
   a.   two / four
   b.   four / eight
   c.   four / sixteen
   d.   eight / thirty-two

5. The instruments that Hartshorne, May, and their associates constructed for the Character Education Inquiry (CEI) can be described as an early form of _____

   _____.
   a.   situational tests
   b.   improvisation techniques
   c.   aesthetic evaluation tests
   d.   self-concept tests

6. The majority of CEI tests were concerned with _____.
   a.   self-concept
   b.   rigidity
   c.   altruism
   d.   honesty

7. The Office of Strategic Services (OSS) devised a number of "lifelike" tests to assess special military personnel during World War II. These tests included_____

   _____.
   a.   situational stress tests
   b.   the "Wall Situation"
   c.   leaderless groups
   d.   all of the above

8. The major reason why situational tests are not used more often is that _____
   _____.
   a. they are illegal
   b. they tend to be validated against fairly specific criteria
   c. they are not nearly as accurate as formal objective tests
   d. none of the above

9. The use of situations that demand improvisation as an aspect of the overall evaluation of a job applicant or fledgling counselor _____.
   a. has become increasingly popular
   b. has been found to be basically unreliable and invalid
   c. is illegal
   d. is ineffective

10. According to Loevinger, the various response sets that are evident in self-report personality inventories are manifestations of one's _____
    _____.
    a. self-conceptualization
    b. impulsiveness
    c. self-esteem
    d. behavioral repertory

11. The construct of self-esteem appears to be _____
    _____.
    a. generally unstable over time when it is assessed with simple, global measures
    b. hierarchical and multidimensional
    c. of little use in predicting academic achievement
    d. unidimensional and consistent

12. The Semantic Differential is basically a technique for the measurement of_____
    _____.
    a. honesty
    b. verbal fluency
    c. evaluative connotations
    d. perseverance

13. The Rep Test is ideally suited for the investigation of_____
    _____.
    a. psychopathology
    b. interpersonal skills
    c. work-related aptitudes and attitudes
    d. the way individuals derive and organize meaning

14. Naturalistic observations have been used most often by _____.

     a.   clinicians in psychiatric hospitals
     b.   child psychologists
     c.   OSS personnel
     d.   counselors

15. Usually, the primary function of an interview is to _____.

     a.   provide an opportunity for observation
     b.   elicit life-history data
     c.   rate the interviewee
     d.   detect roleplaying or faking

16. The _____ is a constant error which reduces the effective width of rating scales.

     a.   halo effect
     b.   error variance
     c.   error of central tendency
     d.   Barnum effect

Miniprojects/Suggested Homework Activities:

1. Survey Chapter 16 one more time and make up your own miniproject. The scope of the chapter is such that it touches on a large number of fascinating topics likely to stimulate your interest and creativity. Examples include (a) emotional intelligence, (b) the nature and measurement of self-esteem, (c) Jane Loevinger's theory of ego development, (d) roleplaying and improvisation techniques, (e) George A. Kelly's personal construct theory and its more recent offshoot—constructivism, and (f) William Owens's seminal research on modal patterns of life-history experiences, among many others. If you do choose to make up your own miniproject, you will find—right in the textbook—a good supply of references with which to start your pursuit of the topic that interests you.

2. Imagine you are in charge of selecting applicants for a prestigious medical school. You have decided to do away with traditional testing, in favor of situational tests. Applicants are being invited in groups of 10 to come to the campus for a two-day period of evaluation. Devise a series of situational tests that might be tried in order to select the top 20 percent of the applicants who would have the greatest chance of succeeding in the program and becoming "good" doctors. How would you evaluate the validity of your tests?

3. Select an appropriate time and place to conduct a naturalistic observation of one person. You might use a coffee shop, a library, or a public park, for example. Devote all of your attention to the person you have chosen to observe for about half an hour and note all of her or his activities, while remaining inconspicuous. Write a detailed word-picture of what you have observed and review its contents to see what evaluative hypotheses, if any, you can gather from your observation.

4. One of the most enjoyable texts that you are likely to encounter in the field of psychology is the book *Nonreactive Measures in the Social Sciences*, 2nd ed., written by Webb et al. (Boston: Houghton Mifflin, 1981). This book—cited on p. 464 of the textbook—presents a number of ingenious applications of naturalistic observation that can be used to conduct social psychological research in an unobtrusive fashion. It is not only well written but—for those fond of the genre—it is also almost as much fun to read as a detective novel.

5. Although most people are not concerned with reliability, validity, or any other psychometric considerations, human beings do spend a good deal of time evaluating each other in countless ways. As a final exercise for this chapter, outline the assessment techniques you knowingly, and not so knowingly, use in your everyday life. Choose a particular aspect of your life, such as your method for assessing a potential marriage partner, boss, or friend, and then evaluate your method.

ANSWERS TO MULTIPLE CHOICE/TEST YOURSELF ITEMS:

1.	a	5.	a	9.	a	13.	d
2.	b	6.	d	10.	a	14.	b
3.	c	7.	d	11.	b	15.	b
4.	c	8.	b	12.	c	16.	c

Part V   Applications of Testing

---

oo   17   oo

MAJOR CONTEXTS OF CURRENT TEST USE

Chapter Outline

Educational Testing
> Achievement Tests: Their Nature and Uses
> Construction versus Choice

Types of Educational Tests
> General Achievement Batteries
> Tests of Minimum Competency in Basic Skills
> Teacher-Made Classroom Tests
> Tests for the College Level
> Graduate School Admission
> Diagnostic and Prognostic Testing
> Assessment in Early Childhood Education
> Concluding Remarks

Occupational Testing

Validation of Employment Tests
> Global Procedures for the Assessment of Performance
> Job Analysis and the Job Element Method
> The Prediction of Job Performance
> The Criterion of Job Performance

Occupational Use of Tests
> The Role of Academic Intelligence
> Aptitude Batteries for Special Programs
> Special Aptitude Tests

Personality Testing in the Workplace
> Integrity Tests
> Leadership
> Instruments
> Concluding Comments

Chapter Summary

EDUCATIONAL TESTING

Achievement tests, which are those designed to measure the effects of a specific program of instruction or training, surpass all other types of standardized tests in the frequency of their use. Achievement tests are often contrasted with aptitude tests and do differ from the latter in that they presuppose more uniformity in antecedent experiences and also in that they are usually given as part of a terminal, rather than a predictive, evaluation. However, neither one of the distinctions drawn between aptitude and achievement tests can be rigidly applied because both types of tests can vary in the kind of learning experiences they presuppose as well as in how they are used. In addition, there can be a good deal of overlap in the content of both types of tests and their respective scores are often very highly correlated.

To avoid the excess meanings associated with the terms "aptitude" and "achievement," measures of cognitive behavior are increasingly being called simply "ability" tests. All such tests sample only what the person knows at the time when the testing is done; they measure level of development in one or more areas but do not reveal how or why that level was obtained. Another aspect of applied aptitude and achievement testing that has brought about confusion is the practice of labeling children whose achievement test scores are lower or higher than their aptitude test scores as under- or overachievers. Actually, under- or overachievement is really a matter of a discrepancy between the scores on two tests taken at different times. When such discrepancies occur, they may be a function of (a) the errors of measurement of the tests, (b) differences in test coverage, (c) differences in the tests' susceptibility to attitudinal and motivational factors, and/or (d) the nature of intervening experiences between the test administrations.

The uses of achievement tests in the educational process are many and varied. Such tests can be used as aids in the assignment of grades, and in the identification of students with academic weaknesses or special learning disabilities, as well as in measuring the progress of those students through remedial work. In addition, achievement tests can be used in the formulation of educational goals, as bases for planning what is taught, and as aids in the evaluation and improvement of teaching.

Multiple-choice questions have been the most widely used, the most thoroughly studied, and the most frequently criticized type of ability-test items. The major criticisms of this item format center on the deleterious effects it presumably has had on curricular goals and instructional methods. These critiques have given rise to a great variety of "performance-based" assessment procedures. Most of the proposed alternatives to multiple choice are open-ended or "constructed-response" tasks that require examinees to generate an answer. The psychometric evaluation of these alternatives is proceeding gradually and the direction of research results differs widely depending on the types of tasks and domains in question. In the meantime, the use of multiple-choice items is still pervasive. Based on direct comparisons of the relative economy, efficiency, and predictive validity of traditional kinds of constructed-response and multiple-choice items, the continued use of the latter appears to be justified. There are, however, many other types of items—as well as other criteria for evaluating them—that need to be considered as assessment methodology evolves.

Several batteries are available for measuring achievement in the major areas covered by academic curricula. These general achievement batteries typically cover a wide range of educational levels and permit comparisons of an individual's standing in different areas as well as from grade to grade. Some of the most widely used batteries are normed concurrently with a test of scholastic aptitude and, thus, also permit comparisons across two types of tests. On the whole, general achievement batteries meet high standards of test development in terms of their norms, reliability, and content validation. The California Achievement Tests, the Stanford Achievement Test Series, and the Iowa Tests series are major examples of achievement batteries that have been normed jointly with the some of the multilevel batteries discussed in Chapter 10.

Another type of instrument used in the educational context consists of tests for the assessment of minimum competency in basic skills. The development of these tests received great impetus from strong societal concerns about the low levels of competence of high school graduates in reading, writing, and arithmetic. Because such tests must reflect the specific curricula they cover, they are usually tailor-made for the school systems or state agencies that employ them, although they may also include components from standardized achievement batteries. Still other competency tests in basic skills, such as the Tests of Adult Basic Education (TABE), have been developed for the growing segment of the adult population that is poorly educated or functionally illiterate.

The largest category of tests used in educational settings is made up of classroom examinations prepared by teachers themselves. Although local classroom tests obviously cannot be standardized, they can be greatly improved by the application of proper test construction techniques. Teacher-made classroom tests should be planned and balanced by drawing up test specifications before any items are written. In addition, teachers should be aware of the many practical rules that exist for effective item writing and should analyze the results of their tests to correct any weaknesses.

The Scholastic Assessment Tests (SAT) Program of the College Board provides an outstanding example of tests that are used in the admission, placement, and counseling of college students. The SAT has undergone continuous development and extensive research since 1926, when it was incorporated into the College Board testing program. SAT Program tests have recently undergone changes in content and format. Their score scale has also been "recentered" using a reference group from the 1990s instead of the former fixed reference group from 1941. The American College Testing (ACT) Program is another widely used assessment tool for college admissions that includes noncognitive components, such as an interest inventory. In addition to the SAT program, the College Board also develops and administers tests, such as the Advanced Placement Program (APP) series, that are used for college admission with advanced standing in a subject.

Graduate and professional schools also use tests to aid in the selection of applicants. The Graduate Record Examinations (GRE) are a well-known example of this type of test. The GRE program includes a General Test, with Verbal, Quantitative, and Analytical Ability sections, and Subject Tests for many fields of study. The GRE scores are fairly good predictors of graduate school performance, especially when they are used in combination with college grades.

Diagnostic tests, designed to analyze the individual's strengths and weaknesses within a specific subject-matter domain, and to suggest causes for her or his difficulties, constitute another category of testing within the context of education. Diagnostic tests typically deal with reading, mathematics, and language functions. Although these tests can help identify individuals in need of additional attention, the clinical diagnosis and treatment of learning disabilities require specialized techniques. A related category of instruments consists of prognostic tests designed to predict performance in specific courses, e.g., algebra. This can be done by gauging the extent to which individuals have acquired the prerequisite knowledge and skills needed for a course or by assessing how well they learn new material similar to what they will encounter in the course. Newer techniques that link assessment and intervention, such as dynamic and curriculum-based assessment, are also being explored, especially in special education settings.

Since 1970, several factors have influenced the development of educationally oriented tests for young children. Among these factors are: research in early cognitive development, the growth of preschool education programs, and concerns about the effects of cultural handicaps on children's ability to profit from school instruction. The largest category of tests in this area are those designed to assess school readiness. This construct refers to the attainment of prerequisite skills, knowledge, attitudes, motivations, and other behavioral traits that enable the learner to profit from school instruction. The Metropolitan Readiness Tests (MRT), and the Boehm Test of Basic Concepts-Revised (Boehm R) exemplify two different approaches to the assessment of school readiness.

OCCUPATIONAL TESTING

Psychological tests play a significant role as aids in occupational decisions both at the institutional level, in terms of the selection and classification of personnel, and at the individual level, in terms of vocational counseling. This section of the chapter deals with the assessment of occupational qualifications from the point of view of employers, while career assessment is discussed in a later section. Although nearly any test may be used by organizations in making occupational decisions, the instruments most frequently employed for this purpose are multiple-aptitude batteries as well as special aptitude and situational tests. Increasingly, personality inventories and biodata measures are also being utilized in employment settings.

The need to ascertain the validity of tests for particular uses is especially urgent in the occupational field because of societal concerns about the possible unfairness of selection devices to disadvantaged minorities and also because of the demonstrated link between productivity and the validity of selection instruments. The traditional view in personnel psychology has been that, ideally, tests should undergo full-scale validation against local criteria of job performance. However, because of the practical difficulties that this process presents, a number of alternatives have been explored. These alternatives include (a) the use of global assessment procedures that resemble the job situation, such as probationary appointments, job samples, simulations, and situational tests; (b) the application of content validation procedures through systematic job analyses and the specification of critical work requirements or job elements; and (c) the prediction of job performance by means of synthetic validation and validity generalization procedures.

The notion that job analyses should focus on critical job requirements led to the

216

development of the job element method for constructing tests and demonstrating their content validity. This method, pioneered by Primoff and his associates, is, in turn, related to the concept of synthetic validation. The latter consists of using the demonstrated validity of certain tests for separate job elements, in combination with the weights for those elements in a particular job, to predict a complex criterion. Validity generalization (VG) procedures, on the other hand, allow the application of prior findings on the validity of a test to a new situation, through meta-analyses. The VG technique, originally developed by Schmidt and Hunter, has found wide acceptance and application in occupational testing. More recently, some of the most promising work in the area of personnel selection has centered on the conceptualization of job performance and the analysis of its determinants and criteria.

Tests of academic intelligence or scholastic ability are an important component of many personnel selection programs because the broad verbal, quantitative, and other abstract thinking skills that they assess are relevant to a wide variety of jobs. Several short tests of academic intelligence, such as the Wonderlic Personnel Test, have been developed for use in industry. Although such tests may contribute substantially to the prediction of job performance, predictive accuracy can be enhanced by the assessment of multiple aptitudes and of additional specialized skills and knowledge required by particular jobs, as well as by the evaluation of temperamental and attitudinal characteristics.

The most extensive use of multiple aptitude batteries has been carried out in the armed services and in civilian government agencies. The General Aptitude Test Battery (GATB), for example, was developed by the United States Employment Service (USES) for use by state employment agencies, and other nonprofit organizations, in the counseling and job referral of a large number of persons. The GATB includes 12 tests and three factorially-derived composite measures. Its scores can be used in a variety of ways, including through the application of multiple-cutoff strategies and of the findings of validity generalization studies. Although a vast body of research has been accumulated on the GATB, political concerns associated with its use have led to developments that make its future uncertain.

Some of the most exciting advances in the construction and evaluation of instruments for personnel selection and classification are those which are taking place as part of a long-term research program with the Armed Services Vocational Aptitude Battery (ASVAB). The Joint-Service Job Performance Measurement/Enlistment Standards (JPM) Project has had as its aim the development of robust measures of performance for entry-level military jobs. It has already resulted in a good deal of support for the ASVAB and its composite scores. Another segment of research on the ASVAB, known as "Project A," is aimed at reevaluating the battery against a wider, and more precisely assessed, range of criteria as well as at expanding the coverage of predictors to include personality and interest inventories.

Many jobs require the assessment of more specialized skills and knowledge through special aptitude tests. The principal areas, described in the textbook, for which special aptitude tests have been developed are psychomotor skills, mechanical aptitudes, clerical aptitudes, and computer-related aptitudes. Even though several of these areas are now incorporated in some multiple aptitude batteries, special aptitude tests, as a rule, provide more extensive normative and validation data for pertinent occupational samples, and allow greater flexibility in their use, than do multiple aptitude batteries. The increasing recognition of the role of social and emotional intelligence in all aspects behavior, including that which is work-related, has started to stimulate the development of specialized instruments designed to assess the interpersonal and intrapersonal skills needed in the workplace.

In the meantime, the use of personality evaluation tools for the purpose of making employment decisions has been flourishing. Recent research with meta-analytic and structural equation modeling techniques has provided ample support for the use of carefully constructed personality tests in the prediction of job performance. At the same time, a great deal of work remains to be done in order to establish the different temperamental and interpersonal requirements of various jobs. For the most part, personality assessment in the workplace has been done by means of the traditional self-report personality inventories described in Chapter 13. However, some specialized techniques already do exist for the assessment of qualities—such as integrity and leadership—that are considered essential in certain positions, and many more can be foreseen in the future.

TEST USE IN CLINICAL AND COUNSELING PSYCHOLOGY

Clinical and counseling psychologists, as well as practitioners in several specialty areas of psychology,[1] engage in the process of psychological assessment. This process involves the intensive study of one or more individuals through a variety of sources of data—such as interviews, case histories, and tests of most types—to arrive at a well-rounded view of those individuals. At the center of this process is a sequence of hypothesis testing aimed at reaching an informed decision about matters of diagnostic and practical significance to the patient or client. Some of the tests used by clinicians are psychometrically weak, and even those whose psychometric properties are sound do not yield sufficiently precise results for individual diagnosis. However, the use of test results as tools to generate leads, in the context of multiple sources of data, provides a safeguard against overgeneralization from isolated test scores.

Individual intelligence tests can provide the clinician not only with scores that reflect the examinee's level of intellectual functioning, but also with qualitative information that may suggest the need for further probing. Many clinicians routinely explore the pattern, or profile, of intelligence test scores for possible indices of brain damage or other abnormalities. Procedures such as the examination of the amount of scatter in test scores, the analysis of the frequency of the salient features of a test profile in base rate data, and the comparison of the

_____

[1]For the sake of convenience, the term "clinician" is used throughout this section of the chapter to denote any professional engaged in the practice of psychological assessment.

score patterns obtained against those associated with particular clinical syndromes, have been used for many years, especially in conjunction with the Wechsler scales. Although these procedures are still the preferred approach to the interpretation of intelligence test data, decades of research on various forms of pattern analysis have provided little statistical support for their diagnostic value. Nevertheless, intelligence tests can provide a wealth of information in clinical cases, if the psychometric data are combined with qualitative observations and other sources of data in a sophisticated fashion, such as the approach espoused by Kaufman. In the meantime, new procedures aimed at identifying and classifying prototypical ability test profiles continue to be explored.

The behavioral effects of brain pathology can vary, in a complex fashion, as a function of the age of the individual, the chronicity, source, extent, and locus of the pathology, and also as a function of experiential factors unique to the affected person. Brain damage encompasses a wide range of disorders with diverse behavioral manifestations, many of which can also stem from factors other than cerebral dysfunction. These facts, which have been increasingly recognized since the 1950s, complicate the diagnosis of brain damage to such an extent that no single technique can be considered totally dependable. Therefore, clinical neuropsychologists typically use corroborative information from a variety of sources, such as electroencephalography and computerized axial tomography (CAT) scans. In addition, there is a whole array of tests that can be used to assess brain damage and to plan and monitor rehabilitation programs. Many clinicians use a combination of tests that assess different skills and deficits in a "flexible" battery approach tailored to individual cases. Others use standardized neuropsychological batteries that provide measures of a number of significant functions. The Halstead-Reitan Neuropsychological Test Battery (HRNTB) and the Luria-Nebraska Neuropsychological Battery (LNNB) are two major examples of the standardized approach to neuropsychological assessment cited in the text.

Another problematic area of clinical assessment is the identification of specific learning disabilities. Although educators have become increasingly aware of the high frequency of occurrence of this type of handicap, the diagnosis and remediation of learning disabilities (LD) have been complicated by the looseness with which the designation has been employed. It is now recognized that the LD population is heterogeneous with regard to the behavioral symptoms they manifest and with regard to the etiology of those symptoms. Children with learning disabilities, by definition, show normal or above-average intelligence, in combination with serious difficulties in learning one or more basic education skills. However, the LD syndrome may occur at any intellectual level and in combination with a great variety of symptoms. Chief among the clusters of symptoms presented are difficulties in perceiving, encoding, and integrating information from different sensory modalities, disturbances in language development, disruption of sensorimotor coordination, attention and memory difficulties, as well as hyperactivity, impulsive behavior, and emotional problems.

The diversity encountered among the LD population, along with the need for highly specific information about the nature and extent of the disabilities in each case, require the use of an assortment of tests and observational procedures for proper diagnosis. Individually administered wide-range achievement tests, such as the Kaufman Test of Educational Achievement (K-TEA), and comprehensive measures of both aptitudes and achievement, such as the Woodcock-Johnson Psycho-Educational Battery–Revised (WJ-R), are especially suitable for the initial assessment of learning disabilities. However, regular achievement batteries and other group tests may be used as screening devices. Individual intelligence tests can also be of help in the intensive study of individual cases. In addition, dynamic assessment techniques, which cover a number of procedures that elicit supplementary qualitative data about an individual through a deliberate departure from standardized test administration, have been gaining popularity since the 1970s. The assessment of learning potential, as practiced by Feuerstein and others, is a particularly promising approach that involves a test-teach-test format in which the child is taught to perform a task that he or she was initially unable to carry out. An even more sophisticated dynamic assessment approach is the multidimensional latent trait model for change, recently developed by Embretson. This work, which already constitutes a significant achievement in psychometrics, combines item response theory techniques, cognitive task decomposition, and computerized adaptive testing to assess and facilitate learning.

The application of learning principles to the management of behavior change has been quite significant within clinical psychology, where this approach is known as behavior therapy or behavior modification. Even though assessment procedures are vital to the definition of the individual's problem, to the selection of appropriate treatments, as well as to the monitoring of results, behavior therapists initially paid little attention to assessment. Since the mid-1970s, however, the importance of assessment procedures in behavior therapy has been increasingly recognized. There are now many physiological, observational, and self-report techniques that can be used in behavioral assessment.

As far as career counseling of individuals is concerned, the two most applicable types of instruments are multiple aptitude batteries and interest inventories, both of which are discussed in other parts of the textbook. However, two additional kinds of instruments—designed specifically for career counseling—should be mentioned in this context, namely, comprehensive programs for career exploration and measures of career maturity. Some career counseling programs have been developed for use in conjunction with multiple aptitude batteries, such as the Differential Aptitude Tests and the GATB; others have been developed completely as career exploration systems. An example of the latter is the Harrington-O'Shea Career Decision-Making System–Revised. Another approach to comprehensive career exploration is represented by the System for Interactive Guidance Information (SIGI-PLUS), which uses an interactive computer program with an extensive database to guide the individual toward effective decision making. The assessment of career maturity—or mastery of, and effectiveness in coping with, the vocational tasks appropriate to one's age level—is yet another technique that can be used in career counseling. The Career Development Inventory, prepared by Super, is one example of the instruments that have been designed to assess career maturity.

Clinical assessment differs from other areas in which psychological tests are used in that the individual judgment of the clinician enters into both the data-gathering and the data-synthesis phases of an evaluation to a unique degree. This situation represents at once an advantage and a potential hazard in the process of assessment and has given rise to research comparing predictions made through clinical judgment with those obtained by the application of statistical procedures. Since the objectivity and skill of the individual clinician in making predictions are themselves critical variables in determining the accuracy of those predictions, no definitive answer can be given to the question posed by such comparisons. Nevertheless, it is recognized that the most effective procedures are those which combine clinical and statistical approaches and that the validity of clinical predictions needs to be continuously and systematically investigated whenever feasible.

The final product of most clinical assessments is a written report, wherein the clinician synthesizes the salient aspects of a case. The content of the report should follow directly from the purpose of the assessment and should focus on interpretations and conclusions rather than on specific data. The organization and integration of data, as well as the use of a writing style and vocabulary appropriate to the report reader, are also crucial to the effectiveness of the clinical report as a tool for communicating assessment results.

Although the contribution of computers to psychological assessment is already quite impressive, much of their potential, in areas such as the application of adaptive (CAT) techniques to personality testing and the integration of data from tests and other sources, is only beginning to be tapped. In personality testing, the currently available applications of computers are confined mostly to the administration, scoring, and narrative interpretation of several traditional tests. However, in cognitive assessment—especially in the area of clinical neuropsychology and related fields—there are many totally new, computer-based instruments already in use. Computerized test interpretation programs can save time and can be more thorough than an individual clinician, but they are also fraught with potential for misuse, especially with regard to the responsibilities and qualifications of users and the availability of information needed to evaluate such services. Some guidance in this area is available at present and more of it should be forthcoming.

Comprehensive Review

STUDY QUESTIONS: EDUCATIONAL TESTING

1. Compare and contrast aptitude and achievement tests.

2. Discuss the problems that have resulted from labeling some instruments as "aptitude" tests and others as "achievement" tests and explain how such problems might be forestalled in the future.

3. List and describe the roles that achievement tests can play in the educational process.

4. Compare and contrast "selected-response" and "constructed-response" tasks, listing the advantages and disadvantages of each for the evaluation of educational achievement.

5. Describe the nature and scope of general achievement batteries, in general, and cite one or two representative examples of such batteries.

6. Discuss the history of tests of minimum competency in basic skills and describe a representative example of a test in this area.

7. List and describe the steps that a teacher should follow in preparing a classroom test.

8. Describe the Scholastic Assessment Tests (SAT) Program of the College Board and specify the major changes it has undergone recently.

9. Describe the Graduate Record Examinations (GRE) in terms of their coverage, scores, and usefulness in selecting graduate school applicants.

10. Discuss the role that diagnostic and prognostic testing can play in the educational context and cite one example of each of these types of tests.

11. Describe the background, content, and characteristics of tests used in the assessment of school readiness.

STUDY QUESTIONS: OCCUPATIONAL TESTING

1. List and describe the kinds of tests that are most commonly used in making personnel decisions.

2. Discuss the importance that proper validation of employment tests has for the employee, the employer, and society in general.

3. Discuss the difficulties inherent in doing local studies of the predictive validity of selection tests and cite the major alternative procedures that have been explored to achieve the same goals.

4. Describe three different types of global assessment procedures that approximate actual job performance.

5. Explain how content validation techniques can be applied to personnel selection tests and discuss the basis for the development of the job element method.

6. Define synthetic validity and describe how it is derived and applied.

7. Discuss the validity generalization approach to test validation pioneered by Schmidt and Hunter and describe the major advantages that result from the use of that model.

8. Explain why the determination of the criteria of job performance is so important and list the major elements of the job performance model John Campbell is developing in conjunction with Project A.

9. Compare and contrast the role of tests of academic intelligence with special aptitude tests in the selection of personnel.

10. Discuss the background, characteristics, and present status of the General Aptitude Test Battery (GATB) of the United States Employment Service (USES).

11. Briefly describe the Armed Services Vocational Aptitude Battery (ASVAB) and the developments that have been taking place with regard to it. Explain why these developments could result in a vastly improved classification instrument.

12. Discuss the concept of special aptitudes, list the major types of abilities traditionally subsumed under this rubric. Cite examples of instruments that have been developed in each of these areas.

13. Explain the role of personality testing in the workplace at the present time and as it is likely to develop in the future.

STUDY QUESTIONS: TEST USE IN CLINICAL AND COUNSELING PSYCHOLOGY

1. Discuss the role and major characteristics of psychological assessment as it is practiced across the various areas of clinical and counseling psychology.

2. List and describe the three major procedures used in analyzing the patterns of scores of intelligence tests.

3. Describe the major features of Kaufman's approach to the interpretation of intelligence test performance.

4. Discuss the historical origins of the field of neuropsychological assessment and cite the major findings of early research on brain damage.

5. List and discuss the main variables that influence the effects of brain pathology on behavior.

223

6. Compare and contrast the "flexible" battery approach to neuropsychological assessment with the standardized battery approach.

7. Discuss the problems associated with the identification of specific learning disabilities.

8. List and briefly describe the types of assessment techniques that can be used to screen and diagnose learning disabilities.

9. Define dynamic assessment, describe its major features as currently practiced, and explain why that approach holds such great promise.

10. Discuss the role of assessment in the context of behavior therapy and describe the three main types of procedures that are used commonly in behavioral assessment.

11. Describe the functions that can be served by some of the comprehensive programs for career exploration cited in the text.

12. Discuss the concept of career maturity and how that concept may be used in career counseling.

13. Discuss the main differences between clinical and statistical predictions. Cite the major findings of the research that has compared the two methods.

14. Explain the function that the clinical report serves in assessment and describe the features that characterize a good report.

15. Discuss the potential contributions and the potential dangers inherent in the use of computers in clinical assessment.

FILL IN THE BLANKS: Key Terms and Concepts in Educational Testing

1. _ _ _ _ _ _ _ _ _ _ _ _ tests are those designed to measure the effects of a specific program of instruction or training.

2. _ _ _ _ _ _ _ _ tests measure the effects of learning under relatively uncontrolled and unknown conditions and include instruments such as general intelligence tests.

3. The categories of tests that were traditionally known as "aptitude" and "achievement" tests are increasingly being referred to simply as _ _ _ _ _ _ _ tests; this more neutral term avoids the suggestion that some tests can measure skills independently of the individual's experiential background.

4. _____ – _____ questions are all those open-ended tasks that require the test taker to produce an answer in the form of words, solutions to mathematical problems, or some other kind of performance.

5. _____ – _____ questions call for the choice of a correct answer out of the options that are provided and include items such as multiple choice, true-false, and matching.

6. _____ _____ batteries are those that measure an individual's performance in the major areas covered by academic curricula and typically permit a comparison of the individual's standing in different areas, as well as over time.

7. The use of _____ _____ tests in basic skills as a basis for awarding a high school diploma arose out of popular concern about the low achievement levels of high school graduates.

8. The basic concept that underlies the development of tests of minimum competency in basic skills is _____ _____ or the possession of the reading, writing, speaking, and computational skills needed to meet the demands of practical situations, such as jobs or the management of one's own life in modern society.

9. The largest number of tests concerned with the content of specific courses or parts of courses are _____ tests prepared by instructors for their own use.

10. In order to plan a test so that its coverage of content areas and instructional objectives will be balanced, ____ _____ should be drawn up before any test items are prepared.

11. A test constructor must decide on the most appropriate ____ ____ for the material to be covered by a test on the basis of the relative merits and practicality of constructed- versus selected-response questions for a given course.

12. _____ tests usually concentrate on highly specific cognitive processes or content knowledge and are designed to analyze an individual's particular strengths and weaknesses within a certain domain and to suggest possible causes for her or his difficulties.

13. _____ tests function as aptitude tests in that they undertake to predict performance, but they also resemble achievement tests because their content frequently consists of prerequisite knowledge and skills necessary for a specific academic course.

14. _ _ _ _ _ _ _   _ _ _ _ _ _ _ _ _ _ is an approach to testing that follows a test-teach-test procedure and evaluates learning potential by observing how well an individual can learn in a one-to-one relationship with a professional who functions as examiner, instructor, and clinician.

15. _ _ _ _ _ _   _ _ _ _ _ _ _ _ _ is a concept that refers to the attainment of prerequisite skills, knowledge, attitudes, motivations, and other behavioral traits that enable the young child to profit maximally from schooling.

ANSWERS TO FILL-IN-THE-BLANKS: Key Terms and Concepts in Educational Testing

1. achievement (tests)
2. aptitude (tests)
3. ability (tests)
4. constructed-response (questions)
5. selected-response (questions)
6. general achievement (batteries)
7. minimum competency (tests in basic skills)
8. functional competence
9. classroom (tests)
10. test specifications
11. item form
12. diagnostic (tests)
13. prognostic (tests)
14. dynamic assessment
15. school readiness

FILL IN THE BLANKS: Key Terms and Concepts in Occupational Testing

1. One approach to personnel selection is to use global assessment procedures that resemble the job situation as much as possible, such as _ _ _ _ _ _ _ _ _ _ _ _ appointments, _ _ _   _ _ _ _ _ _ _, and _ _ _ _ _ _ _ _ _ _ _.

2. The _ _ – _ _ _ _ _ _ test is a simulation technique that has been adapted for testing executives in many contexts; it consists of having the test taker handle a carefully prepared set of incoming letters, memoranda, and such.

3. A(n) _ _ _   _ _ _ _ _ _ _ _ _ is a method, applied in the content validation of personnel tests, that involves the identification of the activities that differentiate a particular job and the specification of the requirements for that job.

4. The concept of _ _ _ _ _ _ _ _ requirements refers to those aspects of job performance that differentiate most sharply between better and poorer workers.

5. The _ _ _ _ _ _ _ _ _ _ _ _ _ _ _ _ technique, proposed by Flanagan as a means of implementing the concept of critical requirements, calls for the description of specific instances of job behavior that are characteristic of satisfactory or unsatisfactory workers.

6. The _ _ _ _ _ _ _ _ _ _ _ method for constructing employment tests and demonstrating their content validity was fully developed by Primoff and others at the U.S. Office of Personnel Management; this method provides for a description of the specific behavioral requirements of a job, from which test items can be directly formulated.

7. The concept of _ _ _ _ _ _ _ _ _ validity can be defined as "the inferring of validity in a specific situation from a systematic analysis of job elements, a determination of test validity for these elements, and a combination of elemental validities into a whole."

8. The _ – _ _ _ _ _ _ _ _ _ _ _ _ is a statistical procedure used by Primoff to compute an estimate of synthetic validity by combining the job element method and multiple regression equations.

9. _ procedures, originally developed by Schmidt and Hunter, allow for the use of existing information on a test in a new situation. This is accomplished through the application of meta-analyses to estimate the extent to which prior validity findings apply to the present situation.

10. The multiple-factor theory that John P. Campbell and his coworkers have been developing in conjunction with the United States Army Selection and Classification Project (Project A) attempts to identify and separate the elements involved in _ _ _ _ _ _ _ _ _ _ _ _ _, including its determinants, consequences, relative costs, and the value placed on each aspect by the organization. This work is of critical importance in arriving at a more careful conceptualization of _ _ _ _ _ _ _ _ for purposes of prediction.

11. The cluster of skills and knowledge developed in the course of formal education, which has been described as _ _ _ _ _ _ _ _ _ _ _ _ _ _ _ _ _ _, consists mainly of verbal comprehension, quantitative reasoning, and other aspects of abstract thinking, and is predictive of performance in a wide range of activities.

12. The _ (GATB) was developed by the United States Employment Service (USES) for use by counselors in state employment service offices; the entire battery of 12 tests can be administered in 2½ hours.

13. The _ Battery (ASVAB)

is a major selection and classification tool developed jointly for use in all the U.S. armed services. This instrument has been undergoing a lengthy investigative effort (Project A) aimed not only at validating it but also at extending the battery by adding new predictors beyond the traditional realm of cognitive functions.

14. _____ _____ tests were developed in order to fill in major gaps in the coverage of intelligence tests by providing for the assessment of more specialized or practical skills, such as mechanical ability.

15. Tests of _____ _____ are typically apparatus tests concerned with manual dexterity and used principally in the selection of industrial and military personnel.

16. _____ _____ tests cover a wide variety of functions which may include psychomotor, perceptual, and spatial skills, as well as information about the sorts of tools encountered through everyday experience in an industrialized society.

17. Tests designed to measure _____ _____ are characterized by an emphasis on perceptual speed and accuracy but may also sample activities such as alphabetizing, coding, and spelling.

18. The recognition of the importance of cognitive dimensions in intrapersonal and interpersonal functioning is likely to stimulate the development of tools to assess the _____ and _____ aspects of _____ in employment settings.

19. Paper-and-pencil measures of trusworthiness, also known as "_____" tests, proliferated in the workplace when the use of polygraphs to make hiring decisions was forbidden by law.

20. _____, which can be defined as the ability to persuade others to work toward a common cause, is one of the most desired qualities in the workplace.

ANSWERS TO FILL-IN-THE-BLANKS: Key Terms and Concepts in Occupational Testing

1. probationary (appointments) / job samples / simulations
2. in-basket (test)
3. job analysis
4. critical (requirements)
5. critical incident (technique)
6. job element (method)
7. synthetic (validity)
8. J-coefficient

228

9. validity generalization (procedures)
10. job performance / criteria
11. academic intelligence
12. General Aptitude Test Battery (GATB)
13 Armed Services Vocational Aptitude (Battery) (ASVAB)
14. special aptitude (tests)
15. (tests of) psychomotor skills
16. mechanical aptitude (tests)
17. clerical aptitudes
18. social (and) emotional (aspects of) intelligence
19. "integrity" (tests)
20. leadership

FILL IN THE BLANKS: Key Terms and Concepts in Clinical and Counseling Use of Tests

1. _____ _____ refers to a process that focuses on the intensive study of one or more individuals—through multiple sources of data—with the goal of making informed decisions regarding diagnosis, treatment recommendations, or many other matters of practical significance to the client(s).

2. The Wechsler scales lend themselves especially well to _____ or _____ analyses because the results of all of their subtests have traditionally been expressed in comparable standard scores.

3. The three major procedures used in analyzing intelligence test profiles are: (a) the examination of the amount of _____ , or variation among subtest scores, (b) the analysis of ____ ____ data about the frequency of certain features within the normative group, and (c) the review of the _____ _____ associated with certain clinical syndromes.

4. One of the major sources of leads derived from the use of individual intelligence tests in clinical assessment is the observation and _____ analysis of idiosyncracies in a person's performance.

5. _____ _____ is a field that attempts to apply what is known about brain-behavior relationships to the diagnosis and rehabilitation of individuals with brain damage.

6. Two of the main variables that shape the effects of brain damage on behavior are the ___ at which the injury is sustained and the _____ of a case, which refers to the amount of time elapsed since the injury.

7. Some clinical neuropsychologists prefer to use different combinations of available tests in a "_ _ _ _ _ _ _ _ _ _ _ _ _ _ _ _" approach, while others choose comprehensive, standardized instruments, such as the _ _ _ _ _ _ _ _ – _ _ _ _ _ _ or the _ _ _ _ _ – _ _ _ _ _ _ _ _ neuropsychological batteries.

8. Typically, children with _ show normal or above-normal intelligence in combination with pronounced difficulties in acquiring one or more basic educational skills.

9. The term _ _ _ _ _ _ _ _ _ _ _ _ _ _ _ _ _ covers a number of clinical procedures that essentially involve the deliberate departure from standardized test administration in order to elicit additional qualitative data about an individual.

10. Among the earliest examples of dynamic assessment procedures is a technique known as "_ _ _ _ _ _ _ _ _ _ _ _ _ _ _ _ _." This technique consists of giving additional cues or time to the test taker, asking the test taker how he or she set out to solve a problem, and/or suggesting a different first step in solving a problem.

11. A relatively new approach to dynamic assessment, exemplified by the work of Feuerstein, is known as _ _ _ _ _ _ _ _ – _ _ _ _ _ _ _ _ _ assessment and involves a test-teach-test format in which the examinee is given instruction on broadly applicable learning or problem–solving skills.

12. The techniques known as _ represent an application of learning principles to the management of clinical problems.

13. The major types of assessment procedures used in the course of behavior therapy are _ _ _ _ _ _ _ _ _ _ _ _ measures, _ _ _ _ _ _ _ _ _ _ _ _ _ _ _ of the target behavior, and _ _ _ _ – _ _ _ _ _ _ _ by the client.

14. The practice of _ _ _ _ _ _ _ _ _ _ _ _ _ _ _ _ involves helping individuals to discern the most appropriate occupational choices, in light of their abilities, interests, and personalities, as well as the requirements of different occupations.

15. The concept of _ _ _ _ _ _ _ _ _ _ _ _ _ _ _, postulated by Super and his associates, refers to one's mastery of the vocational tasks appropriate to one's age level and also to one's effectiveness in coping with those tasks.

16. What a clinician does in assessing a client can be seen as a special case of _ _ _ _ _ _ _ _ _ _ _ _ _ _ _ or interpersonal perception, the process through which anyone comes to know and understand another person.

17. Since the publication of Meehl's classic work on the subject, the question of whether _ _ _ _ _ _ _ _ judgment is more or less accurate than _ _ _ _ _ _ _ _ _ _ prediction has been the subject of a lively controversy in psychology.

18. Through a series of ongoing investigations of the characteristics that moderate the accuracy of clinical judgment, Spengler and his coworkers have concluded that psychologists with lower levels of _ _ _ _ _ _ _ _ _ _ _ _ _ _ _ _ _ _ are more likely to form biased judgments than those with higher levels of it.

19. A report that is seen as "remarkably accurate," due to the fact that it contains general, stereotyped statements that apply to most people, serves to demonstrate the influence of the "_ _ _ _ _ _" effect in a striking fashion.

20. One of the applications of computers to clinical assessment—currently in wide use—is the computerized _ _ _ _ _ _ _ _ _ _ _ _ _ _ _, which is produced by a program with a large database of qualitative interpretive statements linked to specific levels or patterns of scores.

ANSWERS TO FILL-IN-THE-BLANKS: Key Terms and Concepts in Clinical and Counseling Use of Tests

1. psychological assessment
2. pattern (or) profile (analyses)
3. (a) scatter / (b) base rate (data) / (c) score patterns
4. qualitative (analysis)
5. clinical neuropsychology
6. age / chronicity
7. "flexible battery" (approach) / Halstead-Reltan / Luria-Nebraska (neuropsychological batteries)
8. learning disabilities
9. dynamic assessment
10. "testing the limits"
11. learning-potential (assessment)
12. behavior modification
13. physiological (measures) / direct observation / self-report (by the client)
14. career assessment
15. career maturity
16. person cognition
17. clinical (judgment) / statistical (prediction)
18. cognitive complexity
19. "Barnum effect"
20. (computerized) narrative report

TRUE/FALSE and WHY? — Educational Testing

1. Most of the distinctions that can be drawn between aptitude and achievement tests cannot be rigidly applied. (T/F) Why? _____
_____

2. One way in which achievement and aptitude tests *can* be differentiated is that the former measure the effects of learning while the latter measure "innate capacity" independent of learning. (T/F) Why? _____
_____

3. The question of under- or overachievement can be more accurately formulated as overprediction or underprediction from one test to a second test. (T/F) Why?
_____
_____

4. Multiple-choice tests are not only more economical and efficient than essay tests, but can also be more valid predictors of well-established criteria than essay tests. (T/F) Why? _____
_____

5. There is reason to believe that performance-based assessment results in narrowing the gap that exists in the standardized test scores of Whites and those of some ethnic minorities. (T/F) Why? _____
_____

6. One advantage of the typical general achievement battery over independently constructed achievement tests is that the former can provide for horizontal or vertical comparisons or both. (T/F) Why? _____
_____

7. In recent years the focus of interest in evaluating mastery of minimum competency in basic skills has expanded from the school-age population to adults. (T/F) Why?
_____
_____

8. Compared to selected-response items, open-ended questions—such as essays—are easier to prepare and more appropriate than objective questions for teacher-made classroom tests because they do not require advance planning. (T/F) Why?_____
_____
_____

9. Tests, such as those of the SAT and the ACT programs, are excellent substitutes for

high school grades in the prediction of college achievement. (T/F) Why? _____

_____

_____

10. The diagnosis of learning disabilities and the planning of a subsequent remediation program cannot rest solely on the results of a battery of tests. (T/F) Why? _____

_____

_____

ANSWERS TO TRUE/FALSE - Educational Testing:

1.	True	3.	True	5.	False	7.	True	9.	False
2.	False	4.	True	6.	True	8.	False	10.	True

TRUE/FALSE and WHY? – Occupational Testing

1. A full-scale longitudinal validation study is unrealistic in the large majority of industrial situations. (T/F) Why? _____

_____

2. In most instances, the only requirement for a job analysis to serve as an effective tool in validating a personnel selection test is a simple and basic description of the main activities that the job entails. (T/F) Why?_____

_____

3. Synthetic validation and validity generalization allow for the estimation of the validity of a test for a particular job in the absence of local validation. (T/F) Why? _____

_____

_____

4. The use of a single, convenient measure of job performance as the criterion in validation studies is a highly desirable practice. (T/F) Why? _____

_____

5. In spite of the high correlation between performance on tests of academic intelligence and amount of education, the selection of job applicants on the basis of the amount of formal education they have had would not really be fair. (T/F) Why? _____

_____

_____

6. Research on validity generalization has brought about a reawakening of interest in the potential usefulness of tests of general academic intelligence for the purpose of

employee selection. (T/F) Why? _____

_____

7. The findings of the Job Performance Measurement/Enlistment Standards (JPM) Project suggest that the score differences between Black and nonminority examinees on the ASVAB are uniform in magnitude across both paper-and-pencil tests and job-sample tests. (T/F) Why? _____

_____

8. Special aptitude tests contribute very little or nothing, beyond what most standard multiple aptitude batteries offer, to the process of personnel selection. (T/F) Why?___

_____

_____

9. Methodologically sophisticated research conducted in the past decade has provided a great deal of support for the use of personality tests in employment decisions across various settings. (T/F) Why? _____

_____

10. By and large, the most effective tools available for evaluating leadership and selecting high-level executives are paper-and-pencil self-report personality inventories. (T/F) Why? _____

_____

ANSWERS TO TRUE/FALSE - Occupational Testing:

1.	True	3.	True	5.	True	7.	False	9.	True
2.	False	4.	False	6.	True	8.	False	10.	False

TRUE/FALSE and WHY? - Test Use in Clinical and Counseling Psychology

1. Fundamentally, all the activities connected with a psychological assessment involve professional judgment. (T/F) Why? _____

_____

2. Kaufman's method for interpreting the results of intelligence tests emphasizes the uniform application of score pattern analysis to reach decisions about all test takers. (T/F) Why? _____

_____

3. Brain damage may produce different and, in fact, opposite behavior patterns in two individuals. (T/F) Why? _____

_____

4. Research on preschool children indicates that, at that age level, brain-injury tends to affect intellectual functions more massively than later in life. (T/F) Why? _____
_____
_____

5. Neuropsychological tests that assess one or two major functions, such as the Bender-Gestalt and the Benton Visual Retention Test (BVRT), are particularly well-suited for differential diagnosis. (T/F) Why? _____
_____

6. The diagnosis and evaluation of children with learning disabilities have improved greatly as a result of the clear theoretical grounding and deeper understanding of these disorders achieved recently. (T/F) Why? _____
_____
_____

7. In terms of career development, the major task for students at the junior high school level is to demonstrate their vocational maturity by the wisdom and consistency of the ultimate career goals they choose. (T/F) Why? _____
_____
_____

8. Meehl demonstrated that, almost without exception, the routine application of statistical procedures yielded as many, or more, correct predictions as did clinical analysis. (T/F) Why? _____
_____

9. The most desirable format and outline for all clinical reports has become quite standard over the past few decades. (T/F) Why? _____
_____
_____

10. Compared to the current state of development of instruments for the assessment of cognitive functioning, the contribution of computers to the field of personality testing is still at the preliminary stage. (T/F) Why? _____
_____
_____

ANSWERS TO TRUE/FALSE - Test Use in Clinical and Counseling Psychology:

1.	True	3.	True	5.	False	7.	False	9.	False
2.	False	4.	True	6.	False	8.	True	10.	True

Multiple Choice: Test Yourself

EDUCATIONAL TESTING

1. Which of the following is the most commonly used type of standardized test?
   _____.
   a. Achievement
   b. Aptitude
   c. Personality
   d. Interest

2. One distinctive difference between aptitude and achievement tests is that, usually, aptitude tests _____,
   whereas achievement tests_____.
   a. measure the effects of standardized sets of past experiences / reflect learning under unknown conditions
   b. measure innate learning ability / measure what has been learned
   c. are predominantly nonverbal / are predominantly verbal
   d. are used to predict / are used for terminal evaluation

3. The results of achievement tests can be used to_____
   _____.
   a. assess an individual's level of accomplishment in a course of study
   b. evaluate the success of an instructional program
   c. diagnose deficiencies in academic preparation
   d. all of the above are legitimate uses

4. Which of the following is *not* an appropriate use of aptitude and achievement tests?
   _____.
   a. Aptitude tests can be used to predict performance in advanced programs
   b. Achievement test results can be used to evaluate the overall performance of a class of students, or an entire school, compared with other groups
   c. Aptitude and achievement test scores for each student can be compared to identify underachievers
   d. All of the above are legitimate uses

5. In contrast to selected-response items, constructed-response items_____
   _____.
   a. are less reliable
   b. are more generalizable in their results
   c. have become the preferred item format across most educational settings
   d. seem to be more likely to show the effects of anxiety

6. The procedure of norming achievement test batteries concurrently with intelligence tests _____.
   a. assures the validity of the achievement test batteries
   b. permits direct comparisons of scores on the two tests
   c. removes the biasing effects of IQ from achievement test scores
   d. assures the reliability of both sets of tests

7. Tests of minimum competency have been developed largely to _____ _____.
   a. replace existing tests such as the SAT or ACT for admitting students to college
   b. demonstrate basic differences in the innate ability of various cultural groups
   c. identify the strengths and weaknesses of individual students
   d. screen individuals in terms of whether they have achieved "functional literacy"

8. The most important, and also the most frequently overlooked, step in creating a good teacher-made test is _____ _____.
   a. adequate advance planning, using a table of specifications
   b. the inclusion of essay questions
   c. the evaluation of the test after it is given
   d. the development of alternate forms

9. The new SAT I: Reasoning Test _____ _____.
   a. consists primarily of constructed-response items
   b. has replaced the former SAT Achievement Tests
   c. measures verbal and mathematical abilities
   d. is used to assess readiness for graduate school work

10. Tests that are primarily designed to detect problem areas and identify possible causes are called _____.
    a. criterion-referenced
    b. diagnostic
    c. standardized
    d. item-referenced

OCCUPATIONAL TESTING

1. Of the following types of tests, which is *least* likely to be used for the purpose of making personnel decisions? _____.
   a. Multiple-aptitude batteries
   b. Special aptitude batteries
   c. Self-report personality inventories

d.   Projective techniques

2.   When job candidates are asked to perform a task that is actually a part of the work to be performed on the job, under uniform working conditions, the method of evaluation being used is called a _____.
a.   job sample
b.   critical activity
c.   personal analysis
d.   selection analysis

3.   As used in the context of a job analysis, the term "job element" refers to a(n)_____ _____.
a.   aspect of the job that correlates highly with success
b.   specific job behavior that differentiates between good and poor employees
c.   group problem-solving technique
d.   job dimension used in evaluating overall value to the employer

4.   A relatively new approach to the validation of personnel selection tests, which applies meta-analysis to previously obtained data in order to assess the validity of a test in a new situation, is called _____.
a.   Y coefficient
b.   validity generalization
c.   multiple regression
d.   the Work Keys system

5.   Most traditional intelligence tests primarily depend upon _____.
a.   perceptual speed
b.   psychomotor skills
c.   academic-type knowledge and skills
d.   a combination of performance-type skills

6.   Of the following types of job applicants, the ones least likely to be given one of the major types of special aptitude tests discussed in the textbook are_____ _____.
a.   clerical workers
b.   drill press operators
c.   sales managers
d.   assembly-line workers

7.   The Armed Forces Qualification Test (AFQT) is _____ _____.

a. used by all the services to gauge the trainability of potential recruits
b. a subset of the ASVAB made up of subtests on Mechanical Comprehension, Electronics Information, and General Science
c. a composite score derived from the General Aptitude Test Battery (GATB)
d. made up primarily of "hands-on," job-sample type measures

8. Most psychomotor skills tests focus on _____.
    a. manual dexterity
    b. speed of perception
    c. general overall body coordination
    d. spatial relationships

9. The scores on most clerical aptitude tests depend predominantly on_____
    _____.
    a. verbal comprehension
    b. perceptual speed
    c. eye-hand coordination
    d. spatial visualization

10. Current concerns about the use of "integrity tests" in preemployment selection decisions center upon the tests'_____
    _____.
    a. poor predictive validity
    b. emotional effect on test takers
    c. susceptibility to faking and coaching
    d. there are no substantial concerns about the use of integrity tests at present

TEST USE IN CLINICAL AND COUNSELING PSYCHOLOGY

1. Clinicians involved in doing psychological assessments use tests mainly _____
    _____.
    a. as a substitute for a lengthy interview
    b. as the primary source of reliable information about their clients
    c. as a source of hypotheses to explore further
    d. when all other techniques fail

2. A clinical psychologist examining a WISC-III profile is usually most interested in
    _____.
    a. the pattern of subtest scores
    b. the overall score the individual achieves
    c. the reliability and validity coefficients
    d. comparative results obtained by similar individuals

3. One of the most remarkable aspects of brain damage is the fact that _____
    _____.
    a.   its symptoms vary so widely
    b.   it is closely associated with language development
    c.   its effects are usually irreversible
    d.   it seldom affects short-term memory

4. The Halstead-Reitan and Luria-Nebraska batteries are designed primarily to assess
    _____.
    a.   intelligence
    b.   personality characteristics
    c.   brain pathology
    d.   motor-linguistic problems

5. Learning disabilities are usually viewed as _____.
    a.   symptoms of serious brain pathology
    b.   irreversible in most cases
    c.   a handicap that can possibly be overcome
    d.   caused by emotional factors

6. The learning-potential assessment techniques developed by Feuerstein and others are
    characterized by _____.
    a.   their assessment of abilities that were always present but not overtly shown
    b.   a close link between assessment and remediation
    c.   the generalizability of their effects to the child's interpersonal functioning
    d.   the fact that little or no training is needed to use them

7. Which of the following procedures are used in the assessment of behavioral change?
    _____.
    a.   Physiological measures
    b.   Direct observations of target behavior
    c.   Self-reports by the client
    d.   All of the above can be used

8. The _____ is an outstanding example of a
    comprehensive career-exploration program which allows the user to engage in two-way
    communication with the computer and is designed to guide the individual
    systematically toward effective decision making.
    a.   Career Interest Inventory (CII)
    b.   System for Interactive Guidance Information (SIGI-PLUS)
    c.   Enhanced Guide for Educational Exploration (EGOE)
    d.   Work Keys system

9. Given our present state of knowledge, the best overall procedure for synthesizing test data about individuals is _____.
   a. the statistical approach
   b. the clinical approach
   c. the physiological approach
   d. a combination of the clinical and statistical approaches

10. At the present time, computerized test administration probably surpasses the administration of tests by human examiners in terms of _____
    _____.
    a. the precision of task presentation
    b. personality assessment
    c. the evaluation of response sets
    d. all of the above

Miniprojects/Suggested Homework Activities:

Educational Testing

1. The handbook entitled *Educational Measurement* (3rd ed.), edited by Robert L. Linn (New York: American Council on Education/Macmillan, 1989) covers many areas that are, naturally, relevant to educational testing and provide expanded treatments of the topics in this section of Chapter 17. Depending on your interests, you may want to read one or more of the following chapters in that volume:

   ☞ Chapter 8, "The Specification and Development of Tests of Achievement and Ability," by Jason Millman and Jennifer Greene, which—among other things—contains a section on item writing that should prove informative as well as useful to you as a student of psychological testing *and* as a test taker (see Miniproject # 3 below).

   ☞ Chapter 9, "The Four Generations of Computerized Educational Measurement," by C. Victor Bunderson et al., which provides an interesting and informative account of the history, present status, and future trends in the use of computers for educational assessment.

   ☞ Chapter 14, "Certification of Student Competence," by Richard M. Jaeger, which presents a fascinating discussion of the thorny issues involved in competency testing, including the problems of setting standards.

2. Miniproject # 2 for Chapter 5 of this *Guide* suggested the investigation of references

cited on pp. 485-487 in Chapter 17 of the textbook, in connection with the validity data for tests for college and graduate school admissions. If you did not follow up on that suggestion then, it would be just as appropriate to do it at this point. See, in particular, the technical handbook edited by T.F. Donlon (New York: College Board Publications, 1984) on the SAT and/or the most recent *Guide to the Use of the Graduate Record Examinations Program* published by the Educational Testing Service of Princeton, N.J. For the most up-to-date information on the College Board's tests, publications, career search materials, research reports, and news releases, search through its Internet site at the following address:

http://www.collegeboard.org

3. As a follow-up to whatever practice you may already have had writing test items of the multiple-choice variety (see, for example, Miniproject #1 from Chapter 5) and to what you may have learned about item writing rules from the references given in this chapter, locate and review multiple-choice items from several sources. You could, for example, use newspaper or magazine quizzes, study guides (including this one), or old tests you may have in your possession. See if you can spot extraneous clues that give away the answers or help to eliminate incorrect alternatives. Make a list of those, and other weaknesses you can spot, and try to come up with as thorough a list of item writing rules as you can. Compare your list with the one that appears in Table 8.3, "Rules for Writing Multiple-Choice Test Items," on p. 353 of the *Educational Measurement* handbook cited earlier in this set of Miniprojects (# 1A).

Occupational Testing

1. One appropriate avenue to pursue as a follow-up to the information you have acquired on occupational testing is to conduct a survey of the personnel departments of some of the major employers in your area, with the purpose of finding out what instruments they use in selecting job applicants. If possible, choose companies that employ workers in a variety of jobs or choose several smaller companies that could provide information on a representative range of occupational categories.

2. If you have access to test materials through your instructor or through a testing center or lab, locate one of the tests of academic intelligence especially developed for use in industry or one of the special aptitude tests described in Chapter 17. Study the manual and materials for the test you have selected and prepare a Test Evaluation following the suggested outline in Appendix B of this *Guide*. Most of these instruments are relatively brief and easy to study compared to other types of ability measures, such as individual intelligence tests or multiple aptitude batteries.

3. One of the most important general references in the area of occupational testing is the

booklet on *Principles for the Validation and Use of Personnel Selection Procedures* prepared by the Society for Industrial and Organizational Psychology (SIOP, 1987). A review of this publication would help to expand your understanding of what constitutes good practice in the realm of occupational testing.

4. The rapid pace of scientific and technological advances, along with the globalization of economic systems, are creating unprecedented challenges and opportunities in most fields. The volume edited by Ann Howard, on *The Changing Nature of Work* (San Francisco: Jossey-Bass, 1995), contains a wealth of information about what is driving change and about the ways in which work and workers are likely to evolve in the post industrial society. If you have an interest in industrial/organizational psychology as a possible field of work, or even if you are simply planning to be a member of the labor force in the twenty-first century, you are sure to find several chapters in this book of great interest.

Test Use in Clinical and Counseling Psychology

The content of the last part of Chapter 17 spans what is surely the most diversified area of testing. Moreover, many of the topics in psychological assessment are intrinsically interesting and worthy of further pursuit. What follows, then, are only a few out of the many possible suggestions that could be made for follow-up readings and activities to pursue those topics.

1. On pp. 509-511 of the textbook you will find a short overview of psychological assessment and the fields in which it is currently practiced, with references to at least one handbook, sourcebook, or major volume in that field. In addition to the obvious references in clinical and counseling applications of testing, note the citations of works in forensic psychology, neuropsychology, health psychology, assessment of couples, and multicultural assessment, to name just a few.

2. One of the longest running debates in the field of intelligence testing concerns the extent to which profile analyses are diagnostically useful. Investigators and clinicians who believe that pattern analyses *are* worth doing have created a sizable literature concerning the most appropriate methods for such analyses. To sample this literature, as it pertains to current methods of scatter analysis, see "WISC-III subtest scatter as a function of highest scaled score" by J. A. Schinka, R. D. Vanderploeg, and G. Curtiss in the June 1997 issue of *Psychological Assessment* (*9*, 83-88). By the way, this quarterly journal is one of the best sources of information on such matters and on many of the topics discussed in the last part of Chapter 17.

3. The area of neuropsychological assessment is one of the most rapidly growing clinical specialties. Although there is a vast literature that you could access in order to

acquaint yourself better with that field, the book *Neuropsychological Assessment* (3rd ed.) by Muriel Deutsch Lezak (New York: Oxford University Press, 1995), is probably one of the best places to start.

4. Another vibrant field, which is evolving rapidly and is sure to have a dramatic influence in how testing is conducted, is dynamic assessment. In this area, the work of Susan Embretson is unequalled in its originality and methodological soundness. One way to acquaint yourself with her work, including examples of how learning can be used in testing, is by reading her chapter on "Diagnostic Testing by Measuring Learning Processes: Psychometric Considerations for Dynamic Testing," found in pp. 407–432 of *Diagnostic Monitoring of Skill and Knowledge Acquisition,* a book edited by N. Frederiksen et al. (Hillsdale, NJ: Erlbaum, 1990). For an overview of "Dynamic Assessment Approaches," see Carol S. Lidz's chapter by that title on pp. 281–296 of D. P. Flanagan et al.'s *Contemporary Intellectual Assessment: Theories, Tests, and Issues* (New York: Guilford Press, 1997).

5. The controversy that Paul Meehl started in the 1950s, when he concluded that statistical predictions based on actuarial data were superior to those based on clinical judgment, has consumed an awful lot of paper and ink (or toner) on both sides of the issue. More importantly, because it has challenged clinicians to question the bases for their judgments, it has had a healthy influence on psychological assessment. On pp. 527–529 of the textbook you will find a sampling of the literature on this issue, including the recent work of Spengler and his colleagues on the impact of the clinician's cognitive complexity. In addition, you may wish to consult H. N. Garb and C. J. Schramke's (1996) excellent review of judgment research in neuropsychological assessment (*Psychological Bulletin, 120,* 140-153).

6. Report writing is, in most cases, the culmination of the work of the clinical assessment specialist. The best way to become acquainted with what constitutes a good report is to examine a sample of reports directly. If you have access to some, from your instructor or elsewhere—provided that confidentiality can be maintained—by all means avail yourself of the opportunity to read them. Failing that, you might examine one of the books that the textbook cites, such as Norman Tallent's *Psychological Report Writing* (Englewood Cliffs, N.J.: Prentice Hall, 1993). This book, now in its fourth edition, presents the desirable features, and pitfalls, of report writing and includes several examples of reports from a variety of settings as well as a chapter on computer-generated psychological reports.

7. For those contemplating the possibility of a career that involves psychological assessment, it would be an excellent idea to subscribe to an Internet discussion group devoted to that topic. The "assess-p" list, coordinated by David L. DiLalla, Ph.D. from the Department of Psychology at Southern Illinois University in Carbondale, is

an outstanding source of information and discussion—sometimes quite lively—on a huge range of issues related to the current practice of psychological assessment. To subscribe to the list, send the following command:

e.g.,

    sub assess-p yourfirstname yourlastname

    sub assess-p mary smith

to:

    listserv@maelstrom.stjohns.edu

ANSWERS TO MULTIPLE CHOICE/TEST YOURSELF ITEMS:

EDUCATIONAL TESTING		OCCUPATIONAL TESTING		TEST USE IN CLINICAL AND COUNSELING PSYCHOLOGY	
1.	a	1.	d	1.	c
2.	d	2.	a	2.	a
3.	d	3.	b	3.	a
4.	c	4.	b	4.	c
5.	d	5.	c	5.	c
6.	b	6.	c	6.	b
7.	d	7.	a	7.	d
8.	a	8.	a	8.	b
9.	c	9.	b	9.	d
10.	b	10.	c	10.	a

ETHICAL AND SOCIAL CONSIDERATIONS IN TESTING

Chapter Outline

Ethical Issues in Psychological Testing and Assessment

User Qualifications and Professional Competence

Responsibilities of Test Publishers

Protection of Privacy

Confidentiality

Communicating Test Results

Testing Diverse Populations
    The Setting
    Legal Regulations
    Test-Related Factors
    Interpretation and Use of Test Scores
    Objectivity of Tests

Chapter Summary

Psychologists' longstanding concern with professional ethics was first codified formally with the publication of the *Ethical Principles of Psychologists* in 1953. Since then, that publication has undergone periodic revisions and several others have appeared, focusing on various aspects of the profession, but especially those that pertain to the delivery of psychological services.

The latest edition of the *Ethical Principles of Psychologists and Code of Conduct*—henceforth referred to as the *Ethics Code*—was published in 1992. This document contains six general principles that represent the highest ideals to which psychologists aspire and eight sets of standards with enforceable rules for psychologists functioning in various capacities, including testing and assessment activities. In addition to preparing the *Ethics Code,* the American Psychological Association (APA) strives to assist providers of psychological services by monitoring pertinent legal and regulatory developments and by issuing a variety of documents and statements to guide psychologists in their work.

The major responsibility for the proper use of tests rests with the individual user. Qualifications for using tests vary depending on the type of test involved and on other aspects of testing. In general, administrative and scoring tasks may be delegated to properly trained technicians, but appropriate interpretation and adequate communication of test results require the perspective of a psychologist who is qualified by virtue of education and experience in the area of testing. Psychologists themselves should recognize the limits of their competence and provide only those services for which they are properly trained. State licensing laws regulate the profession and help the public to identify individuals who are qualified to practice psychology. For their part, test publishers share in the responsibility to prevent the misuse of tests through their control of the distribution and marketing of test materials.

Two very important aspects of psychological testing practice concern the protection of the privacy of test takers and the confidentiality of test data. Although these issues are related, protection of privacy centers primarily on: (a) the need to obtain informed consent, by making sure that the test taker is aware of the purposes of testing, and (b) ensuring that the information gathered from the test taker is relevant to those purposes. Confidentiality, on the other hand, is concerned with access to test results by test takers and other persons, as well as with the retention of records by institutions and other parties. Proper testing practice also extends to the communication of test results in a manner that is clear to the recipients and that takes into account their characteristics and the context of the communication.

Over the past four decades, societal concerns about the civil rights of ethnic minorities and women have helped to focus much attention on psychological tests. This attention derives primarily from the role tests play in employment and educational decision making and involves the notion that the test scores of minority group members are unfairly lowered by cultural conditions beyond their control. In the realm of employment, the *Uniform Guidelines on Employee Selection Procedures*, adopted by the Equal Employment Opportunity Commission (EEOC) in 1978, have played a crucial role in delineating what constitutes discriminatory practice. However, these guidelines are now dated and in need of revision. In the meantime, many ambiguities remain in this and other areas of test use. These ambiguities require continuous interpretation by the courts which, in turn, are not always properly informed. The essential problem with regard to the testing of minorities lies in differentiating between cultural influences that are limited to the test—which should be eliminated or ruled out—and those that affect both test and criterion behaviors, which may need to be addressed by appropriate remediation but cannot be ignored.

Comprehensive Review

STUDY QUESTIONS:

1. Discuss how the profession of psychology regulates itself internally and cite examples of documents that the APA has promulgated for the use of psychologists.

247

2. Explain the major reasons why the use of psychological tests needs to be restricted to those who are competent in their use.

3. Describe how you would gauge whether someone is a "qualified" psychologist.

4. List three examples of practices concerning the distribution and marketing of psychological tests that are deemed unacceptable and explain why they might be harmful.

5. Discuss how the purpose for which testing is conducted affects the issue of protecting the privacy of test takers.

6. Explain what is meant by "informed consent" as fully as possible.

7. Discuss the issue of access to test results from the standpoint of test takers, parents, third persons, and institutions.

8. Identify and discuss the major precautions that should apply to the communication of test results to the individual test taker.

9. Describe the major legal regulations in the area of employee selection procedures.

10. Cite an example, from the field of employment testing, of a well-intentioned effort to do away with barriers to equal opportunity that has proved to be controversial.

11. Discuss the issue of relevant versus irrelevant cultural factors as it applies to the content of psychological tests.

12. Describe the rationale used by those who view standardized testing as having a positive function with regard to protecting the civil rights of minorities and women.

FILL IN THE BLANKS: Key Terms, Concepts, and Organizations

1. The current _ _ _ _ _ _ _ _ _ _ _ of the American Psychological Association has six general principles designed to guide psychologists toward the highest _ _ _ _ _ _ of the profession and eight standards with enforceable _ _ _ _ _ for those who function in diverse contexts.

2. The group that investigates and adjudicates complaints lodged against members of the American Psychological Association is the APA's _ _ _ _ _ _ _ _ _ _ _ _ _ _ _.

3. The group that is specifically devoted to considering problems regarding sound testing and assessment practices and to providing advice on these matters to other groups is

the APA's Committee on _ _ _ _ _ _ _ _ _ _ _ _ _ _ _ _ _ _ _ and _ _ _ _ _ _ _ _ _ _ .

4. In the field of psychology it is customary to differentiate between _ _ _ _ _ _ _ _ _ , which controls the practice of psychology, and _ _ _ _ _ _ _ _ _ _ _ _ _ , which is concerned with control of the title "psychologist."

5. The diplomate status that the _ _ _ _ _ _ _ _ _ _ _ _ _ of _ _ _ _ _ _ _ _ _ _ _ _ _ _ _ _ _ _ _ (ABPP) confers upon psychologists differs from licensing or certification in that it is a higher level of accreditation and takes into account areas of specialization such as clinical, counseling, and school psychology.

6. The direct control of the sale and distribution of psychological tests and other assessment instruments is in the hands of _ _ _ _ _ _ _ _ _ _ _ _ _ _ , who have in recent years increased their efforts to ensure that tests are used properly.

7. _ _ _ _ _ _ _ _ _ , one of the two key concepts involved in the protection of the privacy of test takers, involves a determination that the information gathered and the instruments used in an assessment are appropriate for its purpose(s).

8. _ _ _ _ _ _ _ _ _ _ _ _ _ is another key concept in the protection of test takers' privacy. It requires that test takers be made aware of the reasons for and intended use of tests.

9. _ _ _ _ _ _ _ _ _ _ _ _ _ _ _ is an ethical consideration that addresses the issue of who will have access to the information obtained by psychologists in the course of their work.

10. The _ (EEOC) is the organization charged with implementing and enforcing Title VII of the Civil Rights Act of 1964 and related legislation.

11. _ _ _ _ _ _ _ _ _ _ _ _ _ refers to the situation that occurs when the use of a selection procedure results in a substantially higher rate of rejection for minority than for nonminority candidates.

12. The notion that organizations should do more than merely avoid discriminatory practices and should make efforts to compensate certain groups—such as ethnic minorities and women—for the residual effects of past social inequities has been known as _ _ _ _ _ _ _ _ _ _ _ _ _ _ _ _ _ _ .

1. Ethics Code / (highest) ideals / (enforceable) rules
2. Ethics Committee
3. (Committee on) Psychological Tests (and) Assessment
4. licensing / certification
5. American Board (of) Professional Psychology (ABPP)
6. test publishers
7. relevance
8. informed consent
9. confidentiality
10. Equal Employment Opportunity Commission (EEOC)
11. adverse impact
12. affirmative action

TRUE/FALSE and WHY?

1. Psychologists in the 1990s need more assistance than ever before to determine and clarify what constitutes ethically and legally proper professional practice. (T/F) Why?

   _____

   _____

2. Licensing laws typically spell out the requirements needed to practice psychology, but lack provisions for enforcement or disciplinary action against violators. (T/F) Why?

   _____

   _____

3. Publication of psychological tests in newspapers or magazines is a good way to promote their use. (T/F) Why? _____

   _____

4. One way to diminish the undue weight that is placed on "high stakes" testing would be to use tests only within the context of a comprehensive assessment. (T/F) Why?

   _____

   _____

5. For purposes of testing effectiveness, it is sometimes necessary to subject a person to a testing program under false pretenses. (T/F) Why? _____

   _____

   _____

6. In clinical situations clients basically surrender their right to privacy in order to obtain

250

help. (T/F) Why? _____
_____
_____

7. The underlying principle regarding confidentiality of test records is that such records
    should not be released without the consent of the test taker. (T/F) Why? _____
    _____
    _____

8. When test records are retained for legitimate use in longitudinal research, access to
    them does not need to be controlled as stringently as it is for other uses. (T/F) Why?
    _____
    _____

9. The acceptance of properly interpreted psychological tests results can, in and of itself,
    be of therapeutic value to clients in the context of treatment. (T/F) Why?____
    _____
    _____

10. Once a selection procedure has been satisfactorily validated, even if disproportionate
    rejection rates occur for minorities, the requirements of the EEOC *Uniform Guidelines*
    can be presumed to have been met. (T/F) Why? _____
    _____

ANSWERS TO TRUE/FALSE:

1. True	3. False	5. False	7. True	9. True
2. False	4. True	6. False	8. False	10. False

Multiple Choice: Test Yourself

1. The standards that psychologists should follow in the exercise of their profession,
    either for research or for practical purposes, are contained in the_____
    _____.
    a.   APA Ethical Principles of Psychologists and Code of Conduct
    b.   Standards for Educational and Psychological Testing
    c.   EEOC Rules and Regulations
    d.   APA Guidelines for the Delivery of Psychological Services

2. Sales of psychological tests should be restricted to those with_____
    _____.
    a.   at least a Master's degree in psychology

b. a Ph.D. or doctoral degree
c. a state license and/or certification
d. appropriate training and experience in the use of the test in question

3. Aptitude and personality testing by mail is _____.
   a. perfectly acceptable
   b. acceptable under some conditions
   c. unacceptable under nearly any condition
   d. acceptable for certain kinds of test takers

4. The privacy of test results, such as those obtained by adults on personality tests, is best protected by_____.
   a. establishing strict laws with severe punishment for those who do not abide by them
   b. never releasing the scores to anyone for any reason
   c. sharing test results only with qualified personnel
   d. informing examinees about the tests and their intended use prior to testing

5. Most examinees will be less sensitive about the privacy of their test scores if they
   _____.
   a. obtain socially acceptable scores
   b. understand their intended use
   c. realize that the score represents only a sampling of behavior
   d. all of the above are true

6. Which of the following legal developments has (have) been instrumental in underscoring the importance of keeping invasive inquiries to a minimum in preemployment testing? _____.
   a. The Soroka v. Dayton Hudson case
   b. The Americans with Disabilities Act of 1990
   c. Both a and b
   d. Neither a nor b

7. Who should make the final decision about the release of psychological test scores?
   _____.
   a. The examinee, or if the examinee is not of age, the parent.
   b. The researcher who collected the data.
   c. The chief executive officer of the institution involved.
   d. The law.

8. Psychological test information obtained on children_____
   _____.

a. should never be divulged to the parents
b. may, in some cases, be communicated to the parents
c. should be shared with the parents
d. should be made available to the child's whole family

9. Of the following, the major problem in educational and psychological testing is_____.
   a. improper test standardization
   b. poor norms that do not apply to a given situation
   c. poor feedback of test results to the examinee
   d. tests that have low reliability and validity

10. In communicating test results to an examinee _____
    _____.
    a. all technical information should be released
    b. the characteristics of the examinee must be considered
    c. no one else should be in the room
    d. normative information should not be divulged

11. Tests on which minority group members score significantly lower than nonminorities
    _____.
    a. should be thrown out
    b. should be modified until average minority scores equal average nonminority scores
    c. may not be biased but instead demonstrate a deficiency
    d. none of the above

12. Speaking about testing that results in decision making of importance to test takers, Samuel Messick has argued that validity judgments_____
    _____.
    a. are essentially value judgments
    b. cannot be made by anyone other than the test taker
    c. do not apply
    d. should be made primarily by legal authorities

13. The EEOC Uniform Guidelines _____
    _____.
    a. recommend the abolishment of testing
    b. apply to tests but not to interview procedures
    c. are based on the current Testing Standards
    d. apply to both private and governmental employers

Miniprojects/Suggested Homework Activities:

If you have done even a relatively small portion of the miniprojects and homework activities suggested in this guide, in addition to studying the entire textbook, you could probably use a prolonged rest at this point. Should you choose to rest, you can start now and read no further than the end of this paragraph. The last suggestion for those who opt for a vacation, yet plan to stay in the field of psychology, is to consider retaining your copy of the textbook for your basic professional library, as it may come in handy in the future.

Those who are still reading this paragraph may find the following suggestions worthwhile:

☞ Generate a list of all the publications cited in Chapter 18 that contain the words "principles," "standards," "code," or "guidelines" in their titles. You should come up with a list of about dozen works that define the proper practice of psychology and psychological testing, from the standpoint of the profession. Note the dates of publication and the publishers of each of these works. Locate and review the ones that interest you the most. Many are available through the American Psychological Association's World Wide Web site and its various links. Miniproject #3 in Chapter 1 of this *Guide* contains the pertinent addresses.

☞ As mentioned in the textbook, every state has some laws that govern the practice of psychology and/or the use of the title "psychologist." Find out what the laws for licensing/certification are in your state and in another state that interests you, and compare them. Applicable state statutes can be located through library research or by contacting the Department of Professional Regulation of the state(s) in question. You may also want to check whether the APA has already published a volume of their series on *Law and Mental Health Professionals* for the state(s) that interest you.

☞ In light of the increasing interplay between the professions of psychology and the law, some institutions (e.g., the University of Nebraska at Lincoln and Catholic University in Washington, DC) offer programs that allow students to combine elements of both in their graduate education, including the simultaneous pursuit of degrees in law and psychology. Naturally, the possibilities of employment for individuals with such joint training are quite good. For further information about these programs, see *Graduate Study in Psychology,* a guide that is published yearly by the APA.

ANSWERS TO MULTIPLE CHOICE/TEST YOURSELF ITEMS:

1. a	4. d	7. a	10. b	13. d
2. d	5. d	8. c	11. c	
3. c	6. c	9. c	12. a	

Appendix A

TABLE OF AREAS UNDER THE NORMAL CURVE

Section 1: How to Use the Table of Areas Under the Normal Curve

Table Headings:

In the first column of the Table $z = x/\sigma$ where x is the distance between any point on the baseline and zero, or the mean, and σ (sigma) is the standard deviation of the normal distribution. The first column lists values of z from 0.00 to 3.70. Column A lists the area of the curve that is encompassed *between* the mean (O) and any z values. Since the normal curve is symmetrical, when z is at the mean (0.00), half of the curve (.5000) is above z and half is below z. If the curve is cut at any point other than the mean, the area in the larger portion is given in Column B and the area in the smaller portion is given in Column C.

Explanation of the Table:

Part One—Diagrams: In Diagram I (Figure 9), we look up a z value of + 1.25 and find the area between that z and the mean to be .3944 (Column A). Because the normal curve is symmetrical, any given z distance subtends the same area above the mean or below the mean. Therefore, in Diagram II, a z value of – 1.25 again gives us an area of .3944 between z and the mean. To find the proportion of the area in Diagram I that falls *above* a z of + 1.25, we subtract .3944 from .5000, and obtain .1056. To find the proportion of the area falling *below* + 1.25, we add .3944 to .5000, obtaining .8944. These values are shown in Diagram III. Diagram IV shows the results with a z of – 1.25. In this case, the larger portion falls *above* z but is also found by adding the value in Column A to .5000 (.3944 + .5000 = .8944) and the smaller portion falls *below* z and is found by subtracting .3944 from .5000. Columns B and C of the Table provide the results of those computations for us. You can verify your results by finding the entries in Columns B and C for the z value of 1.25. You can also, as an exercise, look up and corroborate the areas under the curve that are shown in Figures 3-3 and 3-6 of the textbook (pp. 54 and 67, respectively) for z values of ± 1.00, ±2.00, and ±3.00 in order to make sure that you have learned how to use the Table.

Part Two—Levels of Significance: Up to this point we have dealt with the normal curve merely as a model of a theoretical distribution that can be used to find the position of one measurement from a population or a sample whose distribution approximates the shape of our model. When the normal curve is applied to hypothesis testing, we use it to ascertain the probability that the critical value (z) we have obtained could have resulted by chance. Since z values simply give the proportion in one end of the curve, when we test a hypothesis that permits variation in either direction, we have to double the proportion that falls beyond the z value to find the probability level associated with the critical value obtained. (See, for example, Exercise # 8 in Chapter 4 of this Guide, where the value in Column C of the Table, which is the probability (p) for a z of 2.20, is 0.0139. Because score differences could occur in either direction, p has been doubled to obtain the answer to that problem.) This situation is described as a "two-tailed test," and it is the most common way in which the significance of findings is tested. In contrast, if we had a specific unidirectional hypothesis, as we might in conducting an experiment where we have reason to expect results to fall in a given direction, we would be doing a "one-tailed test." In such cases, if the findings were in the direction that was specified, the p for the critical values obtained would not be doubled.

For further information about the normal curve and its use in hypothesis testing, see pp. 88–90 and 107–111 of the textbook. You may also want to refer to a good basic statistics textbook, such as the fourth edition of David C. Howell's *Statistical Methods for Psychology* (Belmont, CA: Duxbury Press, 1997).

Figure 9 — Diagrams of Areas Under the Normal Curve

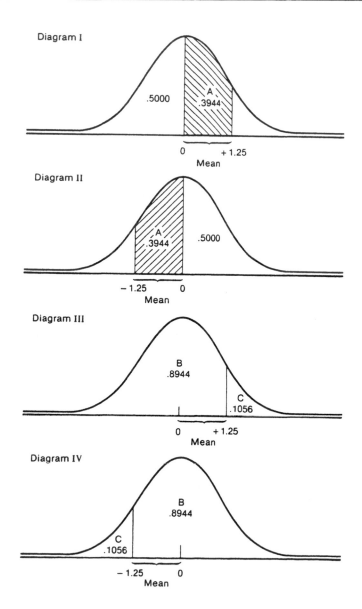

Section 2:

Table of Areas Under the Normal Curve

(1)	(2)	(3)	(4)
	A	B	C
z = x/σ	Area from Mean to x/σ	Area in Larger Portion	Area in Smaller Portion
0.00	.0000	.5000	.5000
0.01	.0040	.5040	.4960
0.02	.0080	.5080	.4920
0.03	.0120	.5120	.4880
0.04	.0160	.5160	.4840
0.05	.0199	.5199	.4801
0.06	.0239	.5239	.4761
0.07	.0279	.5279	.4721
0.08	.0319	.5319	.4681
0.09	.0359	.5359	.4641
0.10	.0398	.5398	.4602
0.11	.0438	.5438	.4562
0.12	.0478	.5478	.4522
0.13	.0517	.5517	.4483
0.14	.0557	.5557	.4443
0.15	.0596	.5596	.4404
0.16	.0636	.5636	.4364
0.17	.0675	.5675	.4325
0.18	.0714	.5714	.4286
0.19	.0753	.5753	.4247
0.20	.0793	.5793	.4207
0.21	.0832	.5832	.4168
0.22	.0871	.5871	.4129
0.23	.0910	.5910	.4090
0.24	.0948	.5948	.4052
0.25	.0987	.5987	.4013
0.26	.1026	.6026	.3974
0.27	.1064	.6064	.3936
0.28	.1103	.6103	.3897
0.29	.1141	.6141	.3859
0.30	.1179	.6179	.3821
0.31	.1217	.6217	.3783
0.32	.1255	.6255	.3745
0.33	.1293	.6293	.3707

Table of Areas Under the Normal Curve

(1)	(2) A	(3) B	(4) C
z = x/σ	Area from Mean to x/σ	Area in Larger Portion	Area in Smaller Portion
0.34	.1331	.6331	.3669
0.35	.1368	.6368	.3632
0.36	.1406	.6406	.3594
0.37	.1443	.6443	.3557
0.38	.1480	.6480	.3520
0.39	.1517	.6517	.3483
0.40	.1554	.6554	.3446
0.41	.1591	.6591	.3409
0.42	.1628	.6628	.3372
0.43	.1664	.6664	.3336
0.44	.1700	.6700	.3300
0.45	.1736	.6736	.3264
0.46	.1772	.6772	.3228
0.47	.1808	.6808	.3192
0.48	.1844	.6844	.3156
0.49	.1879	.6879	.3121
0.50	.1915	.6915	.3085
0.51	.1950	.6950	.3050
0.52	.1985	.6985	.3015
0.53	.2019	.7019	.2981
0.54	.2054	.7054	.2946
0.55	.2088	.7088	.2912
0.56	.2123	.7123	.2877
0.57	.2157	.7157	.2843
0.58	.2190	.7190	.2810
0.59	.2224	.7224	.2776
0.60	.2257	.7257	.2743
0.61	.2291	.7291	.2709
0.62	.2324	.7324	.2676
0.63	.2357	.7357	.2643
0.64	.2389	.7389	.2611
0.65	.2422	.7422	.2578
0.66	.2454	.7454	.2546
0.67	.2486	.7486	.2514
0.68	.2517	.7517	.2483

Table of Areas Under the Normal Curve

(1) z = x/σ	(2) A Area from Mean to x/σ	(3) B Area in Larger Portion	(4) C Area in Smaller Portion
0.69	.2549	.7549	.2451
0.70	.2580	.7580	.2420
0.71	.2611	.7611	.2389
0.72	.2642	.7642	.2358
0.73	.2673	.7673	.2327
0.74	.2704	.7704	.2296
0.75	.2734	.7734	.2266
0.76	.2764	.7764	.2236
0.77	.2794	.7794	.2206
0.78	.2823	.7823	.2177
0.79	.2852	.7852	.2148
0.80	.2881	.7881	.2119
0.81	.2910	.7910	.2090
0.82	.2939	.7939	.2061
0.83	.2967	.7967	.2033
0.84	.2995	.7995	.2005
0.85	.3023	.8023	.1977
0.86	.3051	.8051	.1949
0.87	.3078	.8078	.1922
0.88	.3106	.8106	.1894
0.89	.3133	.8133	.1867
0.90	.3159	.8159	.1841
0.91	.3186	.8186	.1814
0.92	.3212	.8212	.1788
0.93	.3238	.8238	.1762
0.94	.3264	.8264	.1736
0.95	.3289	.8289	.1711
0.96	.3315	.8315	.1685
0.97	.3340	.8340	.1660
0.98	.3365	.8365	.1635
0.99	.3389	.8389	.1611
1.00	.3413	.8413	.1587
1.01	.3438	.8438	.1562
1.02	.3461	.8461	.1539
1.03	.3485	.8485	.1515

Table of Areas Under the Normal Curve

(1) z = x/σ	(2) A Area from Mean to x/σ	(3) B Area in Larger Portion	(4) C Area in Smaller Portion
1.04	.3508	.8508	.1492
1.05	.3531	.8531	.1469
1.06	.3554	.8554	.1446
1.07	.3577	.8577	.1423
1.08	.3599	.8599	.1401
1.09	.3621	.8621	.1379
1.10	.3643	.8643	.1357
1.11	.3665	.8665	.1335
1.12	.3686	.8686	.1314
1.13	.3708	.8708	.1292
1.14	.3729	.8729	.1271
1.15	.3749	.8749	.1251
1.16	.3770	.8770	.1230
1.17	.3790	.8790	.1210
1.18	.3810	.8810	.1190
1.19	.3830	.8830	.1170
1.20	.3849	.8849	.1151
1.21	.3869	.8869	.1131
1.22	.3888	.8888	.1112
1.23	.3907	.8907	.1093
1.24	.3925	.8925	.1075
1.25	.3944	.8944	.1056
1.26	.3962	.8962	.1038
1.27	.3980	.8980	.1020
1.28	.3997	.8997	.1003
1.29	.4015	.9015	.0985
1.30	.4032	.9032	.0968
1.31	.4049	.9049	.0951
1.32	.4066	.9066	.0934
1.33	.4082	.9082	.0918
1.34	.4099	.9099	.0901
1.35	.4115	.9115	.0885
1.36	.4131	.9131	.0869
1.37	.4147	.9147	.0853
1.38	.4162	.9162	.0838

Table of Areas Under the Normal Curve

(1)	(2) A	(3) B	(4) C
$z = x/\sigma$	Area from Mean to x/σ	Area in Larger Portion	Area in Smaller Portion
1.39	.4177	.9177	.0823
1.40	.4192	.9192	.0808
1.41	.4207	.9207	.0793
1.42	.4222	.9222	.0778
1.43	.4236	.9236	.0764
1.44	.4251	.9251	.0749
1.45	.4265	.9265	.0735
1.46	.4279	.9279	.0721
1.47	.4292	.9292	.0708
1.48	.4306	.9306	.0694
1.49	.4319	.9319	.0681
1.50	.4332	.9332	.0668
1.51	.4345	.9345	.0655
1.52	.4357	.9357	.0643
1.53	.4370	.9370	.0630
1.54	.4382	.9382	.0618
1.55	.4394	.9394	.0606
1.56	.4406	.9406	.0594
1.57	.4418	.9418	.0582
1.58	.4429	.9429	.0571
1.59	.4441	.9441	.0559
1.60	.4452	.9452	.0548
1.61	.4463	.9463	.0537
1.62	.4474	.9474	.0526
1.63	.4484	.9484	.0516
1.64	.4495	.9495	.0505
1.65	.4505	.9505	.0495
1.66	.4515	.9515	.0485
1.67	.4525	.9525	.0475
1.68	.4535	.9535	.0465
1.69	.4545	.9545	.0455
1.70	.4554	.9554	.0446
1.71	.4564	.9564	.0436
1.72	.4573	.9573	.0427
1.73	.4582	.9582	.0418

Table of Areas Under the Normal Curve

(1) z =x/σ	(2) A Area from Mean to x/σ	(3) B Area in Larger Portion	(4) C Area in Smaller Portion
1.74	.4591	.9591	.0409
1.75	.4599	.9599	.0401
1.76	.4608	.9608	.0392
1.77	.4616	.9616	.0384
1.78	.4625	.9625	.0375
1.79	.4633	.9633	.0367
1.80	.4641	.9641	.0359
1.81	.4649	.9649	.0351
1.82	.4656	.9656	.0344
1.83	.4664	.9664	.0336
1.84	.4671	.9671	.0329
1.85	.4678	.9678	.0322
1.86	.4686	.9686	.0314
1.87	.4693	.9693	.0307
1.88	.4699	.9699	.0301
1.89	.4706	.9706	.0294
1.90	.4713	.9713	.0287
1.91	.4719	.9719	.0281
1.92	.4726	.9726	.0274
1.93	.4732	.9732	.0268
1.94	.4738	.9738	.0262
1.95	.4744	.9744	.0256
1.96	.4750	.9750	.0250
1.97	.4756	.9756	.0244
1.98	.4761	.9761	.0239
1.99	.4767	.9767	.0233
2.00	.4772	.9772	.0228
2.01	.4778	.9778	.0222
2.02	.4783	.9783	.0217
2.03	.4788	.9788	.0212
2.04	.4793	.9793	.0207
2.05	.4798	.9798	.0202
2.06	.4803	.9803	.0197
2.07	.4808	.9808	.0192
2.08	.4812	.9812	.0188

Table of Areas Under the Normal Curve

(1) z = x/σ	(2) A Area from Mean to x/σ	(3) B Area in Larger Portion	(4) C Area in Smaller Portion
2.09	.4817	.9817	.0183
2.10	.4821	.9821	.0179
2.11	.4826	.9826	.0174
2.12	.4830	.9830	.0170
2.13	.4834	.9834	.0166
2.14	.4838	.9838	.0162
2.15	.4842	.9842	.0158
2.16	.4846	.9846	.0154
2.17	.4850	.9850	.0150
2.18	.4854	.9854	.0146
2.19	.4857	.9857	.0143
2.20	.4861	.9861	.0139
2.21	.4864	.9864	.0136
2.22	.4868	.9868	.0132
2.23	.4871	.9871	.0129
2.24	.4875	.9875	.0125
2.25	.4878	.9878	.0122
2.26	.4881	.9881	.0119
2.27	.4884	.9884	.0116
2.28	.4887	.9887	.0113
2.29	.4890	.9890	.0110
2.30	.4893	.9893	.0107
2.31	.4896	.9896	.0104
2.32	.4898	.9898	.0102
2.33	.4901	.9901	.0099
2.34	.4904	.9904	.0096
2.35	.4906	.9906	.0094
2.36	.4909	.9909	.0091
2.37	.4911	.9911	.0089
2.38	.4913	.9913	.0087
2.39	.4916	.9916	.0084
2.40	.4918	.9918	.0082
2.41	.4920	.9920	.0080
2.42	.4922	.9922	.0078

Table of Areas Under the Normal Curve

(1)	(2) A	(3) B	(4) C
z = x/σ	Area from Mean to x/σ	Area in Larger Portion	Area in Smaller Portion
2.43	.4925	.9925	.0075
2.44	.4927	.9927	.0073
2.45	.4929	.9929	.0071
2.46	.4931	.9931	.0069
2.47	.4932	.9932	.0068
2.48	.4934	.9934	.0066
2.49	.4936	.9936	.0064
2.50	.4938	.9938	.0062
2.51	.4940	.9940	.0060
2.52	.4941	.9941	.0059
2.53	.4943	.9943	.0057
2.54	.4945	.9945	.0055
2.55	.4946	.9946	.0054
2.56	.4948	.9948	.0052
2.57	.4949	.9949	.0051
2.58	.4951	.9951	.0049
2.59	.4952	.9952	.0048
2.60	.4953	.9953	.0047
2.61	.4955	.9955	.0045
2.62	.4956	.9956	.0044
2.63	.4957	.9957	.0043
2.64	.4959	.9959	.0041
2.65	.4960	.9960	.0040
2.66	.4961	.9961	.0039
2.67	.4962	.9962	.0038
2.68	.4963	.9963	.0037
2.69	.4964	.9964	.0036
2.70	.4965	.9965	.0035
2.71	.4966	.9966	.0034
2.72	.4967	.9967	.0033
2.73	.4968	.9968	.0032
2.74	.4969	.9969	.0031
2.75	.4970	.9970	.0030
2.76	.4971	.9971	.0029
2.77	.4972	.9972	.0028

Table of Areas Under the Normal Curve

(1)	(2) A	(3) B	(4) C
$z = x/\sigma$	Area from Mean to x/σ	Area in Larger Portion	Area in Smaller Portion
2.78	.4973	.9973	.0027
2.79	.4974	.9974	.0026
2.80	.4974	.9974	.0026
2.81	.4975	.9975	.0025
2.82	.4976	.9976	.0024
2.83	.4977	.9977	.0023
2.84	.4977	.9977	.0023
2.85	.4978	.9978	.0022
2.86	.4979	.9979	.0021
2.87	.4979	.9979	.0021
2.88	.4980	.9980	.0020
2.89	.4981	.9981	.0019
2.90	.4981	.9981	.0019
2.91	.4982	.9982	.0018
2.92	.4982	.9982	.0018
2.93	.4983	.9983	.0017
2.94	.4984	.9984	.0016
2.95	.4984	.9984	.0016
2.96	.4985	.9985	.0015
2.97	.4985	.9985	.0015
2.98	.4986	.9986	.0014
2.99	.4986	.9986	.0014
3.00	.4987	.9987	.0013
3.01	.4987	.9987	.0013
3.02	.4987	.9987	.0013
3.03	.4988	.9988	.0012
3.04	.4988	.9988	.0012
3.05	.4989	.9989	.0011
3.06	.4989	.9989	.0011
3.07	.4989	.9989	.0011
3.08	.4990	.9990	.0010
3.09	.4990	.9990	.0010
3.10	.4990	.9990	.0010
3.11	.4991	.9991	.0009
3.12	.4991	.9991	.0009

Table of Areas Under the Normal Curve

(1)	(2) A	(3) B	(4) C
$z = x/\sigma$	Area from Mean to x/σ	Area in Larger Portion	Area in Smaller Portion
3.13	.4991	.9991	.0009
3.14	.4992	.9992	.0008
3.15	.4992	.9992	.0008
3.16	.4992	.9992	.0008
3.17	.4992	.9992	.0008
3.18	.4993	.9993	.0007
3.19	.4993	.9993	.0007
3.20	.4993	.9993	.0007
3.21	.4993	.9993	.0007
3.22	.4994	.9994	.0006
3.23	.4994	.9994	.0006
3.24	.4994	.9994	.0006
3.30	.4995	.9995	.0005
3.40	.4997	.9997	.0003
3.50	.4998	.9998	.0002
3.60	.4998	.9998	.0002
3.70	.4999	.9999	.0001

Source: *Statistical Methods for the Behavioral Sciences,* copyright ©1954 and renewed 1973 by A. L. Edwards. Reproduced by permission of David A. Edwards.

Appendix B

A SUGGESTED OUTLINE FOR TEST EVALUATION

<u>Note</u>: The following outline contains basic features applicable to nearly all tests. Additional features are undoubtedly noteworthy in the case of particular tests. In preparing for the evaluation of a test, it would be good to read the *Standards for Educational and Psychological Testing* and to peruse a sample of test reviews in the *Mental Measurements Yearbook* or *Test Critiques* series.

A. <u>General Information</u>

- ▸ Title of test (including edition and forms if applicable)
- ▸ Author(s)
- ▸ Publisher, date(s) of publication, including dates of manuals, norms, and other materials (especially important for tests whose contents or norms may become outdated)
- ▸ Time required to administer
- ▸ Cost (booklets, answer sheets, other test materials, available scoring services)

B. <u>Brief Description of Purpose and Nature of Test</u>

- ▸ General type of test (e.g., individual or group, nonverbal, differential abilities, interest inventory)
- ▸ Population for which test is designed (age range, type of person)
- ▸ Nature of content (e.g., verbal, numerical, figural, motor)
- ▸ Subtests and separate scores
- ▸ Item types

C. <u>Practical Evaluation</u>

- ▸ Qualitative features of test materials (e.g., design of test booklet, editorial quality of content, ease of use, attractiveness, durability, appropriateness for test takers)
- ▸ Ease of administration, including availability of computerized administration
- ▸ Clarity of directions
- ▸ Scoring procedures, including computer-scoring services and available software
- ▸ Examiner qualifications and training required
- ▸ Face validity and test taker rapport

D. <u>Technical Evaluation</u>

   1. Scaling and Norms
- Item response theory model and procedures used, if applicable
- Type of norms (e.g., percentiles, standard scores)
- Standardization sample: nature, size, representativeness, procedures followed in obtaining sample, availability of subgroup norms (e.g., age, sex, region, education, occupation)

   2. Reliability
- Types and procedure (e.g., retest, parallel-form, split-half, Kuder-Richardson or coefficient alpha), including size and nature of samples employed
- Scorer reliability, if applicable
- Equivalence of forms
- Long-term stability, when available

   3. Validity
- Appropriate validation procedures (e.g., content-description, construct identification)
- Specific procedures followed in assessing validity and results obtained
- Size and nature of samples employed

E. <u>Reviewer Comments</u>

▸   From *Mental Measurements Yearbooks*, *Test Critiques*, and other sources

F. <u>Summary Evaluation</u>

▸   Major strengths and weaknesses of the test, cutting across all parts of the outline